CRA
LIPMAN
MAY 14, 1977

SEXUAL ASSAULT:
Confronting RAPE
in America

D0869469

SEXUAL ASSAULT:
Confronting
RAPE
in America

Nancy Gager and Cathleen Schurr

GROSSET & DUNLAP
A FILMWAYS COMPANY
Publishers • New York

Copyright © 1976 Nancy Gager and Cathleen Schurr
All rights reserved

Published simultaneously in Canada

Library of Congress catalog card number: 73–18531
ISBN 0-448-11527-1

First printing
Printed in the United States of America

To all women and children—
especially the victims of sexual assault

ACKNOWLEDGMENTS

Literally hundreds of individuals across the country generously contributed their time, energy, knowledge, and experiences to the making of this book—victims; doctors, nurses, psychiatrists, psychologists, and other hospital and mental health personnel; police officers and officials; attorneys, criminal law specialists, judges, and legislators and their aides; members of rape crisis centers and women working on special rape task forces and investigative groups; and television and press reporters.

Many we interviewed personally or communicated with by phone and mail. Others contributed to our conclusions via their papers and articles. We also benefited immensely from the few pioneers in this still neglected area of sex assaults, who shared their thoughts with us directly or through books and reports, as well as from the increasing media coverage of this subject.

All our sources are either cited specifically in our text, with interviews fully credited, or are listed in the bibliography. To all these individuals we extend our thanks and appreciation. In some cases, of course, our interpretations differ from those of our sources. Any errors of fact or presentation are entirely ours.

Two persons must be acknowledged for their special help over several years: Mary Ann Largen, National Rape Task Force Coordinator of the National Organization for Women, who gave us constant information, advice, and encouragement; and Dr. Joseph F. Skelly, consulting engineer, who assisted with statistical compilations and the graphs and charts in the Appendix.

Special thanks are also due to the following police departments, hospitals and health organizations, and rape crisis centers which took the time and trouble to answer our questionnaires on their specific operating procedures.

Police Departments: Birmingham, Alabama; Phoenix, Arizona; Tucson, Arizona; Little Rock, Arkansas; Los Angeles, California; Oakland, California; San Diego, California; San Francisco, California; San Jose, California; Miami, Florida; Honolulu, Hawaii; Chicago, Illinois; Indianapolis, Indiana; Des Moines, Iowa; Baton Rouge, Louisiana; Detroit, Michigan; Grand Rapids, Michigan; Minneapolis, Minnesota; St. Paul, Minnesota; Kansas City, Missouri; Omaha, Nebraska; Las Vegas, Nevada; Albuquerque, New Mexico; Buffalo, New York; New York, New York; Columbus, Ohio; Toledo, Ohio; Sioux Falls, South Dakota; El Paso, Texas; Fort Worth, Texas; San Antonio, Texas; Salt Lake City, Utah; Norfolk, Virginia; Richmond, Virginia; Madison, Wisconsin.

Hospitals and Health Organizations: Good Samaritan Hospital, Phoenix, Arizona; St. Joseph's Hospital, Tucson, Arizona; St. Mary's Hospital, Tucson, Arizona; Southern Arizona Mental Health Center, Tucson, Arizona; Women's Hospital, Los Angeles, California; University of California Hospital, San Diego, California; D.C. General Hospital, Washington, District of Columbia; Jackson Memorial Hospital, Miami, Florida; City and County of Honolulu Department of Health, Honolulu, Hawaii; Cook County Hospital, Chicago, Illinois; Broadlawns Polk County Hospital, Des Moines, Iowa; Baton Rouge General Hospital, Baton Rouge, Louisiana; Butterworth Hospital, Grand Rapids, Michigan; St. Mary's Hospital, Grand Rapids, Michigan; Hennepin County General Hospital, Minneapolis, Minnesota; St. Paul–Ramsey Hospital, St. Paul, Minnesota; Kansas City General Hospital and Medical Center, Kansas City, Missouri; Southern Nevada Memorial Hospital, Las Vegas, Nevada; Bernalillo County Medical Center, Albuquerque, New Mexico; Edward J. Meyer Memorial Hospital, Buffalo, New York; Medical College of Ohio, Toledo, Ohio; The Toledo Hospital, Toledo, Ohio; McKennan Hospital, Sioux Falls, South Dakota; Medical Center Hospitals, Norfolk, Virginia; Norfolk Community Hospital, Norfolk, Virginia; Medical College of Virginia, Richmond, Virginia; St. Mary's Hospital Medical Center, Madison, Wisconsin; Madison General Hospital, Madison, Wisconsin; Methodist Hospital of Madison, Madison, Wisconsin.

Rape Crisis Centers: Bay Area Women Against Rape, Berkeley, California; Sacramento Women Against Rape, Sacramento, California; Rape Counseling Team, Mental Health Center of Boulder County, Boulder, Colorado; Rape Crisis

Center, Washington, District of Columbia; Tallahassee Rape Crisis Service, Florida State University, Tallahassee, Florida; Chicago Women Against Rape, Chicago, Illinois; University of Maryland Hot Line, College Park, Maryland; Rape Crisis Center, Cambridge, Massachusetts; Women's Crisis Center, Ann Arbor, Michigan; Rape Counseling Center, Neighborhood Involvement Program, Minneapolis, Minnesota; Rape Crisis Center of New Mexico, Albuquerque, New Mexico; New York Women Against Rape, New York, New York; Chapel Hill Women's Assault Line, University of North Carolina, Chapel Hill, North Carolina; Women Organized Against Rape, Philadelphia, Pennsylvania; Rhode Island Rape Crisis Center, Providence, Rhode Island; Roanoke Rape Crisis and Information Line, Roanoke, Virginia; Rape Relief Program of the University of Washington YWCA, Seattle, Washington.

To Our Sisters:

While recognizing the seriousness of rape and its potential for manifold damage—psychological as well as physical—we must not fall into the cliché of regarding rape as "a fate worse than death." Rape victims, like those who suffer other violent injuries, need to deal with emotional effects. But rape must not be considered a lifetime burden, and we should guard against making "permanent" victims of females who are assaulted.

This problem is often overlooked by those who, in their efforts to overcome public lethargy about sex crimes, may unconsciously reinforce concepts of rape as irrevocably "staining," "damaging," and "soiling" women. Rape, atrocious as it is, is not usually the worst thing—short of death—that can happen to a human being. Righteous anger must not blind us to the healthy possibilities of individual assimilation.

Nancy Gager and Cathleen Schurr
Washington, D.C., August 26, 1975

CONTENTS

INTRODUCTION

Rape is a four letter word that was proscribed in polite conversation a generation ago. Even legislatures and judges avoided the word. The statute law was written by a medieval parliament at Westminster. The common law remained for a long time as it was left by antique English judges.

But attitudes toward rape have changed. It is now the subject of articles in the popular press and interviews on radio and television. The United States Congress has debated and legislated on the subject. State legislatures and municipal councils are following the Congressional lead. For the first time in centuries we are questioning the way in which the law has treated both rapists and their victims. The victims themselves, who would have retreated into lifetime seclusion in the past, are coming forward to discuss their experience and what it has done to them.

Granting the broad change in society's general attitudes, what has directed specific attention to the crime of rape?

I believe it is the accumulating evidence of the law's cruelty to the victims of rape. The parents of a young girl have said that their daughter was more pained and injured by her treatment by a prosecuting attorney in a criminal court than by the attack itself. Parents like these have cried out for changes. Then there is the kind of mother like the one who visited me after her daughter was killed in a sex attack. The mother wanted her daughter's death to contribute to a sense of urgency about the need to change social attitudes toward rape.

As is often the case, the public was ahead of government in this matter. Women especially, as victims of rape, became increasingly concerned and active in pioneering studies and programs. A forerunner of today's nationwide movement against rape was Cathleen Schurr, who in 1971 published a series of newspaper articles on the rape situation in Pittsburgh, Pennsylvania. In 1972, Schurr was joined in Washington, D.C., by another professional writer active in the women's movement, Nancy Gager. In June 1973, Gager and Schurr published their investigations on rape in the Washington metropolitan area, and that September testified at the innovative D.C. City Council hearings on rape.

Rape is an extremely complex and emotion-laden subject. My national bill, introduced in the Senate in 1973, was greeted at first with smirks and sly digs. By the time it reached the Senate floor as an amendment to a larger health bill, however, my proposal had twenty-five co-sponsors and was adopted unanimously.

I hope that adoption of this proposal by both houses of the U.S. Congress marks a fundamental departure from the medieval concept of the crime of rape. If it does nothing more than ease the burdens which the victims of rape have been forced to bear in the past, it will be a major legislative success. I am confident that such changes have the potential to do much more, and constitute a major challenge to all of our people to apply the best of our scientific knowledge to the prevention of this crime and the total rehabilitation of its victims.

When I first began work on my anti-rape bill, the first modern legislation on this problem, I was fortunate to have the early articles by Schurr and Gager. Their later work and travel directed toward a national rape project brought them into contact with individuals and organizations working to end rape and help its victims in nearly every state. Now the results of their detailed investigations are available to the general public in this comprehensive, insightful book on rape and related sex crimes: *Sexual Assault: Confronting Rape in America*. Every reader should come away from this book with a new understanding of rape and a fresh determination to end it.

Charles McC. Mathias, Jr.
Member, U.S. Senate

SEXUAL ASSAULT: Confronting RAPE in America

1
EVERYWOMAN
AS VICTIM

Violence against women is endemic in America. It takes many forms—sexual, physical, verbal, and, underlying all, psychological. Of the multiple assaults by men on women, none are more feared, none more vicious or traumatic, than the crimes of rape and sexual brutality.

Rape is the number-one crime against American women today, and it is increasing at a shocking rate. Forcible rape is the fastest growing crime among the FBI's major crime categories, which include murder, aggravated assault, and robbery. Between 1969 and 1974, the number of reported rapes leaped a horrifying 49 percent. Across the nation about 55,000 rapes are now reported annually. This means that a reported rape occurs every ten minutes in this country.

But these figures, compiled by the Department of Justice, are only a part of a gigantic whole, since they include only rapes and not other sex crimes against women. In addition, only rapes reported to the authorities and *accepted* as such are included. Many reported assaults are dismissed and never tallied. For every recorded forcible rape, there are probably five to ten sexual attacks upon females that are not reported. Thus the *actual number* of sexual assaults on females of all ages may reach half a million or more a year, or at least one every two minutes. Each year, the FBI acknowledges in its Uniform Crime Reports that its rape statistics *must* be low, because "law enforcement administrators recognize that fear and/or embarrassment on the

1

part of the victims" cause them and their families to conceal the most profound criminal humiliation of their lives.

Rape—A Working Definition

The word "rape" is one of the most misused words in the English language. For centuries it has been employed symbolically, and its symbolic use—the "rape" of the land; the "rape" of the earth, the sea, or the sky; or the "rape" of a country or economy—has ironically come to carry more weight and drama than its true definition. Historically, the literal definition of rape is specific; it is a crime, usually a felony, in which the criminal (male) compels a victim (female) to submit to penile–vaginal sexual intercourse against her will, with or without the use of force, fear, or fraud. Other forms of forcible sexual assaults, such as oral or anal sodomy by males upon females are excluded from the traditional definition of rape. However, since such sexual attacks on women increasingly accompany the reported *and* unreported rapes, a contemporary definition of rape should include these other crimes, considered by many victims to be more traumatic and humiliating than the historically limited penile–vaginal attacks.

Incest—the crime of sexual intercourse between close relatives—often involves the rape of young children, but it is not part of the statistical picture of what is known as rape. Nor is the dubiously designated "statutory" rape. "Statutory" rape means sexual relations with a female, with or without her consent, who is considered under the age at which she is capable of consent. State laws arbitrarily determine the age at which female children are considered capable of consenting to sexual intercourse and they reflect local and regional prejudices and preferences in attitudes toward females. Delaware said a female of *seven* was capable of giving consent (in 1973 it was changed to twelve) and up until about twenty years ago, Tennessee thought a woman had to be twenty-one before she could legally agree to sexual relations. Many states consider a woman under the age of eighteen to be a child, incapable of giving consent.

On only one aspect of rape do these regional eccentricities fuse in agreement; although married women may be raped by their husbands, no state permits a woman to charge her husband with this crime. Indeed, most American states specifically exclude the male spouse from liability under their rape laws. Within the bonds of holy matrimony, "carnal knowledge," as so many state statutes define sexual intercourse, becomes magically and automatically "lawful," even if force, fear, or fraud is used to intimidate the wife.

This book deals with rape established in the historical context of sexual aggression against females young and old. We shall not be concerned with rape of men *by* men, though some states have begun to revise their sexual conduct laws to apply equitably to males and females.

We shall concentrate on the rape-prone environment that teaches us that women want to be dominated and raped and that all males have the right to be sexually aggressive toward all females. We shall also focus on the many ways in which women allow themselves to be victimized by accepting seemingly minor sexual and social transgressions by males. Thus we are concerned first and foremost with the socially approved female passivity that prevents so many women from making clear choices, including the choice of individual or individuals with whom they will mate. Since until recently the sexuality of women has been defined *only* by men, or disciples of males, many of us still accept this definition of our sexual needs, drives, and fulfillment. As women grow more and more able to make their own choices and decisions, these definitions will change, and we shall no longer need to apologize to men for rejecting them.

Rape—Who Are the Victims?

Any discussion of rape must begin with the object of the attack—the victim. Yet until very recently rape victims were the least studied and understood, invariably given the lowest priority in the few research projects undertaken on rape.

Rape victims are Everywoman—and all too often, Everychild. The tragic fact of man's inhumanity to woman touches every female, whether or not she is directly attacked herself. In hundreds of ways, large and small, the persistent threat of rape insidiously molds a woman's life and continually assaults her emotions. Women hesitate to go out at night without an escort; they fear living alone, working late in lonely offices, hitchhiking (with or without companions), traveling into strange places, doing new and different kinds of jobs, and working in fields and areas traditionally dominated by men. The fear of sexual attack has served to deny personal freedom to women and at the same time to increase their dependency upon men.

Despite the popular fantasy of rape as the crime of a sex-crazed maniac, perpetrated upon a flimsily clad, seductive female stranger, many victims are at least casually acquainted with the offender. Women have been raped by men they loved and trusted—by their fiancés or by men whom they dated (either casually or not so casually). They have been raped by coworkers, bosses, clients, office acquaintances, and men with whom they have only a nodding acquaintance— maintenance men, deliverymen, janitors and guards. As for the rape of women by their spouses, women have been so indoctrinated in the belief that conjugal (sexual) rights apply solely to husbands, that only recently, largely through the impact of the growing women's movement, have they begun to realize that they, too, are sexually victimized.

Contrary to popular opinion, which tends to think of rape victims as young and nubile, victims range from the very young to the very old. Police records show that children have been sexually assaulted in their cribs; grandmothers and great-grandmothers in their seventies, eighties, and nineties have been raped. Rapists attack the rich and the poor, all races and nationalities. Minority women, such as Blacks, Chicanos, American Indians and Orientals, are probably victimized most often. Probably they also report rape the least. Like most crimes of violence, rape occurs most frequently among the poor.

Rape usually occurs indoors, often in the homes and bedrooms of the victims. At other times women have been sexually assaulted in cars, or in public places, such as office buildings, women's restrooms, libraries, parking garages and public parks. Many have been assaulted in front of their young children, their husbands, and their grown sons and daughters. Daughters have been raped before their mothers. Wealthy women have been attacked in their elegant mansions; other women have been dragged out of cars and raped while their dates were forced to watch.

Increasingly women have been raped while going about their daily routine—housewives in their homes doing morning chores, women using facilities in apartment building laundries, students lured into cars while waiting at a bus stop, nurses on the late shift, librarians in book stacks, office workers going to and from their jobs, mothers and homemakers in suburbia, and older women living alone in cities. While statistically there are more rapes in urban centers having a population of over 250,000, sexual assaults are increasing in suburbia.

These victims, the forgotten "who" of rape—the middle-aged and the elderly, the children and the "Third World" women—those who have been silent and ignored are our concern here.

We shall look at "how" and "where" victims are trapped: the ruses, the break-ins, the assaults in public places, and the carefully planned attacks on hitchhikers. Finally, we shall look at the ultimate in cowardice: rapes by pairs, by groups, and by gangs, those male bonding units that provide the spurious courage required to brutalize females.

The following events occurred in various parts of the country. The words are often those of the victims, but some are recounted by a close friend or acquaintance. Since many of the criminals who perpetrated these tragedies have not been arrested or brought to trial, the victims' identities are protected in all cases. Indeed, many victims divulged these incidents reluctantly, and then only after our promise that no one would ever know where they took place. We respect the confidence of these sisters who have suffered so much at the hands of a sexist society.

The Victims: The Middle-aged and the Elderly

My mother wouldn't have talked about it, even if she had lived. But anybody who thinks rape is a sex thing should have seen her. She was almost unrecognizable, beaten and bruised over her whole body. She was raped and strangled in her own home during the daytime. And the suspect is a fifteen-year-old.

—Daughter of eighty-year-old victim

I'm a nurse. I was in the apartment garage getting my car out to go to work. The doors were locked. But a young man who seemed to be in trouble came over to my car, and I rolled down the window to talk to him. He pulled out a knife and forced me out of the car. After he raped me, he beat me with an iron pipe. Rapists are full of hate, especially toward women. It isn't sex they want; it's cruelty and violence.

—Sixty-year-old victim

I was asleep in my bed. I woke in the middle of the night because someone jumped on me. I couldn't see him in the dark. I started screaming. He put a blanket over my head. I thought I was going to be killed. I remember thinking "this is the way I am going to die. . . ." He started doing crazy things, saying "let's see how you like this." He was playing with my breasts and then he made me open my mouth and put his thing in it. He made me keep my hands away from my mouth and he stuck it down so far that I gagged. It was just awful. He turned me over and tried my back end. Then he raped me the regular way . . . when he finished he told me to keep the blanket over my head for half an hour and if I took it off he would finish me. Finally I dared to take the blanket off and called the police. They said I was lucky to be alive. When I went to the hospital I had a lot of bruises on my face, my neck, my chest and back. I had a two-inch stab wound in my abdomen. What did I do to deserve this?

—Sixty-five-year-old mother of three

You'd think you'd be safe in the middle of an afternoon in your own home on an army base. I was alone, bending over the tub washing my hair. He came up behind me and threw a jacket over my head. We struggled; he slipped on the water on the floor; and then he knocked me down. When I screamed, he bit me. I remember begging him, "Please don't kill me!" and I went on screaming and fighting. Then I remembered that struggling can excite this kind of criminal so I just kind of gave up because I didn't want to die. When the telephone began ringing I guess he got scared and ran away. A neighbor heard my screams and called the police. They came right away. They caught him not long afterward. He'd come to the house to rob us; he'd stolen from us before—money and valuables, they found the stuff in his barracks. I'm convinced that talking about the experience so women will know what it's like is important. Holding it in is harmful. Women have been made to feel ashamed and guilty about being raped, as though they were somehow to blame, or that they encouraged it. I feel sorry for women who don't have understanding husbands—as I did—or friends and relatives to talk to. I feel especially sorry for young women who have to convince everybody they didn't "ask" for it. No woman "asks" to be raped. No woman.

—Middle-aged victim, wife of top military official

The Victims: The Children

> We are seeing more abused child patients than ever before
> in the 103-year history of Children's Hospital. . . . We
> must extend our definition of child abuse to include rape,
> molestation, indecent exposure, sodomy, aggravated as-
> sault, kidnapping and homicide. . . . We live in a
> violence-oriented society; we need to teach our fellow citi-
> zens not to flush out their anger and frustrations on our
> children.
>
> —John H. Sharon, attorney, Vice-President of Children's
>   Hospital, National Medical Center, Washington, D.C.

> I was coming home from school on the bus. Two boys got
> on. One was from around the neighborhood, but I didn't
> really know him. He came over and introduced the other
> boy to me. They asked to see me again. I said maybe and
> went home and had dinner. Afterward I left the apartment
> and got into the elevator. They were there. One put his
> hand over my eyes, and the other held a knife at my throat.
> They pushed me out of the building and took me to another
> building in the complex. One boy had a key to an apartment
> there, and they took me inside. They asked me if I had ever
> been touched before, and was I scared. One boy said if I
> cooperated everything would be okay. He said I had three
> choices: jump out the window, get my ass kicked, or give
> them what they wanted. I cooperated. I didn't want to get
> killed.
>
> —Thirteen-year-old victim

> I never thought of those experiences, at the time, as rape.
> I just thought: "That's how things are—just an unwanted
> fuck." The first time I was a virgin. My parents had met the
> guy. They thought he was nice; so did I. He did it on our
> second date in the back seat of his car. He was a foot taller
> than me and weighed about 200 pounds; he about tore
> out my insides. I was afraid to tell my parents because
> they wouldn't have let me go away to college. The second
> time was while I was in college, a black man I was dating. I
> went through a lot of guilt about it. I come from a white

middle-class neighborhood, and I didn't want to hurt a black man by turning him over to the police. Even when I discovered I was pregnant, I couldn't report. I was into drugs, and I knew no doctor or cop would give a damn. I miscarried, fortunately. Then I got counseling and therapy and help from women who weren't shocked by me. It has taken me almost five years to be able to talk about it.

—Victim at fifteen and seventeen

I was about nine years old when my father first began to come to my bedroom, which I shared with my two sisters at night. He would touch my breasts and private parts. This was usually when my mother went to the movies or when she was in the living room with my sisters looking at TV or taking a shower. That same year my father began to put his penis into my private parts. It was very painful to me when he started. My father said this was normal and all girls did this with their fathers to learn how to do it. When I said I was going to tell my mother or someone else about it, he said that what my mother did not know would not hurt her. Sometimes he hit me when I refused. Sometimes he took me in the car, and as we rode, touched my vagina.

—Police statement from fourteen-year-old victim

My mother was an alcoholic and I guess my father was too. But she was very strict. She locked me in a closet when I said bad things and beat me with a stick. When I began to menstruate, my father used to massage my legs at night to relieve the terrible cramps caused by the hormones I had to take to stop weeks of continuous bleeding.

My father's massages soon went beyond my legs, to my breasts and genitals. I felt it was wrong, but I couldn't stop him. I liked to be stroked and loved. I used to go to bed wearing only my pajama tops, hoping my father would come and caress me. One night he came in and the liquor smell was terrible. He ripped off the covers and pulled my legs apart and jammed his penis into me. I thought I was splitting apart and began to scream. He put his hand over my mouth and then a pillow. I began to retch and vomit. The next thing I remember was sitting on the toilet, my father was standing there at the basin, running water over his bloody penis. My mother was standing in the doorway, laughing, drunk or hysterical, or maybe both, I don't know. I remember being angry at her for laughing when he was bleeding so badly. It was only when I tried to get up that I found I was bleeding myself. I couldn't figure out what had happened to me except that I felt ripped apart and there was a hole burning inside me. After a few days my father took me to a hospital and there an old man, a doctor, I guess, scraped my insides and it was terrible. I never talked about it, and I kept it buried and forgotten until it wouldn't be suppressed any longer. After two miserable marriages I got into group therapy. Then the repression of years came to the surface, and I was able to face the horror.

—Victim at eleven

The Victims: Minority Women

All women have a problem establishing their credibility with the police, medical professions, and courts. Dark-skinned women—Blacks, Chicanos, Native Americans and Orientals—have a special problem because of racist attitudes. We know that dark-skinned women get raped more often than white and don't report it rather than subject themselves to further abuse.

—La Donna Harris, President of Americans
for Indian Opportunity

I was beaten and raped in a state away from my home. I went to the police even though the man had threatened to kill me if I told. The cops asked a lot of awful questions, like how did I like it and was he any good? The cops kept asking me if my boyfriend was the rapist, I guess because I was honest enough to say that I had had sex with my boyfriend. They seemed to think that because I wasn't a virgin it couldn't be rape and I should charge him only with assault and battery. They caught the rapist but he left town before the trial. At the hospital nobody treated me any better. I had to wait two hours before anyone would see me. When I asked about VD and pregnancy, they told me to see a private physician. The hospital was angry because I had no cash to pay them. As a result of all this, my boyfriend refused to marry me. If you're Chicano and on welfare, nothing can help you.

—Twenty-three-year-old victim

I know a case in which the police caught three men *in the act* of raping a black woman who had been a prostitute some twenty years before. At the hearing, the judge dwelt on her former life, not on the rape by the three men. The men were exonerated.

—Black attorney

I was raped at knifepoint in my apartment. I decided quickly that nonresistance would save my life. The police kept referring to the rape as "making love." I refused to go to the general hospital which takes rape victims; as a minority woman I knew I wouldn't get good treatment. The hospital they took me to gave me specialist help, which was good. For months that rapist's face kept popping up in front of me; my fiancé married someone else. He couldn't understand why I didn't have any bruises. I still can't sleep nights. I'm afraid of everything. And I can't afford to move from the apartment where it happened.

—Thirty-one-year-old victim

She was fifteen. She lives in a black community which prides itself on its "upper class" image and refers to poor blacks as "niggers." She was raped twice. Her mother wouldn't talk to me because she was so ashamed. I got the story from a black policeman and a black inspector. The day after I printed the story—without naming names but indicating the section of town to point up the lack of police protection there—my paper was flooded with angry telephone calls from residents. They said I had given their neighborhood a "bad name," and that the girl had "brought it on herself."

—Black woman, newspaper editor

He was a white truck driver from a nearby town. He grabbed my sixteen-year-old daughter on a street corner while she was waiting for a bus. He took her away out in the country and made her do terrible things, and then he raped her. My husband said there wasn't any point in reporting it to the police—white people think all Indian women are fair game. We're second-class citizens; that's what we're born for. They think it doesn't mean anything to us, but my daughter hasn't been the same since it happened.

—Chippewa tribeswoman

It was my first week on the force; there weren't many black cops around town in those days. A black woman came staggering into the station house. Her dress was ripped to shreds, her face was black and blue, and there were bruises and blood on the rest of her body. She said she'd been raped. Nobody listened. She got jailed for disorderly conduct.

—Black precinct chief

Trapping the Victim: The Knock on the Door

Apparently, in the eyes of the court, allowing a male into your home implies consent for him to have sexual intercourse with you. The courts apparently see that opening your front door to a man means that the vagina is opened to his penis. As brash and boorish as these conclusions may sound, we must understand they constitute the thinking of the society and the courts, not of women. One man can visit another in his home, beat him up in an argument, and the male victim can charge him with assault. Yet a woman who has been raped in her home by a male friend need not press charges because no court will believe she did not consent.

—From *Stop Rape*, pamphlet published by
Women Against Rape, Detroit, Michigan

He lived a few doors down the street from me, and I'd known him for several years. My kids knew him well. He was married, about twenty years older than me, with three children. Both he and his wife were very religious; they went to church and did a lot of praying. One night he knocked on my door around 9:30 P.M. He said his wife had locked him out and he wanted to use my telephone. We talked at the door. He said he felt bad and needed something to drink, so I let him come in and made him a cup of tea in the kitchen. Afterward the newspaper headlined the story with something about a "tea party" turned into rape!

He kept staring at me. I was wearing pants and a T-shirt; and he said I ought to put some clothes on. I guess he meant a bra. I went into the bedroom, and he followed and threw me down on the bed. I screamed and the kids came running. They began to yell, and he told them he'd kill them if they didn't shut up. I wouldn't take my pants off like he said, so he ripped them off me. He weighs about 180 pounds. I weigh 110. He started to choke me and cut off my breath. I got terrified and thought he's killing me, I am dying and he will kill my kids too (they were still yelling and screaming). He grabbed me by the pubic hair and threw me down on the floor and asked if that hurt. He seemed pleased when I said yes. I don't remember how long it lasted, or when he left, but finally I was alone and the kids were still screaming and I got to the phone and called a friend.

I went to court. There were endless postponements. First the defense tried to make me out as mentally incompetent and that I should see a court-appointed psychiatrist. That motion was denied. In court they tried to make out I didn't resist enough. But they had a sworn deposition from the examining doctor who said the strangulation marks on my neck were the worst wounds he had seen—outside of gun and knife wounds—in some thirty cases of rape. I'm divorced, so the accused's attorney subpoenaed my boyfriends for the past year and a half, but they didn't testify because they had nothing bad to say about me. The defendant's wife testified that I had been "flirting" with her husband and that I didn't supervise my kids, but the state attorney objected to that and it was stricken. (Later I found out that her own kids—they're five, seven, and eight—were picked up for shoplifting about three weeks before the trial.) The jury—nine women and three men—reached its verdict in about an hour. Not guilty.

Hating is a terrible thing, but after going through that circus in the courtroom it comes easy. . . . I was the one on trial. I never even had a traffic ticket, but my rapist had been arrested twenty-six previous times. Why can't the jury know things like that? Why weren't they told that he refused to take a lie-detector test, and I wanted to take one? For a man to brutally rape a woman in front of two small children and then walk away a free man is a sad reflection on society.

—Raped by "religious" neighbor

I answered the doorbell of my apartment at 8:30 one morning. A man there said he had information about my television set which had been stolen the day before. I let him in. When he got inside, he grabbed me around the neck and forced me into the bedroom. He put tape across my mouth, tied my wrists and legs, and put a blanket over my head and turned me on my stomach. He raped me anally. He threatened to kill me if I made any noise. I would have fought him but I was afraid for my kids; they're all pre-school age. After he left my five-year-old son came into the room holding a kitchen knife and said, "I was going to stab that man who was hitting you." He helped me get untied. . . . They never caught the rapist.

—Victim, mother of three

It was six o'clock on a summer evening, and I was getting ready to go to work. A young man, about sixteen, knocked on the door and asked if "John" were home. I said no and tried to shut the door. He pulled a knife, and despite my struggle, forced his way in. He searched the apartment, then blindfolded me and ripped my clothes off. He told me what he was going to do to me and ordered me to act like his "girl friend" and to tell him how much I liked everything. He talked a lot. First he raped me vaginally. Then he took me into the living room and put me on the floor on my stomach. He had rectal sex with me. It hurt so bad and he was so brutal, I cried and cried. He told me to shut up, except to say how much I liked everything he did. I thought I was going to die, and I wanted to die with dignity, not yelling and screaming. He shoved me into the bedroom and put a knife in my ribs and demanded that I "kiss his ass"—literally. Finally, he had an orgasm and I could stop. He tied me to a chair, still blindfolded, and left through a window.

I called the police from a friend's apartment because the rapist had cut my telephone wires. I phoned my office and left a message saying I couldn't go to work. (The next day my supervisor said I should have called her at home because my absence had caused a real problem in the office!) I went to my cousin's home for the weekend; I couldn't face going back to my apartment. I was in shock for a week. I was suspicious of everyone and paranoid with fear. Still I reported it, and the police found the man. The court case dragged out over most of the next year and I was in a bad state. I always had to have someone with me in the apartment or to walk me to the bus. In court, when the defense lawyer questioned me I fell apart. All the feelings I had had the night of the rape came back to me. The result was a hung jury. The defense lawyer kept saying I was blindfolded; how could I prove it was the same man? I had to prove it had actually happened. I was on trial, not him. I couldn't go through it again. I wish I'd never reported it. I was a virgin when it happened.

—Nineteen-year-old victim

He lived in my apartment building, and I kept meeting him in the elevator and the laundry room. He introduced himself, and one evening after several months of casual conversations, I accepted his invitation for a drink and dinner at his apartment. When I got there he said we'd go out for dinner and after a couple of drinks he began making advances. I left, telling him he had misinterpreted me. A couple of weeks later he knocked at my door and said he wanted to apologize. As soon as he was inside, he hit me in the face and called me "slut" and "whore." He knocked me down, tore off my pants, and despite my struggles, raped me. I got free and ran for the door. He grabbed me from behind, forced me to my knees, and jammed his penis up my anus. When he finished, he said, "I'm leaving now, slut!" The detective said it would be easy to get a conviction for assault, but because I let him in, it would be practically impossible to get a conviction for rape. I broke my lease and moved away. And I dropped the charges. What was the use? Men can do anything they want and get away with it. Women are always to blame. It's a lousy world.

—Raped by a neighbor

We had moved into a new apartment the day before. My husband had left for school, and I was about to go to work. Just before 8 A.M., a man knocked on the door and said he was an inspector there to check out the walls and ceiling. I let him in. He was over six feet tall and weighed close to 200. He seemed official. I went into the bedroom to get a coat and purse. When I came back into the living room, he had picked up a knife for cutting linoleum and rope from some packages. I screamed and he forced me back into the bedroom. He tied my hands with the rope and gagged my mouth with a bedsheet. Then he began tearing off my clothes, but suddenly stopped and asked where my money was, I told him it was in my purse in the other room. He told me to lie still and left me.

I got up and banged my head against the window until the glass broke. Some construction workers down below looked up and saw me. My hands were still tied and the gag was in my mouth. The rapist heard me and came back from the other room with the knife in his hand. He was going for me when he heard footsteps running up the hall stairs.

He ran out and the door locked behind him. He passed the construction workers on the stairs. They asked him what was going on and he said, "That girl's crazy," and dropped the knife and the cap he was wearing. He got away. Several men came to my door. My hands were tied and I was terribly embarrassed to be undressed in front of them, but at least I was still alive. The construction workers called the police for me. The man hasn't been caught, and I don't open the door any more without being sure who's there.

—Twenty-year-old attacked by "building inspector"

She was brought up in a small town where people left their doors open, their cars unlocked, and helped people in trouble. Later she lived in a big city housing complex with her husband and two children. One morning she answered a knock on her door. A young man, wearing construction worker's clothes, asked to use her phone because his "car had broken down." She let him in and he made a phone call. Afterward she mentioned that she and her husband wanted to sell their own car. Two days later the man returned to the apartment before her husband had left for work. He asked if he could bring a friend around that evening who might want to buy their car.

A few minutes after her husband had left for work, the man returned. When she opened the door, he confronted her with a knife and said that unless she submitted to him sexually, he would hurt the children sleeping in the next room. Terrified, she acquiesced. After raping her, the man left. She waited a day before telling her husband, feeling guilty for having let the man inside. Her husband was furious when she told him and they went to the police. But the police refused to act. They said she had admitted the criminal into the apartment and she had no cuts or bruises. Her word would not stand up in a court trial. Deeply depressed, the couple returned home.

Four days later the husband encountered the rapist on the street outside their apartment. Assuming the woman had not told her husband, the criminal started to approach him but fled when he saw the husband's angry face. A week later there was another knock on the apartment door. A man's voice said he was a mechanic come to repair the dishwasher. Trembling with fear, the woman refused to let him inside. The dishwasher was not broken, nor had she called a mechanic to repair it. Looking out a side window shortly afterward, she saw the alleged "repair man" talking on the sidewalk to the man who had raped her the week before!

Later that month, with his wife on the verge of a nervous collapse, the husband put his wife and children on a plane for Florida to stay with relatives. He found a job in another state and his family joined him. They will never return to the state where she suffered such brutality—not only by the rapist, but at the hands of the agencies of law enforcement.

—Reporter's notebook

Trapping the Victim: Breaking and Entering

Some of these fellows—the rapists—seem to get a big kick out of breaking and entering to do their dirty work. Obviously, it isn't sex they're after with the crazy chances they take. Besides, a lot of them, maybe most of them, have sex easily available—at home, on the streets, with friends.

—Police officer

I lived on the ground floor of an apartment complex. I woke up one night to find a strange man standing by my bed. I started screaming. He said he wouldn't hurt me, but I screamed again, and tried to get up. He pinned me down on the bed, and I saw a penknife in his hand. I don't think he really meant to hurt me, but in the struggle he cut my head. He said, "I've raped five women this week and three of them are alive because they were smart." I tried to argue him out of it. I told him I work for a judge in the law courts and he'd never get away with it. But I couldn't stop him. Afterward he had the nerve to say, "There that wasn't so bad, was it?" and I said, "You must be insane. You break into my apartment in the middle of the night and you think it isn't so bad for me?" Then he began questioning me about when I had to leave in the morning—he seemed to think I would let him stay the night! He was a weird kid, about nineteen. I heard later he was on mescaline.

I called the police as soon as he left. He had got in by cutting through a screen in the window. A few days later I moved out of the apartment. The police caught the rapist about two weeks later, when he tried to get into my old apartment again. One night after midnight a policeman who lived in the complex came down to empty his garbage and saw this fellow using a glass cutter on the same window where he'd gotten in before. The police officer caught him and arrested him. He turned out to be a G.I. from a nearby army base, and he came to the trial in full dress uniform. Despite two signed written confessions, the jury acquitted him on all three counts—rape, breaking and entering with intent to rape, and breaking and entering with intent to steal.

I can't express the utter amazement, shock, and subsequent depression I felt in this verdict. This criminal is now walking the streets. The detectives and attorneys had warned me, but I thought we had a foolproof case; he had confessed and I was positive of his identity. But his attorney produced a parade of seedy "relatives" who swore he was with them the night of the rape, and the jury took their word to mine. If one of my sisters told me she had been raped, I would take her to a doctor myself and advise her under no circumstances to report the crime.

—Victim, legal secretary

The police know him well—they call him "Gentleman George." He'd been operating in my district for about two years. He went cruising around a twenty-block area in my neighborhood every night for months. For some reason the police can't catch him, even though they think he's responsible for dozens of rapes.

I live on a second-floor apartment with a balcony. Normally, I never open the balcony windows at night, but on this night I did because the temperature was up to 90 degrees. Later the police told me the rapist had got in earlier and turned up the heat so I would be forced to open my window. He was a real pro. I'm a light sleeper, but he was in bed with me before I even knew he was in the apartment. He came in from the balcony, picked up a kitchen knife, and covered my face with my own poncho from my closet. There he was on top of me, naked. He even knew my name. Police say he makes a point of calling his victims by their first names. It's terrifying.

I screamed and he told me to be quiet. As soon as I stopped screaming, he dropped the knife. That's when I started fighting and screaming some more. The rapist picked up his clothes and ran to the balcony. Other tenants saw him running naked across the parking lot. The neighbors heard me and called the police. They came in a few minutes. It was the most terrifying experience of my life. I had a black eye, scratches and bruises. I was hysterical. The police had to wait three hours before I could answer questions. Still and all, I guess I was lucky. I might have been injured for life. Or I might have got killed. But "Gentleman George" is still at large."

—College student

Trapping the Victim: Rape in Public Places

Rape may be a private, lonely crime, but it often occurs in very public places—in community and apartment house laundries, city offices, and parks. Nurses and airline stewardesses have been attacked on their way to and from work; I know a librarian who was raped at knifepoint after having been forced from the library stacks to the public toilet by her assailant.

—Reporter's notebook

I was raped by a total stranger in my own office where I was working over the weekend. The inner and outer doors to the office building were supposed to be locked. My own office door was locked while I worked. But he caught me in the hall as I was leaving. He had a black ski hood over his head and a long knife in his hand. He forced me into the ladies' room and raped me on a dirty cot next to the wall while he kept the knife at my throat. Afterward he said he was "sorry" and he "had to do it that way." He took money from my purse and blamed me for leaving the door to the building unlocked. As soon as I got home I called the police. The policewoman who talked to me made it clear she didn't believe me. The hospital attendants also said they thought I hadn't resisted enough. Dear God, is a woman supposed to be killed before they will believe she was afraid for her life?

—Victim, raped in her office

I was attacked in the laundry of the apartment where I live. The man lived in another building in the complex. I had seen him there doing his laundry before, but we had never spoken. On this particular evening he asked me if I was married. I said yes, and he grinned and said, "But you don't wear a wedding ring." I said, "You do, but it doesn't seem to make any difference," and turned to leave. He grabbed me from behind. He was tall and heavy and he had my neck in a stranglehold. I jerked away and got free, but he came after me and slapped me. I slapped him back, and he let fly a stream of obscenities. I think my fighting back threw him off. He hadn't expected a fight. He yelled at me, "You goddamn whore, you know you want it, you know you like it, you bitch, you bitch . . ." Then he grabbed my hair and I bit him, but he forced me to the floor, calling me "whore" over and over again. He weighed at least 200 pounds, and he was over six feet tall. I must have gone into shock. I don't remember how I got back to the apartment. My husband wasn't there, and I don't remember calling the police. The court case was ludicrous. Dismissed on a technicality. After it was all over one of the assistant district attorneys asked me if the assault was "with my approval?"

—Anti-rape task force leader

She was raped one morning while walking her two large dogs in a small elegant park near her exclusive District of Columbia townhouse. She was middle-aged, strong and athletic, the wife of a high state department official. Four teen-agers jumped and yoked her from behind. Three of them dragged her up a steep bank and repeatedly raped her, while the fourth held her dogs and stood watch. The humiliation she suffered later at the hands of hospital attendants caused her to make a public outcry, and the publicity resulted in improved hospital procedures. She has since left the country. Her assailants were never caught.

—Reporter's notebook

I had worked late and on the way home stopped to pick up something at the drugstore. I parked my car in the shopping center parking lot, near the store. Since it was so close, I didn't lock it. When I came out of the store and got into the car, a man rose up from the back seat and at gunpoint ordered me into the back seat, where he blindfolded and gagged me. Then he drove a long distance, to a wooded area. He raped me twice on a blanket which he spread on the ground. I never reported. I was afraid I could not positively identify him. The next day I saw my gynecologist and he agreed with me. Now I feel guilty about not reporting, leaving the rapist free to hurt other women. Emotionally, I've never recovered from the rape.

I'm afraid of all men; I can't work overtime any more and I'm afraid of the dark. I can't go to sleep without several lights on.

—Parking-lot victim

Trapping the Victim: Rape on the Highway

So tempting a target is the hitchhiker that some criminals regularly patrol roads frequented by hitchhikers, usually near universities and colleges. Many highway rapists prepare for their victims in advance, removing inside car door handles and hiding male accomplices on the rear floor out of sight. The actual assault site often has been selected in advance.

—West Coast detective

My girl friend and I had both hitched a lot. . . . We'd been on the road for about two weeks when it happened. Two men in their forties picked us up, gave us a long ride, and took us to lunch. Then suddenly one of them opened the glove compartment and took out a gun. At gunpoint they took us to a motel. The big guy—he must have weighed over 200 pounds—got in one bed with me. I kept resisting until he started to strangle me. He forced me to give him a blow job, and he kept saying, "You really like this, don't you? You really enjoy it, don't you?" and he threatened to attack my friend who was in the other bed with the other man unless I did everything he wanted. Afterward they told us they always worked that way —driving around, picking up girls, and spending money on them with meals and Cokes and then having sex with them. That's what he called it. We called it rape. But we didn't report it. My friend was only fifteen, and my family would have had a fit. Besides, the police don't care about people like me. They say if you hitch you're asking to be raped.

—Eighteen-year-old victim, high school dropout

Highway rapists enjoy a certain advantage. Hitchhike rapes don't command much attention by the police or the courts. Juries don't have sympathy for the girl who hitches. Neither do judges. They seem to think that if a girl thumbs a ride, she's asking to be attacked. I've hitched all over Europe and this country. I know the danger, but I don't intend to stop. What kind of justice is it when you lock up the victim of a crime instead of the criminal?

—Law student

I know victims trapped on the highway while trying to be helpful. The man would park his car at the side of the road with the hood up indicating engine trouble. In one case, he flagged for help and asked the woman to drive him to a service station. Then he pulled a gun on her and raped her. Another time the woman stopped to offer help, and while she was looking at the motor he flashed a knife. Both crimes were committed in daylight hours. It is an appalling commentary on today's society. Today's Good Samaritan, if she's female, is a potential rape victim.

—Reporter's notebook

In Boulder, Colorado, in 1972, nearly 70 percent of all rape victims were hitchhikers; in Boston, 33 percent. Almost a third of the Berkeley, California, rapes during the first two months of 1973 were hitchhikers. Many victims are brutally murdered—many of them chronic and fearless hitchhikers.

—Newspaper account

She was hitchhiking with two male companions from Ohio to Florida to attend a rock festival. They were picked up at midnight on a major highway by three men in a station wagon who were drinking beer. One of the drinkers suddenly took a pistol from the glove compartment, pointed it at the girl's two companions, and ordered her into the rear of the station wagon. Two of the beer drinkers then raped her. As soon as the hitchhikers were let out of the car, fortunately near a phone, the girl and her companions notified the police. In the court trial, the defense attorney's main argument was that the victim had by her "life-style"—hitchhiking with two male friends, and her occasional use of drugs—outlawed herself from the protection of rape laws. The jury convicted. One defendant appealed. Appellate Judge Daniel T. Prettyman of Maryland affirmed the conviction, stating, ". . . no matter how loose the morals of a woman may be, she still enjoys the privilege of bestowing her favors upon those men of her own selection and not upon others whom she does not select."

—Court records, *Bailey* v. *State*, 294 A. 2d 123 (1972)

Trapping the Victim: Pairs and Gangs

To rape a girl in company with other men presumably says something about shared maleness and shared sexuality, about camaraderie and about the place of women in relationship to men . . . the apparent increase of such activity may indicate a growing masculine need to establish sexual identity and sexual superiority. . . .

—Ph.D. Gilbert Geis, sociologist

I had recently been divorced. I went fishing with two men with whom I had worked for years. I trusted them. They ended the outing by beating me up and raping me. I didn't report. They told me that if I went to the police they would stick together and claim they both had had sexual relations with me for years. But I went to a doctor because I had been so badly beaten.

—Raped by "old friends"

Gangbang Calendar: Friday morning—two men arrested at the racetrack for abducting and raping a fifteen-year-old girl and holding her captive for a week in various city apartments. Friday afternoon—eight youths grab sixteen-year-old high school student walking home from school, drag her into a car, and repeatedly rape her. Following Tuesday afternoon—six female members of a street gang kidnap two teen-age girls, drag them to a basement where ten youths rape and sodomize them. Tuesday evening—nine youths abduct thirteen-year-old girl on the street near her home, take her to their gang headquarters where they all rape her.

—Newspaper accounts

I was a virgin. I thought I was going out with one fellow from the college, but there were two others in the car. I was so scared I was numb. I submitted because I was afraid to do anything else. Besides, there were three of them, all stronger and bigger than I was. The police told me I had no grounds to prosecute because I couldn't prove I was forced. There was no gun and I wasn't beaten. It taught me that there was nothing good in sex for a woman. After that I just put out because I knew that if I didn't fellows wouldn't ask me out. For years I never told anyone, and my guilt grew and grew. It wasn't until I had become a member of the National Organization for Women and began to trust other women for the first time in my life that I found out other women had had the same experience. All of us felt it was our own fault because we'd done something "dumb." Instead of concentrating on the rapists we had turned it in on ourselves. We'd all been trained to give in to someone bigger and stronger. Besides, everything works in the man's favor; if we submit out of fear, he turns around and says we asked for it—and the police and the courts believe him, not us.

—Gang-raped as college freshman

My girl friend and I were at a party and these two fellows asked to drive us home. But there were a couple of other guys in the car; they were all pretty drunk. They took my friend home, but they refused to take me home. Instead they took me to this motel. They threw me down and tore my clothes off and raped me. I never stopped crying even when they hit me. I asked them why they didn't get someone willing, like a prostitute; but they said they didn't want a prostitute, they wanted me. So one after another they raped me. I kept crying and screaming, and finally after it was all over, they carried me back to the car and drove me home.

—Twenty-year-old gang victim

These personal stories represent only a fraction of those we heard while researching this book. While the circumstances of the rapes vary, all the victims share to some extent the damaging psychological effects of the assailants' hatred and brutality. In most cases rape, a traumatic experience in itself, is followed by soul-shattering despair and discouragement. This despair is often unexpressed and lies festering, deeply suppressed, and unrecognized by the woman herself until years afterward.

The problem extends beyond the sexual assault to a society that encourages sexual aggression by men and endorses passivity among women. It is this socially approved passivity that so often results in the victimizing of women. This passivity has nothing whatever to do with the recently invented "victim precipitated" forcible rape. This term is an academician's substitute for the popular myth that "women bring rape upon themselves" and part of the ancient process whereby male rapists receive, if not total absolution, at least partial forgiveness.

The more subtle forms of sexual subjugation— spurious forms of belittlement and familiarity such as baby, honey, gal, doll, sweetie, sugar, dearie, and, now, the highly polarized "mama" (reminding recalcitrant women, perhaps, of biological obligations?) and all the other casual physical intimacies that men characteristically allow themselves, even with women who are total strangers—are a form of verbal and social rape insofar as women are unable *easily* to reject them. Not until we can free ourselves from unquestioning, quiet, guilt-ridden acceptance of these seemingly innocent familiarities can we begin to reduce the more blatant crime of rape itself.

The following story illustrates how this socially conditioned passivity and guilt get in the way even of a strong woman who refused to be made into a rape victim:

Sarah is a graduate student, agile and athletic, well able to take care of herself in the many foreign countries where she has traveled alone. Her mother is a nationally known professional woman, her father a high government official. Her parents were away when Sarah received an invitation to a cocktail party given by a man whom we shall call Walter, a wealthy industrialist friend of her parents. At the party, he pressed her to stay after the other guests had left because he had something "important to say to her, alone." The thought that this relic of another generation would attack her never entered her mind.

But after the guests had left, Walter threw himself on top of Sarah, his bald head glistening with sweat, while he hoarsely declared his sexual intentions. She weighed about 95 pounds; he weighed at least twice that. She struggled furiously; but the more she fought, the more violent he became. During the struggle the phone rang, and Walter, ever loathe to let pleasure interfere with business, paused to answer it. Sarah seized the moment and raced for the hall.

Wrenching open the apartment door, she had second thoughts. Walter was an old friend of her parents, a successful and prominent businessman whom she had known since childhood. She had rejected him. She must have embarrassed him; she felt sorry for him. So just before she raced for the stairs—faster than waiting for the elevator, her alerted mind told her—she paused and called back over her shoulder: "Nothing personal, Walter!"

Sarah's experience illustrates the fact that rape is a crime of intimidation—and some women are more easily intimidated than others. It is a bitter commentary on a society that has trained its women to apologize for refusing to be made into victims.

2
THE CHILDREN: TRAINING OUR DAUGHTERS FOR SILENCE

He is twice as big as I am . . . I can't fight him. I've seen him beat the hell out of my mother who's as big as he is.
— *Twelve-year-old incest victim*

When they told me Viola had been dishonored, I said I didn't want her back in the house, I was so shocked.
— *Father of child raped by neighbor*

I blame her more than I do him. It went on for a year before she told me.
— *Mother of preadolescent sexually abused by her father*

Nowhere among all the sexual crimes is the tragedy more outrageous—or more muted—than in the sexual abuse of children. These victims of adult sex offenders, most of whom are little girls, are society's least protected children. They are doubly victimized: first, by family and parental neglect, and second, by the country's consistent refusal to admit the dimensions of the problem.

The sexual abuse of children is simply unthinkable to a civilized person, who finds it easier to comprehend the despair of a battering parent (we have all raged at our children) than the actions of the sexual molester. And the usually silent child victim is a reminder of society's

29

inability, or unwillingness, to protect its defenseless young against the enemy within.

Information on the incidence of sex crimes against children is skimpy. While testifying before a United States Senate committee hearing in 1973, Dr. Vincent de Francis (director of the Children's Division of the American Humane Association, a national standard-setting agency on child abuse) estimated that some 100,000 children are sexually abused each year. Other estimates of child victims reach five or six times that figure. Nearly ten years ago, sociology professor Dr. John H. Gagnon, then a sex researcher at the late Alfred Kinsey's Indiana University Institute of Sex Research, calculated that as many as half a million little girls were sexually victimized in one way or another every year. More recent estimates go as high as a million cases annually. New York City, one of the few cities for which statistics are available, has some 3,000 cases each year. Officials in Santa Clara County, California, assert that the sexual abuse of children is much more common than child battery but that it comes to light much less often. Experts agree that the sexual victimization of children is probably far more prevalent than is popularly believed.

The reason for the silence is obvious. Little girls, like their mothers before them, learn at an early age to endure being sexually used. A few experiences with the disbelief, shock, shame, embarrassment and anger of those closest to them provide good training in silence.

The sexual abuse of girl children by adults runs from indecent exposure, molestation, carnal abuse, and impairing morals to sodomy, incest, and rape. Because these crimes are so personal and because they relate to areas in our culture that are interlarded with taboos and violent emotional impact, child victims often are exposed to traumatic stresses and tensions. The disastrous effect of silence and fear imposed by threatening adults—whether it comes from those close to the child, or from society at large—is beyond measure. Those who have worked with child victims (social workers, public health nurses, psychological counselors and others) indicate that child victims suffer enormous blocks in terms of suppressed terror, fear, guilt, shame, and loss of self-esteem.

But as in the case of grown women who are sexually victimized, other segments of our culture (notably certain social scientists, criminologists, psychiatrists, and psychologists) have tended to minimize the traumatic effects of such abuse. They insist that the deleterious effect on child victims has been exaggerated, both in terms of personality "development" and later adult "adjustment." Some even argue that sex relationships with an adult when the child is very young are actually beneficial.

These proponents of adult–child sex relationships are refuted by other experts such as Dr. Harry L. Kozol of Massachusetts. Dr. Kozol is director of psychiatry for the Department of Mental Health for the Commonwealth and director of the Center for Diagnosis and Treatment of Sexually Dangerous Persons at Bridgewater, Massachusetts. The center and its associates have studied some 3,700 sex offenders over the past ten years. Dr. Kozol says:

> In my experience a demonstrated sexual interest of an adult in a child of either sex is extremely ominous. Adult child molesters appear to suffer from an obsessive compulsive disorder which almost inexorably causes them to repeat their offenses. It is virtually certain that a child molester will repeat his molestation time and again.

Physical Damage

The few existing reports of the sexual abuse of children are singularly noncommunicative about the physical injuries of the children. Doctors, social workers, psychologists, and others in counseling fields have tended in their reports to speculate exclusively on psychological damage and to make only passing reference to the physical.

Apparently, therefore, we must direct attention to the obvious—the conspicuous difference in size between a grown male and small girl. The tiny vagina of a small girl cannot easily accommodate the full-grown penis of an adult male. Adult women who were sexually assaulted in childhood use expressions like, "I remember he tore my insides out," and, "It felt like I was splitting apart," indicating that, unlike the memory of a normal experience such as childbirth, the pain is remembered and felt with anguish long after the event.

Child victims suffer physical damage ranging all the way from vaginal lacerations, perineal tears or ruptures, severe bleeding and hemorrhage, to multiple bruises, abrasions, and bites, which may contain infection-causing dirt particles. There are also other obvious physical results of assault such as venereal disease or pregnancy to which young children, as well as adults, are vulnerable. Medical treatment for the child victim must be adapted to the little girl's size, as Dr. Vincent J. Capraro, clinical professor in gynecology and obstetrics at the State University in Buffalo, New York, points out. He urges doctors to use "proper small examining instruments" with little girls. Lacerations should be repaired under general anesthesia, he says, using "very fine catgut and very small needles." If a needle of the size used for adults is used on children to repair vaginal tears, the opening may be reduced "as much as 50 percent," Capraro warns. This advice to physicians and the medical fraternity is clear evidence of the special physical vulnerability of the young female.

But while Dr. Capraro may be genuinely concerned for the well-being of victims, he, like most members of his profession, sees future damage to the child victim predominantly in terms of what he calls "psychosexual" adjustment and adult psychosomatic "complaints." This orientation thus focuses on alleged "mental" attitudes and on the victim's sexuality, ignoring the fact that sexual assault may also result in physical injury.

Physical damage from childhood rapes can be far more serious and permanent than medical and health professionals indicate. This injury is in addition to the emotional traumas which send many young girls into mental hospitals for years—even for the rest of their lives. As grown women, victims may suffer painful complications in childbirth, lasting discomfort or distress in the bladder and anus, or spasmodic rigidity and accompanying pain in adult intercourse. None of these can be swept under the easy catchall rug of "emotional problems" or "psychosomatic ailments," which physicians and psychiatrists use to evade and ignore the very real physical agonies of raped children.

Many child rapes—apparently an increasing number of them—are accompanied not only by "ordinary" cuts, bruises, and broken bones but also by ghastly forms of sadism. Some children are murdered at the time of the attack; others die later of their injuries. One twelve-year-old girl, raped by the husband of a woman friend she was visiting, was left in a Detroit alley with a severely fractured skull and multiple lacerations. After a year in the hospital and a second year in a nursing home, she died.

In Chicago, workers in the Department of Human Resources encounter so many appalling cases of child assault that personnel are no longer assigned exclusively to juvenile victims. Said one veteran worker, "We'd never before had to plan funerals for children or to deal with the rape of youngsters. It was turning our own people into nervous wrecks."

In Washington, D.C.'s police headquarters, we were shown photographs of a nine-year-old girl who had been raped by her mother's "boyfriend" and then burned with cigarettes all over her buttocks. She now lies silently in a hospital bed, not speaking to the policewoman who brings her toys and tries to comfort her, shocked into the escape of psychosis. Another child

visited by a social worker friend had been literally
ripped apart in a family gang rape by her father, brother,
and two uncles. She required twenty-seven stitches in
her vaginal area. She spends her days humming word-
lessly to her doll, a vacuous smile on her small face.
Such examples, and some even more unspeakable, can
be given by the thousands and from every state in the
union.

The few existing studies on the sexual abuse of children agree on one fact: the number of child victims is
disproportionate. During the 1960s, in Washington,
D.C., Dr. Charles Hayman, then associate director for
Preventive Services of the Department of Human Resources, Health Services Administration, and public
health nurse Charlene Lanza collaborated on a project
study of the sex assault cases they had followed through
District of Columbia General Hospital and the police.
Their figures provide sad proof of the large percentage
of child victims.

In a single year (September 1965 to September 1966)
more than half the female rape victims referred by the
police for medical treatment were children under seventeen years old; 24 percent of these were under thirteen. In a longer period (September 1965 to June 1969),
13 percent of the victims were nine years old or younger
(the youngest was six months old); another 23 percent
were ten through fourteen years old. These figures include, of course, only the reported rapes, perhaps 10 to
20 percent of the actual total.

In the light of such facts (and other cities give similar
impressions of prevalent rapes and sexual atrocities
against children) it is inexcusable that so little attention
is paid to this crime and that so little money is spent to
ameliorate the sufferings of child victims. "No lasting
effects" is the simplistic phrase used by psychologists,
sociologists, and the medical fraternity to dismiss these
young patients as "cured" once the last stitch and
bandage are removed.

Molestation—A General Crime

One element of the sexual use of children by adults seems to be fairly generally established: it knows no economic or social boundaries. Contrary to popular opinion, incest and rape—and lesser sexual molestations of children by adults—are not confined to the ghetto. Children who are neither culturally deprived nor economically disadvantaged have been molested.

"I've seen patients who were sexually molested or abused from all walks of life," says Dr. Belinda Straight, a psychiatrist at Children's Hospital in Washington, D.C. "I've treated State Department children who have been overseas in the care of a non-English-speaking caretaker where the abuse happened over a period of time without the parents' knowledge. It can happen anywhere."

Even men who are supposedly community "leaders," members of prestigious professions, are guilty of sex offenses against their daughters. Almost half of Philadelphia psychiatrist Dr. Joseph Peters' private therapy patients, all of whom were childhood victims, were raped by their own fathers. One of these men was a minister; another was a judge; and still another was an architect. "These were men these young girls loved and trusted," says Dr. Peters, now director of the Center for Rape Concern at the Philadelphia General Hospital.

The A.H.A. Studies

As we have indicated, studies in the field of sexual abuse of children are few; those which exist usually focus on offenders rather than victims. Exceptions include two studies in the late 1960s by the American Humane Association, which is funded through the Children's Bureau of the U.S. Department of Health, Education and Welfare. The larger of these projects, "Protecting the Child Victim of Sex Crimes Committed by Adults," was directed by Dr. Vincent de Francis and deals with some 263 New York City child victims of a broad range of sexual crimes committed by adults. The other study, "Child Victims of Incest," was directed by the A.H.A.'s Yvonne Tormes and focused on some twenty child victims of incest.

An overwhelming number of the victims included in the first study were girls (the ratio was ten girls to one boy). The incest victims in the other study were *all* girls, since the research focused on the most commonly reported type of incest, that between father and daughter. Victims of the various sex crimes ranged in age from infant to teen-ager; the median age was eleven years. Offenders were preponderantly male—97 percent—ranging in age from seventeen to sixty-eight.

The most prevalent crime against these girls—45 percent of the total, or 114 cases—was rape or attempted rape. Carnal abuse, defined by New York law as any indecent or immoral practices with the sex organs of a child, made up 19 percent, or 49 cases. Impairing morals accounted for 12 percent, or 30 cases; sodomy accounted for 14 percent; and incest accounted for 9 percent.

In 75 percent of the cases the offender was known to the girl or her family; he was her own father, stepfather, mother's lover, brother, uncle, or "friend" of the family. Only 25 percent of the offenders were strangers.

In 60 percent of the cases, the children were coerced by direct force or threat of bodily harm; 25 percent were lured into being victims by relatives or friends playing on the child's affection or loyalty.

More than a third of the assaults took place in the family home; in almost a third of the cases the children were subjected to repeated offenses, usually incest, ranging over periods of a few weeks to seven years.

As in the case of older victims of sexual abuse, the emotional impact on the victims is difficult to assess. The A.H.A. researchers determined that two-thirds of the children were emotionally damaged by the experience and that 14 percent were said to be severely disturbed. Twenty-nine children became pregnant as a result of an assault.

In more than two-thirds of the homes, the parents were found to be "inadequate," failing to provide elementary emotional, moral, and physical care and protection. They were families for the most part already badly disrupted by severe emotional problems such as alcoholism, drug addiction, and violent physical abuse.

Incest

Father–daughter incest is the most commonly detected sex crime within the family. In *The Silent Sin*, Dr. John Woodbury and Elroy Schwartz claim that the number of Americans who have been involved in incestuous experiences runs as high as "twenty million, that is, one in every ten people." From this they deduce that sex within the family is "far more common and *far less traumatic* than we have always been led to believe." (Italics added.) We agree that the incidence of incest is probably vastly greater than the sparsely reported cases. The prevalence of a criminal phenomenon, however, is no proof of its "less traumatizing" effect upon the victims.

Yvonne Tormes, who directed the 1968 A.H.A. incest substudy, for example, found her subjects severely oppressed by the experience, observing in the girls "symptoms of depression and a heightened sense of guilt, with very low self-esteem." She writes:

> The victim of incest is especially vulnerable.
> The child's feelings of guilt are often too enormous
> for the ego to accommodate and serious emotional
> damage, to the point of schizophrenia, may result.
> The home offers little if any protection to the child
> not only because the perpetrator has easy access
> but also because the other parent, usually the

mother, is frequently aware of the situation and either condones it or is immobilized by fear of physical injury to herself, or by fear of losing her husband completely.

One thirteen-year-old girl who ran away from home after being repeatedly molested by her father, confessed to the police. But when her father was arrested she frantically sought his release, saying she had lied. Later she admitted to a project worker that her father had indeed molested her sexually, but she was overwhelmed with guilt for having gotten him into trouble and for "upsetting the whole family."

Another child, repeatedly victimized by her father, sustained herself well until she faced police and court action. There, like many adult rape victims, the forced repetition of her story and the endless recounting of the details of a socially condemned activity enhanced the fear, confusion, and guilt she already suffered, and she became further isolated from her family and friends. She felt she was on trial instead of her criminal father. And she was utterly crushed by the heartless how-could-you-do-this-to-us? attitude of her family. In the end, although she was the victim, she felt she had been punished—"exiled" to a foster home—while her mother and father seemed, to her at least, amiably reconciled.

In the Tormes investigation all the victims came from intact families, all were sixteen years old or younger, and all had come to the attention of legal authorities. The incestuous acts all took place in the home, *seventeen of them while other members of the family were in the house.* The study confirmed earlier findings: incest is rarely a single occurrence, and in most cases before the behavior is uncovered, it has become "a permanent component of the family structure."

The incest families are patriarchal in character, though perhaps it would be more accurate to say that such families are usually totally dominated by a male despot. The mother, on the other hand, is fearful, dependent, and passive to the point of self-annihilation. Often she is totally immobilized by the situation, unable to take any kind of constructive action. By superior initiative and brutality, the husband has nullified her roles of wife and mother, and she has been deprived of self-fulfillment even within the family. "Even prior to tolerating incest, she seems to have tolerated an increasing amount of deviant behavior—violent and non-violent—from her husband, and her forbearance seems to have encouraged his progress to the incest offense," Tormes says.

Physical Abuse

What the wives and families of sex offenders endure before they can bring themselves to take action against the father is a measure of the powerful effects of total patriarchal domination of the family. (An interesting sidelight is that only two of the twenty father–offenders in the Tormes study had records of violence outside of the home; a man's home apparently *is* his sexual castle.)

Thirteen mothers and daughters gave these examples of fatherly behavior: he broke a radio over the mother's head; he burned the children with hot irons; he chased the mother out of the house with a gun on three occasions; he locked the mother or children in closets while he sexually abused the child victim; he kept the family out of the house until very late at night; he threw knives, bottles, and other heavy objects at the mother or children; he forced sexual intercourse with the daughter in the mother's presence, or with the mother in the children's presence; he tried to strangle the mother with a handkerchief; he forced the daughter to submit to a crude abortion that resulted in a debilitating illness.

Families apparently learn to cope with the progressive patterns of deviance; abject submission to the father–offender seems to inspire him to greater rages and new methods of terror. Often it is not until the family members fear for their lives that they can bring themselves to report him. Still, in families where the father's violence was a constant occurrence or occurred only when he was drunk (every weekend) dutiful wives continued to describe their husbands as "wonderful" husbands and fathers and as "affectionate, sweet and tender"!

Says attorney Nan Huhn of the District of Columbia Corporation Counsel:

Sexual abuse goes hand in hand with physical abuse. In many cases, girls are beaten when they resist. Fathers say they are teaching them the facts of life. The mothers, forced to choose between their children and their husbands, are often too terrified to act. The two biggest reasons the kids don't come forth are that they are afraid the father will find out or that no one will believe them. The longer it goes on, the harder it is on the children emotionally.

Many fathers justify incest on the ground that it keeps the daughter from "taking up with undesirable characters" or that it "makes a woman out of her," thus giving a rationale for incest which shifts it from criminality to "duty" and "responsibility." Under these two headings children are battered into submission in many other areas; but it is only in the sexual area that the female child victim is judged guilty of complicity.

As with the battering of children, where so many abusive parents were themselves the victims of physical abuse from their parents, child molesters often come from families in which they and their siblings were sexually victimized. One psychopathic father, later imprisoned, who had impregnated his thirteen-year-old daughter and repeatedly raped two other daughters, reported that he had started having sex when he was seven or eight years old with his nineteen-year-old aunt; his own brother had been sexually involved with their sister during adolescence. In this family, the mother might have protected the two younger daughters by reporting her husband, but she was afraid of him. She failed to tell authorities that her husband had fathered their child's baby until four years after the baby was born. As in most cases where the mother is said to "contribute" to the abuse, the mother, too, had been sexually abused as a child.

Biological "Normality"

One common explanation of sexual aggression against young females is that it is biologically "normal": animals do it. The attitude has been best expressed by anthropologist and Kinsey associate Dr. Paul H. Gebhard, now director of the Institute for Sex Research at Indiana University, and others, in *Sex Offenders*, a classic study issued some ten years ago:

> The horror with which society views the adult who has sexual relations with young children is lessened when one examines the behavior of animals. . . . It is common and biologically normal. . . . Disregard for age, sex, and species need not be regarded as biologically pathological; it is precisely what we see in various animals, particularly in certain monkeys.

Of course, this analogy scarcely proves that what's good for monkeys or other mammals is necessarily biologically "normal" for human beings, female or male. We see a lot of things in monkeys, including the eating of fleas and other insects. Dogs and cats and cows ingest the placenta after birthing their young. Some mammals tear each other apart with their teeth from time to time. None of these, to our knowledge, is recommended for humans on the basis of biological normality.

Sexual activity between consanguinous adult animals and their immature offspring is a biological fact, of course; among horse, dog, and cattle breeders it is specifically engineered to produce offspring. But the mating is cross-sexual; that is, mothers with sons, daughters with fathers. Only within the human family is cross-sexualization a male-dominated actuality. Female sex offenders within the family are so rare as to be almost nonexistent; sex offenders are preponderantly male both inside and outside the family—child victims are preponderantly female. It would seem clear from this that something besides biological "normality" is in operation; namely, the sexism characteristic of the deeply entrenched patriarchy in our society.

"Functional" Incest

Certain social researchers studying data on incest second-hand, namely through the "literature," have invented categories of incest and given them titles like "functional," "pathological," and "accidental."

The inventor of the "functional" category is Dr. Christopher Bagley, sociologist–researcher at the Institute of Psychiatry in London. He is worthy of comment only because his review of a number of studies on incest —some of which date back more than half a century —has led otherwise progressive thinkers, such as California psychologist Richard Farson,[1] to conclude that the "dangers of incest have been highly overrated."

Bagley asserts in "Incest Behavior and Incest Taboo" that children have sex desires and aspirations from a very young age and enter "not unwillingly" into intercourse with parents of the opposite sex. Kids have no "natural" revulsion to incest; they may participate in it over a number of years and the "opposite-sexed parent seems to be a covert but significant figure in the child's sexual life." As the child grows, the sex relationship becomes taboo and the relationship then becomes

[1]Cofounder, chairman of the board, Western Behavioral Sciences Institute at La Jolla, and author of *Birth Rights*.

nonsexual—though exactly how this miraculous trans-
fer is accomplished is not made clear. Such a conclusion
does suggest, however, that incest is something to be
outgrown, like hives and eczema.

Bagley explains the "functional" aspect of incest as
follows:

> When a family member is socialized in the norms
> of incest, whether it is seen by the family to be
> functional for the survival of the family or because
> it is desired for some other reason by some domi-
> nant family members, the evidence from case his-
> tories shows that incest can be accepted by the
> younger partner with equanimity. (Emphasis
> added.)

In this scheme "functional" incest stems from a "defect" in the family (such as the wife's illness, desertion,
or death) that makes it impossible for the father to lead a
satisfactory married life. Since all of the families in
Bagley's second-hand study were explicitly patriarchal
(Swedish, German, or Mormon), and in some cases still
feudal (Japanese), it would seem to indicate that the
child's "calm" acceptance of incest entirely benefited a
dominant patriarch. To interpret an act that clearly benefits only the elite members of a community as therefore
"normal" is like saying that slavery is acceptable to
slaves because it serves the white male masters.

None of the incest studies contain examples of incestuous relations between mothers and sons or other male
relatives, whether or not the father has deserted or is
chronically ill, dead, or maybe just plain unbearable.
"Functional" incest for the preservation of family is a
prerogative of the dominant males of the clan only; if
perhaps the wife's invalidism or other recalcitrancy is
not excuse enough, other disenchanting qualities—
such as being too old, too fat, too thin, or too tired—
may be invented for her. By extension, of course, this
concept of "functional" incest as accepted "with
equanimity" by the girl victim can easily be applied to

other "dominant" family members, namely, uncles, grandfathers, growing sons, or anyone else considered eligible to join the all-male gangbang.

One of the disarming naivetés constantly expressed by the incest apologists—or the because-it's-there-it's-normal devotees—is what they describe as the "easy" acceptance by young girls of a sexual relation with their fathers. Bagley cites the case of a psychotic father who over a four-year period had incestuous relations with his two adolescent daughters, neither of whom told the other or the mother and who seemed to accept the relations with their father as "special favor on his behalf." This illustrates, according to a secondary source cited by Bagley, the "tendency for girls to accept, *passively or with eagerness,* the sexual advances of the father, without denouncing him to his wife."[2] (Italics added.)

But what child does not accept patterns of behavior—good or bad—set by parental teaching or example? The children of thieves usually learn to steal; young slobs at the table commonly learn bad manners from older slobs; and children reared in a family of fighters usually learn to fight. Girls learn passivity from passive mothers; or they learn submission from watching their mothers acquiesce under the verbal or physical intimidation of dominant males. Similarly girl incest victims fail to betray their fathers because the fathers customarily hold the reins of power even without resorting to physical violence. Verbal threats, veiled hints, and other forms of moral blackmail work secretly and just as effectively on victims as physical brutality and violence.

Somewhere to the right of the "normality" apologists for incest are those like psychiatrist Karl Menninger who suggest that early sex with adults may actually contribute to mental health. Arguing that children are not irreparably ruined by exposure to such experiences

[2]F. S. Capiro, author of *Variations in Sexual Behavior* (full cite unavailable).

at an early age, Menninger refers to a follow-up study done by two well-known Freudian psychiatrists on adults who had been child victims. Because these adults had turned out to be "distinguished and unusually charming and attractive in their outward personalities," Menninger concludes that early sex doesn't have to be harmful.

Dr. Menninger explains that early adult–child sex relations are:

> . . . traumatic only when connected with deep hostilities . . . but when the experience actually stimulates the child erotically, it would appear . . . that it may favor rather than inhibit the development of social capabilities and mental health in the so-called victims.

But Dr. Edward H. Weiss, also a psychiatrist, and Georgetown University professor and chairman of a D.C. medical subcommittee on rape, told us in an interview that sexual attacks can:

> . . . trigger a lot of problems, with the possibility of long-range damage to the victims. It is our feeling that the hidden injury to the child may be emotional and not show on the surface. The long-range effects on the personality may be far more devastating than the physical effects of the crime itself.

The callous assurance with which male investigators have dismissed "unsettling effects" on young girl victims contrasts sharply with the observations of two women working in the field. Dr. Ann Wolbert Burgess, a psychiatric nurse, and Dr. Lynda Lytle Holmstrom, a sociologist, together conduct a victim counseling program at Boston City Hospital and have written a useful guidebook, Crisis Intervention and the Rape Victim, deriving from their work. They report that young girls exhibited behavior all the way from uncontrollable crying to fidgeting and restlessness; they were shy, scared, frightened, and subdued; some were barely able to answer questions. In later stages, long-term reactions included physical symptoms, nightmares, and phobias about being alone or being in the neighborhood where the assault occurred. Some became truants from school—a common reaction seen by many others dealing with child victims of sexual attacks—or were mortally afraid to go back to school after the attack. Many were unable to get along with schoolmates or to perform schoolwork, and many developed lasting sexual fears. "Only a few victims developed no symptoms; most had mild to moderate symptoms," Burgess and Holmstrom report. "The syndrome of behavioral, somatic, and psychological reactions is an acute stress reaction to a life-threatening situation."

Unlike the theorists who draw conclusions from reading the "literature" on adult–child sex, these two investigators report on detailed conversations with child victims that clearly show the painful difficulties many girls experience in school after they have been victimized. One twelve-year-old suffered under the verbal attacks of peers who usually referred to her as "Susie slut" when they were not calling her "ass hole," "prostitute," or "bitch."

Others who work with victims, such as Women Organized Against Rape in Philadelphia (half of whose rape victims are children), report serious effects of rape that do not manifest themselves until long after the crime. For example, one youngster who seemed to have survived the crime without unusual difficulty threatened to drop out of school months after the attack. A sensitive and alert social worker uncovered the relationship to the crime and was able to help the child.

All those who have worked with young victims agree that it is essential to help parents respond constructively to the child's pain. WOAR's experience is that parents are usually in a state of crisis themselves when a sex crime is discovered; they must be helped to accept the crime in a way that does not communicate panic, fright, or horror to the child, thereby contributing to or creating trauma. Given the social mores surrounding adult–child sex and the confused, conflicting attitudes toward sexuality in general, this is often difficult if not impossible. Manifestations of parental and family anxiety (and ignorance) undoubtedly contribute to the child's lasting injury. But this is no reason to conclude, as have so many writers in the field, that children are *more* damaged by the reaction of those around them to the crime than they are by the event itself. These reactions are, after all, secondary to an offense; without the initial crime there would be no reaction, negative or positive. To understand the crime, we must look closely at the society that spawns it—a society still espousing a double standard of sexuality and still saturated with hostility toward females.

The "Seductive" Child

The double standard of sexuality espoused by society is especially noticeable in the so-called technical literature of the social "scientists." For example, the term seductive originally applied to *males* who lured and enticed females to submit to "defloration." Psychiatrists, psychologists, anthropologists, sociologists, and criminologists—reversing the actor and the acted-on—now apply the terms almost exclusively to the female. Aided and abetted by the Bible and Freud, these students of social function conceive of seduction as being organically and pejoratively female.

Technical literature is overburdened with reference to the "seductive" female child, or something called the "Lolita" syndrome, wherein dirty old men are led astray by five-year-old sex fiends. This, of course, works to shift the focus (and the blame) from the adult male offender to the female victim. It also effectively ignores all other facets of a child's personality except her sexuality. Thus in "Psychotherapeutic and Legal Approaches to the Victimized Child," a survey of child sex victim studies during the 1950s and 1960s, Leroy G. Schultz finds young female victims described variously as "collaborative," "nonobjecting," "encouraging," "fully participating," and "seducers" (the last term being applied to some 20 percent of 185 court cases in 1956).

These designations are all highly loaded—and none more so than the overused "seductive"—when used in connection with sex crimes. Its constant repetition in the elitist journals of psychiatry, child care, sociology, criminology, law, and medicine helps to fix it firmly in the minds of professionals in these fields—who then go on to spread the word to the public at large. The fact is that the exact meaning of "seductive" is unclear; investigators (male *and* female) who use it make certain assumptions about female personality based on Freud and other sexists before and after him, which lead to further confusion.

We should remember that words dealing with alleged female aggression and excesses in sex are of recent origin. "Nymphomania," for example, came into the language in the eighteenth century, a time when women were believed to have *no* sexual desire. The nymphet or "Lolita" theory of female nubility favored in the sociological literature is of very recent origin. Vladimir Nabokov's novel *Lolita,* was first published in Paris in the mid-1950s and in the United States three years later. Social scientists were quick to seize upon another pejorative sexual implication for the female; "nymphet," through the French "nymphette," and the sociologist's "Lolita" both mean any nubile, prepubertal female. It is interesting that the focus is upon Lolita rather than upon her elderly pursuer, who is, after all, the quintessential, prototypical dirty-old-man of legend and the Nabokov satire centers on *his* sexual preoccupations. (Perhaps as social scientists grow more aware they will invent a male equivalent of the "Lolita" syndrome, and the dirty-old-man will be elevated to the "Horny Humbert" theory of *male* sexuality.)

The fact that some child victims appear to invite sexual molestation is not conclusive evidence of anything except perhaps the sexual orientation of the observers (some of whom may overidentify with Lolita's d.o.m.). A preadolescent may endanger herself, for example, by accepting a ride from a neighbor or neighbors, but to define that action as "precipitating" a sexual assault is as preposterous as maintaining that banks "seduce" criminals into robbing them because they keep money.

In the family situation, where intimate contact is frequent and often inescapable, the child victim of a relative or family friend (Lolita's "dirty old man" was her stepfather) is at the mercy of the adult, not the other way around. Our children are raised in such a way that they can rarely refuse physical attention from adults. As Dr. Richard Farson puts it, in *Birth Rights:*

> *Parents have insisted that children accept all forms of affection from relatives and friends —being picked up, fondled, hugged, kissed, pinched, tickled, squeezed—leaving children little experience in saying no. . . . They are not informed about sexual matters, do not understand their own sexuality or that of others, and thus cannot cope effectively in this area. We keep them innocent and ignorant and then worry that they will not be able to resist sexual approaches.*

Most experts in the field of child care, however, ignore the innocence and ignorance of the child—not to mention the fear—finding more comfort in the mysterious sexual power of the young female child over the adult. Thus Dr. C. Raymond Kiefer, director of Child Mental Health in Indianapolis, Indiana, opens his guide to office counseling with the reminder that the child often plays some part in encouraging the sexual situation: ". . . little girls run out of the house to show their pretty bodies to a wider world; little boys get into urinating contests . . . repeated sexual involvement with the same person says clearly that at some level the child *wanted* the relationship to continue." (Italics added.)

Some authorities, subscribing to what may be called the genital theory of female delinquency, go further. This hypothesis has been nourished by patriarchal society in the church and in the law, where, as we shall see, it has been carefully incorporated into Anglo-American laws of evidence. Here it is summed up by child psychiatric specialist Dr. Peter Blos, in his article "Preoedipal Factors in the Etiology of Female Delinquency" published in *The Psychoanalytic Study of the Child,* contrasting male delinquency with female. The boy's delinquency, he asserts, has "elements of keen interest in reality; we recognize his fascination with the struggle waged between himself, people, social institutions, and the world of nature." Thus a boy in conflict with his father might get drunk, destroy property, or steal a car—actions Blos further describes as "an attempt at progressive development."

The girl, on the other hand, says Blos, "takes revenge on her mother, by whom she feels rejected, by seeking sexual relations" and finds "bodily outlet in genital activity. The pregenital instinctual aims . . . relate her delinquency to perversion." Put more simply, destroying property, getting drunk, or stealing is evidence of growth and development, while sexual activity, if female, is evidence of perversion. It is only a step away to the "seductive" female child, enticing her innocent father/uncle/brother/grandfather into her bed.

But seductiveness lies largely in the eyes of the beholder. D.C. public health nurse Charlene Lanza has been dealing with child victims for many years. "I don't think the average preadolescent youngster is looking for sex; certainly the child victim is not expecting it," she says. "The young child may have feelings of need for the total encompassing love of a male figure. If she is not getting this love she might act in a way that others might interpret as seductive, but it is not *sexually* seductive. It's a different picture when you talk of teen-agers, by the way."

Vincent de Francis concurs: "Many child victims are extremely deprived, emotionally. They hunger and crave affection and are likely to accept it from any source, under any condition, and almost at any price."

As to a little girl's repeated involvement sexually with an adult, Lanza points out that if a father or other adult relative initiates sex with the child when she is very young, "the child thinks that is the normal thing to do, so the behavior will continue, sometimes over long periods of time. The child doesn't discover it isn't 'normal' until she gets out into the world and finds out 'everybody' doesn't do it. Her feelings may then become badly disoriented."

And at this point the really innocent child may suffer severe anxiety. Author Germaine Greer tells of one of her friends who had "enjoyed" sex with her uncle all through her childhood but never realized there was anything unusual about it until she went away to school. There the acute, overanxious reactions of teachers and psychiatrists forced her to fake symptoms until she felt guilty about not feeling guilty.

That a girl seems to be a willing participant in sex with an adult does not mean that she knowingly consented to it at any level. The adult male may have coerced her by threats, by lures, by gifts or favors, or by some other enticement. Yielding or making a concession to an adult male cannot be equated with valid consent, because at the outset, the child cannot envision what that consent really means. As de Francis reminds us: "Children are protected by law against consenting where, because of age, they are deemed incapable of making an 'informed consent,' that is, consent based on full and complete understanding of all the implications of the consent."

The Doctrine of "Community" Response

There is no doubt that the "community" response to a child victim can mean the difference between permanent damage to the child's psyche and survival after a potentially traumatizing occurrence. By "community" social scientists usually mean those immediately around the victim—parents, relatives, neighbors, friends and others—and also the larger society with its remote and unfamiliar institutions of law enforcement and justice. The guilt and fear that these two elements of the "community" can induce in a child *can* be worse than the criminal act itself.

The anger, rage, disbelief, or just simple refusal to listen to a child as she struggles to tell what has happened to her must inevitably leave scars. And parents are often more concerned with protecting themselves and their "good name" than they are about the effects on the child. Sometimes parents react by becoming hysterical or by physically attacking the child victim; others punish her verbally, dismissing the story as untrue, or worse, unimportant. Some parents have attacked the offender in front of the child; others have threatened officials if the criminal is not instantly sentenced.

But these negative reactions are only part of the picture; it is not useful to assign to "community" response—as so many social workers and other social theorists do—the *bulk* of responsibility for a child victim's trauma. Despite all the psychiatric arguments for the "normality" of incest and other forms of adult–child sex, such relations are tabooed culturally, legally, and morally in our society. It is spurious to argue that innate sexuality in a girl makes sex with her father a "normal" action, whereas her mother's lack of support when the crime is discovered is more harmful to her than her sexual submission to the adult male who has used her. Obviously, rejection by those close to her can cause enormous injury to a child's psyche. But that rejection is caused by the crime itself and by society's attitudes toward it; the social conditioning of a human being revolves not only around actions and nonactions toward her, but also on the social responses to these actions.

Some mothers and fathers go overboard to prove that the crime is not traceable to parental neglect or inadequacy; others blame themselves unrealistically—some mothers to the point of suicide. Some parents cruelly blame the child, like the mother who said in front of her nine-year-old daughter: "She has been taught since the day she was born never to get into anybody's car except her father's. She knew better; it was stupid for her to do it . . . and when you do something wrong, you have to do unpleasant things afterward. Court is part of the punishment."

Other parents inflict their own punishment on the victim, in one case keeping the daughter under virtual house arrest: "Because of what happened, she can't go out or see any of her friends for a month. As for the phone, there's only one friend we'll allow her to talk to."

Another mother said she was very angry and gave her daughter a good beating. Another said of her raped child that she had "brought it on herself. She had no business going with him. She should have come straight home." And one mother of an incest victim said it was the daughter's fault: "She looked for him. She used to sleep with me but she moved to the couch in the living room because she wanted to be near her father." The mother of an eight-year-old who reported being molested by her father slapped her face and called her a "bad girl." Seven years later—after the former child victim had attempted suicide—the mother reported the molestation. Another mother, told by all four daughters that their father was manipulating their breasts and vaginas, insisted he was merely trying to show "affection." Many cases are not reported until the daughters become pregnant by their fathers.

The frustrations of children who try to persuade their families to believe them are endless: "I can't talk to my parents; they would never understand. . . . I try to talk to them and the TV is going and they want to watch. I get so mad and upset so I can't talk to them." Or: "My mother doesn't care. She doesn't think there was anything wrong." Or another adolescent, in a foster home after being incestuously abused by her father: "My mother knew. It had been going on for years. I saw her a couple of times after he went to jail and all she did was complain about the trouble I've caused the family."

Not all the family reactions are deleterious. As one mother said: "I believe this is like a wound. If you let the sun and air at a wound, it will heal. If we talk about the incident, it will heal. In one way it is embarrassing, but then I have always believed things should be talked about."

And the kind and sympathetic grandmother who made the child understand that she was loved and no one thought "less of her that it happened . . . at Christmas she wanted a piano. I couldn't buy her a real one, but I bought a small one and you'd think I bought her the moon. She plays it all the time. . . . That really helped her feel better."

Children in the Courts

Beyond the family, the child victim faces special problems with the official world—police, special officers, prosecutors, the court, and its officers. Over and over again the child must repeat the details of the crime to strangers. In court, before a jury of twelve more adult strangers, often in the presence of the offender himself, the child must tell her story one last time through an adversary interrogation.

Few representatives of the judicial process are expert at techniques needed to interview children, but they are gentle when compared to the ingenious attorneys who defend the accused. These attorneys tend to defend the criminal by what amounts to putting the child on trial. They often attempt to show that the child is malicious, incompetent, "seductive," or lying for a variety of reasons—the same techniques used so often with older, more mature victims.

Suggestions that the adversary system be amended in order to protect children in judicial situations, however, are resisted by American lawyers and criminologists. Other countries—among them some of the Scandinavian nations, Israel, France, and West Germany—have developed more humane methods of handling the situation, using a surrogate for the child in court when a court appearance is deemed potentially damaging to the child's mental health. In Israel, for example, a social worker may be cross-examined in place of the child. American attorneys recoil at this practice, saying it violates basic American rights of the accused, including equal protection of the law, the right to exclude hearsay, the right to cross-examine witnesses, and the right of the accused to face his accuser (even if that "accuser" is only in the third grade).

Those who deal regularly with the psyches of child victims feel it is cruel and unnecessary to put a frightened and embarrassed child in front of unfamiliar people and have her repeat what happened to her while facing her assailant. Psychiatrists like Dr. Weiss instead advocate private questioning in the judge's chambers; an adult surrogate for the child during court examination; or if the child must appear in court, the use of child specialists, social workers, or doctors to conduct the questioning.

Some criminologists and attorneys assert that 80 to 90 percent of all criminal defendants plead guilty without a trial, and that therefore most child victims do not have to appear in court. Nevertheless, in some jurisdictions children may be forced by law to testify in court without their consent against the offender. According to Professor Schultz: "Regrettably the law . . . may force the child victim to testify against the offender without the child's consent, and the *victim* may be placed in detention until the trial," (italics added) an obvious potential for additional trauma for the child. This can happen when the criminal is considered to be a threat to the community and the victim's testimony is essential to conviction. While Schultz asserts that the imprisonment of child victims is fortunately "rare," it should not happen at all. Also, when the issues of what Schultz and others categorize as the victim's repeated involvement or "participation or seduction" (generally with victims over fourteen) arise, defendants may demand a trial in order to "impress" the jury with the victim's "contribution." Her "participation" of course may have come as a result of bribes (money, candy, gifts) or threats. And the definition of that elusive female "seductiveness" is still largely a matter of subjectively determined male-oriented interpretation, leading easily to conclusions of victim guilt.

The concept of victim guilt dies hard, especially when the victim is female. Renowned criminologists (such as Hans Von Hentig, Marvin E. Wolfgang, and their disciple Menachem Amir) are especially devoted to the concept of the female victim's guilt and "seductiveness" and have set up their own standards for determining such involvement. Needless to say this whole *gestalt* works for the benefit of the male offender, since most men, including learned criminologists, cannot agree on a firm, immutable definition of "seductive."

No one will argue that young girls (or young boys for that matter) are always entirely innocent of involvement in sexual activities with adults. Certainly the belated recognition that even infants and young children are capable of sexual stimulation and orgasm makes them sexually receptive at a much earlier age than was believed heretofore. But a recognition of early sexual capabilities is insufficient reason to assign motives, let alone blame or guilt.

Perhaps the newly created National Center on Child Abuse and Neglect can eventually shed some further light on this and other realities of adult–child sex relationships. Even though the 1974 enabling legislation for the Center appears to limit its concern for sexual (and other) abuses of children under eighteen to "a person responsible for the child's welfare," this multimillion-dollar new Health, Education and Welfare Department funding agency should at least be able to provide some broad guidelines in identification, prevention, and treatment. Just how much help will be available to sexually abused children—in a country far more comfortable dealing with battery than with sexual offenses against children—remains to be seen.

Learning the "Shame"

Criminologists, in developing sophisticated theories of "victimology," seem not to know that few women reach adulthood without experiencing some sort of sexual molestation in childhood at the hands of an adult male or males. And few seem to be aware of the full implications of these experiences.

Sociologists and their friends in the legal system prefer to rely on psychiatric speculations with regard to the female life experience—such as Freud's "polymorphic perverse" (or a "tendency" for victimization among all women), the female propulsion to "passivity and masochism," and a "universal desire" among females to be aggressively handled in sex relations.

Given these foundations, it is an easy step to publication of psychoanalytical theories that females "universally" wish to be forcefully seduced by strangers (why strangers?) and, finally, that all females long to be raped. These psychiatric fantasies have been voiced for so long and so often and in such important places that many men and, alas, many women, have come to believe them. When applied as universals to female children, such conjectures are singularly harsh and unnecessarily cruel.

Women's personal childhood experiences refute these claims. Although many of us would prefer not to acknowledge it, most women, either subconsciously or consciously, live with concern over being sexually used (or abused). From the time little girls begin to walk we are taught to be wary, though often our teachers are vague as to what we should be wary of, with veiled and mysterious warning of evils we cannot imagine. We are taught from infancy that certain areas of our bodies are secret, private, dark, and hidden places—not to be touched, not to be displayed, never to be revealed. Indeed, the very word for the female genitals—*pudendum*—comes from a Latin word meaning "that of which one ought to be ashamed." The plural form (*pudenda*) applies to both sexes; but common usage and contemporary dictionaries carry on the tradition of assigning "that of which one ought to be ashamed" *first* to the female.

Little girls soon learn that curiosity, touching, fondling, or enjoyment of their erogenous areas is shameful. And if their own families are sexually permissive, the outside world is not. Men, even a sex researcher like Alfred Kinsey, are puzzled by this. Kinsey reports in *Sexual Behavior in the Human Female* that he finds it "difficult to understand why a child, *except for its cultural conditioning,* should be disturbed by having its genitalia touched, or disturbed by seeing the genitalia of another person." (Italics added.)

It is precisely that cultural conditioning which has effectively taught little girls to be disturbed in such instances. And when Kinsey observes that "the emotional reactions of the parents, police, and other adults . . . may disturb the child more seriously than the contacts themselves," he is simply commenting on the results of that cultural conditioning in action. The entire culture is conditioned to feel embarrassment and shame over sexuality, and when the language itself incorporates a judgmental concept (that female genitalia are shameful) we can be certain that the indoctrination is very deep indeed.

Kinsey's dismissal of concern about sex crimes against children as "hysteria" over sex offenders shows a callous disregard for female sensibility and a curious lack of comprehension of what it means to grow up female in our society. One of the things it means is that those around us may react with violence, shame, or incredulity when we recount tales of sexual molestations—especially if the offender is a family member or a close friend.

Blood ties are strong; protection of those close to us is something inculcated in us from birth. Often without understanding the nature of the crimes against her, a little girl senses that the world outside will disapprove. It is better to keep the secret. But this does not, as some male theorists like to think, make us "willing participants."

As children we are so deeply indoctrinated with the "shame" of our own sexuality that when we are sexually used or abused, we often become conflicted and confused about what has happened. Besides, someone is likely to have said or implied that what happened was our own fault and that somehow we, and not the offender, "did something bad." If we encounter disbelief or opposition from parents or others close to us, we react to the "shame" with silence. "I didn't want to get my parents in trouble," said one little girl who kept silent for months after her stepfather's assaults on her had been revealed by a relative.

"After the third time, I gave up trying to get my mother to believe me," a professional woman told us recently. Molested when she was six by the family doctor and at eleven by a neighbor, this woman was finally sexually mauled by her uncle, an assault she did not reveal until many years later.

Another career woman recounting her childhood experience remembers that her parents were more outraged about her remaining in a city park sleigh riding long after she was supposed to come home than they were about the fact that a stranger had sexually assaulted her. As an adult she derives little comfort from the insistence of social theorists that the pain she suffered at the hands of her parents did her more harm than the experience itself. A few years later she was molested again by another stranger, and she kept it to herself.

It may be that sexual molestation by adult males of female children—and the subsequent negative "community" response—are key factors in preparing women for their adult sex roles. Socialized to feel shame and guilt about female sexuality, trained to passivity and silence, girl children grow up accepting all forms of subordination to the boys and men around them. It is, as feminists point out, excellent training for victimization . . . and silence.

Few women reach adulthood without experiencing some form of sexual molestation (as Kinsey and others have recounted), if not from the males in the immediate family, then from others. Sexual molestation is progressive; it goes on through the peeping-tom episodes by the boys in the school yard (give-you-a-nickel-to-look-up-your-skirt; a dime-if-you-take-your-pants-off); the "pantsing" and "depantsing" rituals of childhood; and on up to the clumsy pawing and fumbling of adolescents. In all these occurrences, the girl's role as victim is clearly delineated.

Because the girl has been taught from infancy that her genitals are something of which she "ought" to be ashamed, whether she feels that way or not, she does not usually fight back (even to the extent of "telling" on her persecutors). Generally she has also been carefully and subtly trained not to fight back; the danger of arousing male hostility is too great. To deal with a masher by hitting him, screaming at him, or even reporting him to someone in authority is to bring shame upon herself. It is too embarrassing. It will call attention to her; she will have done that unforgivable "female" thing—made a "scene." Even verbal assertiveness for females is potentially threatening. Most girls and women sense, if only subconsciously, the perils of arousing male animosity and violence. If there is any doubt about this, try responding aggressively and negatively, if you are female, to the next strange man who calls you "dear," "doll," or "honey," across the sales counter. Try answering the next passing male stranger who calls out, "Baby, you're looking good today!" by growling: "A lot better than you!"

Try replying to easy uninvited familarities with a scowl—the male hostility and anger it evokes are remarkable. Curiously, this hostility usually translates into the sexual: "Stuck up bitch. I wouldn't screw you if you were the last dame in the city" and "You stink. I wouldn't lay you even if you had a *smile* on your puss" and "You're nothing but a two-bit broad; who needs your kind?"

It is difficult for many men, no matter how understanding, to empathize with the feelings and reactions of women in such situations. Good men protest innocence or insist that such unwanted attentions signify a "compliment" or that perhaps the female who objects is not "getting enough"—again the male propensity for translating humiliation into sexuality.

But some women are refusing to be victimized any more, and they are teaching their daughters that sexual familiarity from males is not their responsibility; it is the man's. They are teaching girls to believe in themselves and to know that the man who lays a hand on a strange female knee in a darkened movie house is accountable for his action—not the owner of the knee. And perhaps, as more and more young females grow up believing in their own sexual autonomy, the horrendous task of wiping out the sexual victimization of little girls will be on its way.

But caution must also be taught to children in a violent society, especially since children are naturally less wary of strangers than adults and lack experience and judgment. To instill awareness of potential dangers without terrifying or overly alarming the child should be the aim of every parent and others charged with child guidance. But ignorance of the reality of rape is as harmful as too many warnings. As one mother put it, "If you live in an area with rattlesnakes, you teach children to be cautious. You don't pretend rattlesnakes don't exist." Parents usually apply this common-sense approach to hazards such as fire, traffic, and poison ivy; but until recently thay have said too little to their daughters about avoiding sexual molestation and assault.

Children should be taught caution, not fear. Children should be taught a new definition of "stranger." A stranger is anyone whom the child does not know really well, no matter what that stranger—he or she—says. Parents and teachers could use a representative list of acquaintances, semi-acquaintances and would-be acquaintances to help the child understand the "stranger" concept.

The following rules (provided by the Akron, Ohio, Police Department) form an excellent checklist for parental and teacher guidance for children. They should be posted in the school or at home:

—Never accept a ride in a car from a stranger or from someone you don't know very well. Sometimes these people will have plausible excuses. They may ask, "Will you show me where the Wilsons live? I can't seem to find their house," or, "Your mother sent me to bring you home." No matter what they say, *never get into a car with anyone who is not a good friend.*

—If a stranger stops his car to talk to you or ask directions, never get close enough for him to be able to grab you.

—Never take shortcuts through lonely alleys, dark streets, or wooded areas. Don't play in empty, abandoned buildings or around new construction where there is no one to help you.

—Never play near public restrooms. If you have to use the toilet, go in quickly—with friends or an adult—and leave right away. Men looking for children often wait around such places.

—Unless you are with one of your parents, don't talk to strangers while playing in the park or shopping. Above all, *never accept any treats from a stranger.*

—If a teen-ager or adult sits down next to you in a theater, be alert. If he talks to you or tries to touch you, get up right away and tell the usher or manager.

—If you go door to door for a school or club project, always take a friend with you. Even if *both* of you are invited into a stranger's house, refuse politely. Do all your business outside.

—If you are at home alone, or baby-sitting, never let anyone into the house. If you must open the front door to talk to someone, make sure the screen door or the storm door is locked or that a chain latch is firmly in place. Even if he says he has a package to deliver or that he is a friend or relative, don't let the stranger in. If he is a friendly person, he'll respect you for being careful.

—Always let your parents know where you are going and what time you expect to be home. If you're going to be late, call your parents. In this way, if you do not arrive home when you are expected, your parents can act quickly and alert the police that you may be in danger.

—Never let a stranger stroke your hair, straighten your clothes, or touch any part of your body. If he should try, run away as fast as you can.

—If a man frightens you or starts to chase you, run fast, scream as loudly as you can, and head for the nearest house or building where there are adults who can help you. If you can find a policeman, go to him as quickly as possible.

—Try to keep your head. Remember what the man looks like and what kind of clothes he is wearing. If he is driving a car, notice the color, and, if at all possible, try to get the license number. If you don't have a pencil, try to scratch the number on the sidewalk with a stone, or write it in the dirt, with a stick. If you can do these things, the police will have a good chance of catching the man and keeping him from bothering other children. *But remember that none of these things is as important as your safety.*

3
THE POLICE:
THE MAN IN THE STREET

If a woman has a knife at her throat, she might as well relax and enjoy it.
—High-ranking police official, Ann Arbor, Michigan

The policeman who talked to me really was nice–almost like my brother. He seemed to understand how bad I felt, and he drove me down to the hospital himself.
—Rape victim, Denver, Colorado

When you report to the police, you're a piece of evidence only–not a human being in trouble and needing help.
—Rape victim, Washington, D.C.

Going to the Police

What happens when a woman is raped? As we have seen, in many cases the woman tells no one about the assault and keeps the "secret" to herself for years or even for a lifetime. Some women go through life with a terrible burden of unexpressed guilt and fear because they felt that no one would listen sympathetically, that no one would help. Other victims confide in a relative or friend, who may or may not sympathize, and go no further. From all the evidence, the vast majority of rape victims never report the crime to any social authority.

The minority who do report usually turn first to the police. Some phone the police immediately after the rape; many wait several hours or even days or weeks before they gather the courage to describe this "socially unacceptable" assault. The standard procedure of all police departments is to send the nearest patrolman or precinct officer to the scene of the attack to question the victim, get her to medical treatment (generally in a public city or county hospital) and to gather preliminary evidence. Unfortunately, at this point many rape cases are arbitrarily dismissed as "unfounded" by the patrolmen on the beat, who decide that the report is false or that there is too little evidence to proceed further. Or the patrolmen may call in the department's detectives, and they then dismiss the case. But if the investigating officers feel an assault actually occurred, they try to identify and arrest the assailant—or assailants—and build up a good case for court prosecution.

The way in which police procedures are carried out varies enormously from department to department, and even from policeman to policeman within the same department. Only a few cities—such as Washington, New York, Denver, and Tucson—have separate sex squads or sections; most departments lump all sex crimes under the homicide or juvenile offenders units. One of the greatest gaps in current police methods is the lack of training given to police officers in handling rape victims. Characteristically, trainees receive only two or three hours of information about sex-crime techniques. Many departments give no special rape training at all—and certainly none in the essential area of how to deal with rape victims in a careful, sensitive manner. As a result, not only are many victims traumatized further but much evidence may be lost in the process; and these mistreated victims in turn discourage other rape victims from going to the police.

The handling of sex crimes against both children and adults is an extremely complex and difficult job, requiring high levels of skills and human understanding. Few officers today possess the maturity or training to achieve such qualifications. After a policeman is summoned to a rape scene, he should give priority to aiding the victim, although too often he does not. In the ideal situation, she will be asked only a few brief questions about what happened, where the crime occurred, and a description of the assailant, before being rushed to sympathetic medical and psychological care. The victim will be questioned later in much greater detail after her medical examination, which should be given as soon as possible both to help the victim medically and emotionally and to gather necessary evidence.

Investigative methods are outlined in the uniform police training manual issued by the International Association of Chiefs of Police, which stresses: giving the police department dispatcher an immediate description of the assailant and his direction of flight, apprehending the assailant as soon as possible, determining if a crime has been committed, protecting the crime scene, controling the onlookers, interviewing witnesses for details, and preparing the required reports.

The ways in which such guidelines are actually carried out can be vastly different from the idealized versions. Darlene Cole, a D.C. Rape Crisis Center founder and herself a rape victim, described the police insensitivity common to many locales:

> *So many different people see the rape victim that it becomes almost like a party. And a lot of the police are very voyeuristic about whether the woman secretly enjoyed the rape, how it felt, whether she likes sex a lot—asking insulting and unnecessary questions like that. The police need a great deal more specialization so that only a few people with special training will see the victim.*

Victims report being leered at, humiliated, and harassed by the policemen they called for help. To many women, the police often seem more interested in explicitly sexual details than in catching the rapist. "Are you a virgin?" "Did you like it?" "Did you climax?"

"What were you wearing?" are police questions repeated by rape victims throughout the nation—in urban, suburban, and rural areas alike. Women are often asked things like, "How long were you on the floor?" "What verbal response did you make during the rape?" "Did his language excite you?" "How much prior sexual experience have you had?" Such questions have little to do with finding the rapist and much more with human curiosity or satisfying the officers' vicarious sexual urges.

Ironically, while the police are primarily responsible for preventing rape, responding to victims, and solving cases, most of them are male; and like other "men in the street," they share the prevalent social attitudes condoning rape. In effect, many policemen—though certainly far from all—show rape victims the same inhumanity shown by the rapists themselves. Hundreds of victims echo the reaction of the woman who said, "The way the police treated me was as bad as the rape itself."

Policemen are apt to dismiss sexual attacks in certain social situations as "no rape at all" or "if she asked him in for a drink, she had it coming." Or, at best, the policemen may consider a case impossible to prove, even if they fully believe a rape happened. One center worker observed, "God help you if you're raped by someone you know, especially someone you know well, like a boyfriend or a fiancé. The police can't believe a man you know can rape you. To them, it's just a 'lovers' quarrel."

A young California actress described what happened when trusted friends introduced her to a man at rehearsal and she accepted a ride home. On the thruway, the man began talking about all the "swinging" actresses he knew and suggested they go to a motel. The young woman refused and asked to be taken home or let out. The man said, "Okay, jump," drove by her exit, and sped onward. The actress became frightened and began begging him and crying, but he only laughed and told her not to play shy, "You want it as much as I do."

She was helpless as he drove on at 80 miles an hour, despite her screams, threats, and pleas. After an hour he finally stopped at a motel, and she pretended to give in and phone her roommate about being late. Instead, she called the police.

Ten minutes later, while she was struggling with the man in the room, the police arrived. The assailant told them, "I don't know why she pulled this. She *wanted* to come up here." The woman denied it and demanded that charges be brought for attempted rape. The police refused to believe her, saying, "Now, why don't you just calm down and let him take you home?" She was furious and screamed, "This man tried to rape me. *I want protection!*" The police grinned and let the man go, winking and slapping him on the shoulder as he left. They took the actress back to wait for the morning train, making cracks about "girls who go to motel rooms with men." A lawyer later advised her there was nothing she could do.

Another woman asked a man up to her apartment for coffee after a date, something countless numbers of women have done without expecting to be assaulted. Abruptly he grabbed her and pushed her down on the couch. As she struggled futilely against his greater weight and strength, he shook his clenched fist in her face and growled, "Settle down, you bitch, or I'll knock your fucking teeth out!" The woman was terrified and gave in. The man left immediately afterward, and the woman went to the police and told them she'd been raped. "But I didn't have any marks on me, and they didn't believe me," this victim recollected. "Finally the lieutenant decided to bring the man in for questioning. Do you know, that bastard looked me straight in the eye and claimed, 'You were perfectly willing, honey —remember?' The police let him go. They said there was no case."

This is a common story. As many men have learned, if you don't beat a woman up or bruise her too much, you can rape with impunity. Few people believe the victim in such a situation. Michigan's Women Againt Rape concluded from their experiences, "Policemen often appear to get a lecherous pleasure in writing out rape reports. Police go on the assumption that it didn't really happen, if a woman is not noticeably physically injured. The treatment a woman receives after she has been raped indicates clearly that she has stepped out of her place in reporting a rape and asking for justice. The policemen responding to the call provide the first level of harassment. They apparently seek vicarious pleasure from having the woman recount over and over again the details of the rape when their initial report usually doesn't require the information they are eliciting."

An appalling example of police callousness—one which could be duplicated in many places—was told by New York Women Against Rape (NYWAR), a feminist crisis center. A Spanish victim phoned and said she had been assaulted by a neighbor who helped her carry home a heavy load of groceries. Once the man got inside her apartment, he attacked and raped her. Another neighbor heard her screams and called the police. When the patrolmen arrived, the woman was still being raped and was bleeding from multiple blows. "When the rapist opened the door to the police, he claimed that everything was 'okay.' The woman denied this, begging the police to arrest the man for rape. The policemen refused, saying she had no chance of getting a conviction since she had let the man inside her apartment. They let the man leave, taking no action against him. The police did not even offer to take the woman to the hospital for medical treatment." Because the victim was Spanish, the police automatically judged her a liar and refused to help—a case of racial as well as sexual discrimination.

Minority women are especially oppressed by the police. In New York City, 60 percent of rape victims are estimated to be black or Spanish women. NYWAR members say that "Black women really get the raw end of the deal with the police." Some minority victims report being propositioned and physically as well as verbally manhandled by the police officers who question them. Mae Walker, who worked with Harlem victims, agreed with others that "more rapes are committed on Third World women than any other group, and they are reported least."

Accounts of rape cases given to us by California police officers working in Mexican and black areas revealed the same racist–sexist bias. Their contempt for these lower-class "basically lazy" people was obvious. Rape is common in such communities, they said; people are not shocked or alarmed: "These girls who get raped have generally the same story. She went to the party with Frank, and they started taking reds (barbiturates) or drinking. After the party she and Frank went for a cruise. He started getting friendly, and it ended up in a rape. Usually it's a boy–girl friend experience."

The ages and life-styles of women also prejudice police against them. Hitchhikers are often dismissed as "hippies asking for trouble." Teen-agers are routinely disbelieved. For example, one Maryland teen-ager was raped by a policeman who picked her up when she was intoxicated. A Prince Georges County special task force studying rape problems, which later investigated this case, reported, "She was taken to the police station, questioned for a few hours, and then released without medical treatment or examination when the detectives decided her story was inconsistent and no crime had occurred. The girl said she had to repeat her story four or five times during the interview and was told each time she was lying. She claimed her words were twisted to make it seem she had provoked the assault. After being questioned, the girl signed a statement admitting consent. Immediately afterward, the teen-ager reported to a member of this task force that she had signed the statement just to get away from the police questioning." We found rapes by policemen in a number of cities.

A thirteen-year-old girl in Maryland was raped at knifepoint on her way home from school by an eighteen-year-old neighborhood youth. When her parents found out, they took her to the police. Later the family told the special task force that the police interview was very upsetting to them all. Their daughter was embarrassed when she had to write out a detailed statement of the attack. She did not know what some terms meant. The police criticized the mother for not giving her child more sex information—the girl was too naive, they said, to be a good victim–witness. The parents felt that "the police make the victim feel like the guilty one."

Doctors are often aware of police maltreatment of rape victims, although few speak out publicly. One exception is Dr. Dorothy Hicks, head of a Miami hospital rape center. Said Dr. Hicks:

> *Usually a rape victim who reports the crime or seeks medical attention is subjected to degradation and humiliation at the hands of police officers and hospital personnel. Most police officers have a stereotyped view of a rape victim's reactions. They expect her to be hysterical. If she is calm, although it may be a sign of shock, they are likely to believe rape never took place. Equally absurd, if a woman shows no signs of being badly beaten, the police often decide she has been a willing participant.*

Many women have encountered police disbelief and contradictory attitudes toward resistance. At a Seattle rape rap group, victims exchanged their disillusioning experiences. "Police advise you not to fight," one woman said bitterly. "Just lie back and enjoy it—*enjoy it!* Then when you are raped, they ask, 'How come you didn't resist?' When it happened to me, one officer said, 'Tell me the truth. Don't all women secretly want to get raped?' " Officers often blame victims who, in their view, step "out of bounds" or "titillate" men. Said one Los Angeles officer, "Plenty of women ask to be raped by the way they act, by the way they dress and walk and play on a man's feelings."

Too often, instead of being supported and understood by the police at a time of trauma and shock, victims are treated with a lack of respect and regarded scornfully. Typically, officers tell a woman, "Weren't you asking for this, honey? Looks like you enjoyed it. Come on, sweetie, now tell us, just exactly what were you doing on the street so late at night? What were you wearing, that cute little number you got on now?" The victim's self-doubts are reinforced, and she must then go through grueling hours of repetitive, often insulting, and patronizing questions.

To skepticism may be added sheer ignorance. Like most of the population, policemen often have little knowledge of female sexuality. A New York detective long on the force discussed the murder of a sixty-eight-year-old close friend of one of us. When asked if she had been sexually molested, he lowered his voice, looked slightly embarrassed, and said: "No, she wasn't. You see, she was elderly, and when you're senile the vagina shrinks and rape is impossible." This astonishing notion, a new version of "rape is impossible," would have been news to the thousands of women in their eighties and up who are raped.

The importance of immediate and continuing police empathy for the victim has been stressed by the few medical and psychological groups studying rape. The D.C. Mental Health Committee stated that initial "sympathetic support and reduction of emotional trauma" by the police is "the most critical phase for the victim. . . . We would like to underline very strongly that *the police examination, both the timing of it and the exploratory nature of it, take into due account the emotional suffering experienced by the victim.*" The Ann Arbor center summed up the major police role in sex crimes as "the apprehension, identification, and preparation for prosecution of the rapist. This should be done with the least possible trauma to the victim. At present, most police forces are a very long way from this goal."

Fortunately a number of police departments are exceptions to such widespread harassment, sexism, voyeurism, indifference, or, at best, veiled contempt for rape victims. In Denver, Colorado, where a special public task force made strong recommendations for citywide improvements in combating and prosecuting rape, a National Organization for Women (NOW) group praised the police: "Officers work hard to arrive at the truth and to present a tight case to the D.A.s. Actual reports of women indicate that the police treat victims with the utmost dignity and sympathy in difficult questioning." A Denver crisis center worker added:

> *All the victims I have talked to have been very impressed by the empathy and competence with which they were handled. Detective Frank Kennedy, of the Special Rape Investigation Unit, is certainly working beyond the call of duty. After interviewing several victims, he pieced together a good description of a dilapidated old car one rapist was using. On a hunch he spent every night for several hours after work driving up and down capital hill streets looking for the car. When he found it, he found the rapist.*

In Alexandria and nearby Arlington, Virginia, NOW investigators also commented favorably on police responses, finding them generally sensitive to the emotional needs of rape victims and open to suggestions for improvement:

> *Alexandria detectives apparently do not make snap judgments about the validity of rape reports. All time and work necessary to a thorough investigation are given, and they appear to avoid pro-*

vocative and unwarranted questioning of victims. Most victims who dealt with the Arlington police reported positive feelings about their treatment by detectives. Some patrolmen were also found encouraging and sympathetic.

Obviously, police departments differ greatly, as do the personnel within these departments. Despite many examples of police ignorance and insensitivity, victims' reactions vary widely. One young Boston victim felt the police were "outstanding. I have the utmost respect for this police force. They've been unbelievably kind. My feeling is, what can I do to repay them?" Boston Hospital counselors were told by victims that "the police made me feel better," or "they were helpful." A Pittsburgh policeman told us, "Remember, most of us are fathers, sons, and brothers. We care about our women—and we really want to get those guys."

Yet even when the police are genuinely trying to help, their ingrained condescension toward women may add to the victim's humiliation and rage. Most male officers lack sensitivity—and the training—to relate to victims in a nonsexist way. As one young woman described her experience:

The sex squad officers saw me as a daughter, I think. They were middle-aged white men. I was a white college student who went to school with their daughters. So they came on in a very paternalistic way. The precinct officers seemed to believe me, but they were terribly insensitive when they brought me home from the emergency hospital. They spent the whole time discussing other rape cases, which made me pretty sick.

Such subtle sexism can add to the victim's profound sense of helplessness, vulnerability, and weakness. The measure of "good" police treatment is usually assessed, when at all, in simple terms. Attitudinal research, as in all areas of rape, remains inadequate and unsophisticated.

In 1974 the Ann Arbor Women's Crisis Center undertook a pioneering survey to determine whether police treatment of rape victims was in fact nonsupportive and insensitive. The women designed a questionnaire to be given anonymously to rape victims by phone. The results tended to confirm the national impression of mixed police behavior. Half of the women who had reported their rape to the police said they received good treatment, while the other half felt they did not. But nearly one-half the rapes reported in the survey were not reported to the police. Victims usually gave fear as their reason—fear of bad police treatment, of parents or husbands finding out, or of retaliation by the rapist. Thus in this survey only 25 percent of the victims *known* to the Crisis Center approved of the police. One woman said about the officers she saw, "They treated *me* as the criminal. They said my pants were too tight."

Hundreds of stories can, of course, be told on both sides—both for and against police methods, behavior, and attitudes. Other women have mixed experiences. The victim's reaction is usually closely attuned to the treatment she receives from particular police officers. The different reactions produced by policemen who are kind and humane, or rude and arrogant, are illustrated by this victim's typical story:

> *The first two officers who arrived were really nice. They apologized for seeming gruff but explained they had to ask some questions and hoped it would be okay with me. The questions didn't bother me. But then the sergeant came and did dumb things. He held up my nightgown and said, "Is this all you were wearing?" Then he realized I had been in bed asleep when the guy broke in. It was a short nightgown and I almost felt I had to apologize for what I wore to bed. He also wanted to know why I hadn't*

defended myself, and I asked him, wouldn't he rather be raped than dead? He didn't answer that.

Another case demonstrates the understandable ambivalence of victims about being questioned in sex assaults and their resentment over feeling neglected as suffering human beings. Said the victim of a gang rape:

I guess I am really torn between what they had to do and my own needs at that time. I get confused about their duty and feeling their interest is not in me but to find those guys—which, of course, is their job. But they made me constantly repeat myself, like I had to prove everything over and over. Then when I went down to the station to look at pictures, the officer couldn't have been nicer.

Such cases show how essential it is for police investigators to treat the victim as an intelligent person with the right to know why certain questions must be asked. It is harrowing, frustrating, and demeaning for the victim to be asked questions which are never explained, although this is common practice. Such depersonalization is also less productive for the police, since the angry, embarrassed, or frightened victim may evade, repress, or even lie about intimate details that seem irrelevant to her. *A failure to provide information to victims is self-defeating for the police,* since widespread community ignorance and fears about police responses are a major reason why so few sex crimes are reported.

Procedural Guidelines

A few police departments issue procedural outlines to prepare the victim for the necessary steps in her personal treatment and the investigation of her case, although more generally she is told very little or nothing of what lies ahead.

The Washington Metropolitan Police Department's brochure gives a good idea of some positive police methods and how they can be sympathetically presented to rape victims. Four areas are covered: the Interview (of the victim), Crime Scene, Police Assistance Regarding Medical Examination, and Follow-up Investigation. Other sections describe Medical Procedures, Court Procedures, Defense Attorney's Contacts with Victims, and a final Conclusion asking for cooperation and expressing concern for the victim. Such clear explanations are a great help to both victims and police officers. They provide a sample of standards still lacking in most departments:

> Interview: *The initial interview with the investigator is one of the most important phases of the investigation. Due to the confusion, embarrassment, and numerous interruptions, which often occur, the investigator will request that the interview with you be conducted in private, away from all other friends, relatives, neighbors, witnesses, and police officers, unless you desire someone to be present. The questions asked during this interview are not meant to be embarrassing in any way but this information is necessary for presentation in court to prove the elements of the offense. The questions will usually be brief during the initial interview.*
>
> Crime Scene: *The crime scene will be processed by the Crime Scene Examination Section, upon direction of the investigator of the Sex Offense Branch. It will be necessary for the investigator to obtain your clothing that was worn at the time of the assault. Hair samples will also be taken. These items, along with any other recovered evidence, will be sent to the laboratory for analysis.*
>
> Police Assistance Regarding Medical Examination: *You will be requested to have an examination by a physician as soon as possible, at the hospital*

of your choice. However, if you are transported to a hospital other than D.C. General Hospital, you may be billed for hospital services. Transportation will be provided to and from the hospital by the Sex Offense Branch Investigator. A friend or relative may accompany you to the hospital, if you wish.

Follow-up Investigation: *You will be issued a card which gives the time and date you are to report to the Sex Offense Branch Office and the name of the investigator assigned to the case. Upon arrival in the Sex Offense Branch Office, you will be assisted by an investigator in some or all of the following procedures:*

1. *A detailed signed statement.*

2. *Construction of a composite drawing with a police artist.*

3. *Photographing of all injuries.*

4. *Viewing of photographs of known sex offenders.*

5. *Obtaining elimination fingerprints.*

6. *Interview with a Public Health Nurse.*

7. *If the subject is identified, you will accompany the investigator to the United States Attorney's Office to obtain a warrant.*

Interviewing the Victim

The preliminary interview at the crime scene, or as soon as the police are informed, can be crucial for both victim and investigators. Questions clearly and sympathetically asked may elicit key information leading to a rapid arrest and preservation of vital evidence. Contrarily, crude and arrogant interrogators can so frighten the victim that her responses will be limited and important facts will go unreported (aside from the further injury done to the victim herself).

This first interview should be short and cover only essential points: a brief description of the attack and the attacker; his name if known to her, his friends, his place of work, where he lives; a physical description of the assailant (including any information on height, weight, clothes, race, voice, accent, scars, distinguishing characteristics, and so on); any weapons used, threats made, key phrases, etc.; general description of the rape scene (such as the type of car if it occurred in one) and other pertinent factors; and any possible witnesses. After this initial brief interview, carried out with as much privacy and courtesy as possible, the police officer should speed the victim to immediate medical attention. Then he or his partner, or the more specialized investigators, can continue their probe of the crime scene, question other witnesses, and gather physical evidence for the crime lab.

The *detailed interview,* which should be made only after the victim has received medical attention and psychological support, must again cover these questions and go into further detail in each area. Again, an atmosphere of sympathetic concern for the victim as an injured individual against whom a crime has been committed is essential to the interview. If inconsistencies appear, the victim may have to repeat certain sections of her story. But the interviewer should explain the need for such intensive questioning and treat her with respect as an intelligent person. The victim should never be threatened, shouted at, cursed, disparaged, teased, provoked, insulted, hounded, or treated in any other demeaning way. Police destroy their own dignity and credibility by making aspersions and innuendoes against a victim, even if they genuinely doubt her report. Experience and intelligent assessment, not browbeating, are the tools of true professionals.

The use of a standardized form for rape interviews has often been suggested to resolve the interwoven problems of sensitivity, consistency, relevance, and thoroughness. Undoubtedly such a form would often help, and a number of departments have developed interviewing guidelines. But *most important* are the skill and courtesy of the questioning officer, personal elements that can never be replaced by any list of questions, no matter how excellent it is. In many cases, rigidly following a set of preconceived questions might upset a victim and lead to superficial answers. The interviewer who is in tune with the victim's mood and reactions will adapt his questions to the circumstances and to the person and will sympathetically draw from her the most pertinent information. This is not to disparage forms, but rather to view them with some caution. Accuracy and honesty, from the police interviewer as well as from the victim being interviewed, are also essential factors.

Use of Policewomen

Interviews are often more productive if the police officer is a woman rather than a man, as women and police themselves are coming to realize. Although women are conditioned to regard males as authority figures—and many policemen claim victims prefer to be interviewed by a man—a well-trained policewoman can overcome this obstacle and offer woman-to-woman understanding and psychological support which victims cannot find in a man. Policewomen also have less sex prejudice. One Manhattan attorney observed, "Police are skeptical about the authenticity of a rape report because they are men. I've talked to policewomen who are not as skeptical as their male colleagues about legitimacy." However, some policewomen (especially "oldtimers") echo male bias against victims as "rape bait." Said one, "The majority of rapes happen because the woman does something foolish. . . . So many silly little girls, dressed the way they are, lead a man on, then think they can back out."

More and more policewomen, however, feel strongly that victims do not "invite" rape and that female police officers can be far more effective with victims than their male colleagues. "Women will give female detectives information they say they won't give to men," said New York's Lieutenant Julia Tucker, former commander of the first all-woman section on sex crimes. "Many policemen are embarrassed in sex cases. They just don't know how to come across with the right questions." Her successor, Lieutenant Mary Keefe, shares this concern over the clumsiness of male interviews. "Frequently the male officers come on too strong," Keefe noted. "That inhibits the victim from following through with her complaint, to see that the perpetrator gets his conviction."

Few policemen have any understanding of the complexity of emotions felt by rape victims, just as they have little understanding of women in general. They tend to see sex cases in simplistic terms, and want simple, clear-cut reactions from victims. Conditioned to be mistrustful and impatient with women, most male officers lack both sophistication and patience. They may also be secretly shocked and embarrassed themselves, which they cover up by being brusque. Or they may feel guilty at near-rape relationships with women in their own lives or simply because they are men and may have fantasized rape themselves. Or they may feel terribly inadequate in dealing with the situation, both the victim and the crime. The major problem seen by many feminists is that most police officers are male, "and men look at rape as primarily sexual, while women see it as primarily violent—an act of terror," said D.C. rape center spokeswomen. "Police questions are often not like those asked in other violent crimes, but deal basically with sex. Policemen typically try to find out if the victim is sexually active. If she says yes, she is encouraged to drop the case. If the woman was raped in her own bed, they want to know if her nightclothes were 'alluring.' "

New York City has one of the country's highest sex crime rates, and the women's movement has pressed hard for reforms in this city. As a result, an innovative all-female Sex Crimes Mobile Unit, helped by local

women's organizations, has been set up by the NYC
Police Department as part of its special Sex Crimes
Analysis Section, which is headed and mainly staffed
by policewomen. The Mobile Unit—which travels to
different neighborhoods—contains a rape-prevention
demonstration by policewomen, charts, warnings, advice to prospective victims, and a small room for confidential discussions between city women and the
friendly, matter-of-fact policewomen. The department
maintains some twenty-five policewomen in the city's
five boroughs and twenty-five women at headquarters.
These women are backed up by over fifty policemen and
a twenty-four telephone service. Policewoman Terry
Enterlin explained their functions: "All a woman has to
do is have the nerve to come to us, and we'll carry the
ball from there. We'll fill out a complaint, counsel the
woman, and go through all the necessary procedures
with her, all the way to the D.A. and the courts."

New York's all-woman section was started in 1973 in
response both to the chilling rise in the city's rapes over
two years—nearly 36 percent—and to the recognized
fact that rape victims are often reluctant to talk to men
officers. The unit tries to interview the victims as soon
as possible for vital information to determine how,
when, and where the rapist strikes and to identify and
apprehend him. At least seventy complaints come in
each week. Most are from young women in their twen-
ties but victims can be any age. With the help of detectives, the unit is making a concerted attempt to collect
data in a consistent way in order to find meaningful rape
patterns and to develop better investigative techniques.
The NYC Police Department is also pioneering in a
Police Foundation funded study based on interviews of
350 victims to learn how to respond better to rape calls
and how to improve interviewing methods.

Sergeant Carolen Bailey of St. Paul, Minnesota, is
another young, dynamic, and self-confident policewoman who believes that women are better at questioning victims and just as good as men in tracking down

rapists. "A policewoman can do anything a policeman can," said Sergeant Bailey, the sole woman in the homicide and sex section of St. Paul's Police Department. "We should have women on patrol to respond to all rape calls," she said in a 1973 interview, "but right now we don't have any." Sergeant Bailey questions all rape victims personally and has found most of them cooperative. "They are usually extremely upset right after the attack," she said, "but the next day they have calmed down. I always tell victims who are too upset that we can talk later. I also make certain they know that they don't have to prosecute. But I tell them it's very important at least to report the facts to the police so we can build up an M.O. [modus operandi or method of operation] on the rapist."

A 1974 study by a Pennsylvania State University sociologist revealed that policewomen who move up through the ranks have greater leadership potential than their male counterparts. Dr. Barbara Price, former research director for the university's Police Executive Development Training Institute, tested 253 men and women police officials on the eleven personality traits commonly used to indicate leadership. Dr. Price concluded: "The tests showed that women police executives are significantly more emotionally independent, intellectually aggressive, and flexible in their attitudes." The policewomen "scored consistently higher" in five of the eleven traits, tied with the men in five others, and trailed in only one—persistence. "The women came out ahead in the areas of emotional strength," said Dr. Price. "They were able to handle confrontations better—both alone and with the help of others. The women also showed they could meet the challenge of new situations better, and they are more self-confident."

Physical Evidence

Collecting and interpreting physical evidence is an essential part of sex crimes investigations. The police should clearly and sympathetically explain the need for preserving this evidence to the victim. The immediate reaction of most rape victims after the assault is to wash themselves thoroughly and destroy their contaminated clothing. Many shower repeatedly and take vaginal douches, trying desperately to cleanse themselves of the mental anguish of feeling dirty and "used." Disgust, shame, guilt, horror, revulsion at self and others, fear of disease and pregnancy—all these emotions are mixed with the need to wash away the knowledge that one's body has been invaded and brutalized by another. Tragically, few policemen are trained or able to empathize with the victim about these feelings; they do not put themselves in the victim's place (such as by imagining themselves sodomized). Instead, they add to her guilt by blaming her for washing and "destroying evidence" by removing, through douching, live sperm in her body. Despite the victim's discomfort, all cleansing should be delayed until she can be thoroughly examined for material evidence.

In addition to gathering physical evidence at the crime scene and from the victim herself that will aid in tracking down the assailant, the police are concerned with supporting the following legal charges: that sexual penetration, however slight, occurred; that force was used in the assault; and that the victim was forced into a sexual act against her will. The victim's physical condition is considered basic. As the standard police manual states, "Penetration of the vagina is the prime condition of the act, and the male need not experience an emission. Thus, the act of penetration, not the degree of completeness of the act, is the necessary element." Feminists are trying to widen the laws to include penetration of any part of the body as rape; e.g., anal and oral, and by objects other than the penis. But most laws and courts still focus on penile–vaginal crime.

In the hospital results, the police look for proof of tissue damage in the vaginal area (see Chapter 4). In addition, smears and wet specimens are taken from the vaginal passage to check for sperm. While evidence of sperm usually helps the case in court, it proves nothing other than that the victim had sexual intercourse recently (time estimates vary greatly according to individual physiological factors). This is one reason why police question victims about when they last had sexual relations. The absence of spermatozoa in rape cases, however, is far from rare. Some rapists are sterile or have had vasectomies; ejaculation may be interrupted; the victim may have washed away the evidence; the testing may be poor or inadequate; and so on. Many rapists are actually impotent and cannot climax in an assault, or they assault the victim in perverse ways.

The victim's entire body is also examined both for injuries and for foreign materials useful as evidence, such as fibers, lint, dirt, grease, vegetation fragments, etc. Bite marks on face, neck, and breasts are frequent. The thighs may show evidence of force. Samples of the victim's pubic hair are examined in the police laboratory for foreign hairs which may reveal the sex, approximate age, and race of the rapist, as well as the part of the body from which they came (although a specific individual cannot be identified). The pubic combing is often bewildering and obnoxious to victims and *must* be tactfully explained. Hair specimens are also taken from the victim's head for comparison purposes. Fingernail clippings may provide skin scrapings of the rapist.

The victim's clothing and her surroundings, if known, are closely examined for semen, blood, fingerprints, and other physical evidence. Clothing should be collected before it is washed or destroyed and carefully handled to preserve evidence which only lab tests can discover. Weapons are also often used to terrorize rape victims or, fortunately less often, to injure them. If a weapon is not left at the scene of the attack, a description may lead to the discovery of such incriminating evidence on a suspect or in his residence or car. Automobiles, where many rapes take place, may provide important evidence.

A thorough physical examination of a suspect, when possible, is as important as that of a victim. Usually the assailant has plenty of time to remove any evidence of his act before being arrested. Yet police and doctors report that in many cases he has not bothered to clean or wash himself, and thus may unwittingly have preserved crucial evidence. Semen is often found on the penis, pubic hair, or clothing of the accused, as well as evidence of vaginal skin cells on his penis. His clothes may also have physiologic fluids or hairs from the victim. Such known materials, when compared to those found on the victim, may provide a strong chain of corroboration. The suspect's general body surface may also show signs of injuries if a struggle occurred, such as scratches and bites on his hands and arms or scratches on his face and neck, all of which are common in rape.

Police skills in gathering physical evidence, making technical studies, and piecing together even minute clues are extremely important to catch the assailant and prove the crime. Most police departments, however, lack good cross-checking systems to make full use of such physical clues, and instead use a kind of "Dick Tracy" verbal checkout between individuals. Instead of a computerized or even manual system that would turn up repetitions of important evidence—such as the make or color of a car used in different rapes—detectives may casually rely on their own and others' memories: "Say, Joe, wasn't a green car used in that James Street rape last year?" Filing methods are also often antiquated. On the positive side, a few departments have modernized methods and sophisticated personnel to find and match evidence. But all too often, sloppy and inadequate work by policemen at the scene prevents an arrest or ruins a rape case in court.

Los Angeles prosecutor Aaron Stovitz, a veteran of rape trials, voiced the lawyers' typical complaints (police complain as bitterly about attorneys' ineptitudes):

The police usually don't have the time, manpower, or inclination to thoroughly investigate a rape before they dump it on us to prosecute. Time and again, we get a good case we could have won if the cops hadn't blown it at the scene of the crime. Either they don't question the victim enough, they don't take pictures of all the evidence—or maybe they just don't spend enough time collecting evidence before they run out and arrest some guy. That precludes any further leads that could strengthen our case. Besides that, half the time they arrest the wrong guy altogether.

Finding the Rapist

Establishing the assailant's identity may involve very simple or very complex factors. He may be picked up at or near the scene of the crime and be immediately identified. He may be brought in soon afterward and identified by the victim in a police lineup. He may be painstakingly sketched by the police artist or similarly formed from a composite kit which enables an arrest to be made. He may be caught through his use of a telltale M.O. (*modus operandi*), such as raping in a certain building or area, using a certain disguise or story for false entry, and so on, or he may leave repetitive clues which eventually give him away. It is important for the police to broadcast a rapist's M.O. as soon as possible. This is illustrated by the capture of an assailant who had been flagging down women on a freeway in the early morning hours posing as a stranded motorist; one woman spotted him and phoned the police in time for him to be picked up. Evidence tying him to a recent rape was found in his car, and he was positively identified by two victims.

Identifying the attacker can be very traumatic for a victim, and too often the police are insensitive, even callous, in setting up such encounters. One hospital nurse who had been brutally raped suffered severe hysterics when she was brought in to identify a suspect. She assumed she would be in a dark room and he would be in another, as in the movies; instead, she was suddenly brought face to face with the man who had raped her. Another victim was asked to view a lineup of five suspects, each standing in front of a number. Her description indicates important nuances of circumstance and reaction to which police are often oblivious:

You know what it looked like from watching television. What you don't know is what it felt like and how hard it is to identify someone under those conditions. The lights on the men were very bright. When he attacked me he had come out of the shadows. He honestly didn't look the same. I had to remember what I had seen and see it all again in this light and this place. . . . I was cold and alone and afraid. Afraid I would identify the wrong man. Afraid he would jump through the glass and kill me when he heard my voice. Afraid I would be sick right there and ruin the control I was fighting so hard to keep.

In her report, "Forcible Rape: A Consideration of the Basic Issues," Cynthia Jackson, an analyst with the Justice Department's Law Enforcement Assistance Administration, also pointed out:

The process of identification of the offender can be a difficult one for victims. In some states, if the police apprehend a suspect within one hour of the offense, he can be returned to the scene of the offense for identification purposes. In rape cases, requiring a victim to identify her assailant so soon after the assault can be terrifying. However, going to the police station to review mug shots or a lineup can be very embarrassing because the victim is aware that most of the police personnel in the room with the photographs and areas around the lineup viewing room know that she is a rape victim.

Another problem is that the victim is often not told of developments in her case, such as whether suspects have been arrested, the results of medical tests, whether evidence has been found, or if an arrested suspect is out on bail. Many victims are frightened of being attacked again, and if they have reported the assault, of the rapist's revenge. This terror should be easy to understand, especially if the victim learns that the man she accused is still free or has been released. Yet police may show no concern for her natural feelings of anxiety.

The police, in turn, feel that nobody understands their problems and that their "objective" attitudes are justified by the realities of rape. Explained one detective:

> The average police officer simply tries to view the rape in the same way he knows a suspicious, doubtful jury will look at it later in court. Police reflect the attitudes of the court. Only about 2 percent of all victims will call us immediately. Most rush home first or they sit around for hours, calming down, getting over embarrassment, calling relatives. Some women don't call us until the next day. Obviously, the longer a woman waits to report, the more it reflects on her veracity as a witness. We figure if it didn't bother her any more than that, why should it bother us or any jury? And what would you think if a woman who said she was raped was calmly drinking coffee when you arrived? If it's a guy who's a neighbor, a friend, or an old lover, we have to be careful. You'd be amazed how many times a woman tries to get revenge for some reason or other.

Many victims are well aware of such police cynicism. As one New Yorker said, "My date tore my clothes to shreds and raped me, but I never reported it. I knew it was hopeless. The police would have said, Well, you invited him up." A young California hitchhiker who had been raped eleven times by three young students who forced her to go to their apartment was convinced by the two officers not to bring charges—they said they believed her story, but probably no jury would. Such incidents are commonplace. The difficulty and humiliation of convincing first police and then judges and juries that a rape has occurred keep many victims from reporting in the first place. As a result, the vicious circle of silence and social complicity grows larger and tighter, and America's women are caught in the deadly noose.

The Least Reported Crime

A major handicap in police prevention and investigation of sex crimes is the appalling lack of information about both rapists and victims, although at long last the Department of Justice is beginning to assemble more extensive data. No one really knows how many rapes and sexual assaults occur yearly. The FBI figures of about 55,000 forcible and attempted rapes each year are merely a surface indication. Official estimates generally range from five to ten times this number; some experts feel that only one in twenty sex assaults is ever reported. Rape crisis centers tend to support the highest estimates, and most women working with victims believe that at least 90 percent of actual rapes are never reported. In 1965, the National Opinion Research Council conducted victimization studies for the President's Commission on Law Enforcement and the Administration of Justice. Based on Council percentages, Professor William Brown of the New York State University's School of Criminal Justice concluded that in 1968 *well over half a million women and children were sex victims.*[1] In 1975, with even official figures climbing sharply, the total is even higher.

FBI statistics are further limited by including only forcible and attempted rapes of adults, not children.

[1] "Police–Victim Relationships in Sex Crime Investigations." *The Police Chief*, January 1970.

Rape is defined as forced vaginal intercourse—which leaves out anal rapes and other types of sexual assaults that are increasingly common. The FBI also depends entirely on local police departments for its data, and many of these agencies are notoriously unreliable in collecting information. Dr. Duncan Chappell, then Associate Professor of Criminal Justice at the State University of New York at Albany, and his assistant, Susan Singer, made comparative studies (published in 1971 and 1973) of data in Boston, Los Angeles, and New York police files. They reported a poor level in quality and quantity of information on all aspects of rape, with very little detail on either rapists or victims. Comparisons between different departments were further hampered by a lack of standardized definitions. The researchers concluded:

> *It is patently obvious that what each department regards as the kind of case to be classified as forcible rape and forwarded to the FBI* Uniform Crime Reports *for tabulation as such is far from equivalent.* . . . The need for standardized police reporting methods for the entire nation seems so obvious to us that the absence of such measures, given the nature of public and political concern about crime, appears almost incomprehensible. (Emphasis added.)

The lack of comprehensive crime complaint forms in most departments is a great hindrance to investigation as well as reporting. A few departments, such as Los Angeles, have recently developed detailed computerized forms on the criminal's personal description and M.O. A police-community study group in Buffalo, New York, began work in 1974 to assess national police forms and to design a form especially for rape and rape victims. As Chappell and Singer pointed out, the development of such a form "should receive the highest priority. The use of such a form could aid in preventing clues being missed, and assist with the systematic gathering of evidence in rape cases by providing more effective screening data with which to identify at an early stage in an investigation whether or not a complaint is well founded."

A public health investigator in Kentucky who researched rape in rural areas told the National Organization for Women that she had found an incredible lack of ethical standards in official reporting. "Some counties reported no rapes in their 1973–1974 crime statistics," she said. "Yet private physicians in those same counties admitted they had treated dozens of cases in that period." There is no reason to believe that nonreporting by either agencies or individuals is peculiar to any region. Even the FBI reports show suspiciously low figures in many areas, or even reports of no rapes—a highly unlikely event for such places as Waltham, Massachusetts; Amsterdam, New York; Ashland, Kentucky; or Belleville, New Jersey—all cities with 50,000 to 100,000 people. A Bethesda, Maryland, doctor told us that in his forty years of practice, including work in a community clinic, "I don't believe I have ever had a single rape case where they went to the police. When I ask them why, they say, 'Who wants that hassle?' The girls tell me the police harass the victims. Apparently the cops just don't believe them. And the women say it doesn't do any good to tell the police—they never catch the men."

There are probably eight basic reasons why so few rapes are reported or, if reported, do not show up in the statistics:

1. Women are brought up to be ashamed and guilty at being raped. Husband, families, friends, and neighbors, it is feared, would treat them as outcasts if they knew (as too often happens). This is probably the major cause of women not reporting.

2. Women fear police, hospital, and court harassment, as well as embarrassing publicity.

3. Police departments fail to publicize and explain procedures in rape cases, provide a sympathetic reception for sex complaints, or encourage victims to report.

4. Police often don't believe women when they do report. Or they try to act as lawyers themselves and advise against bringing a charge.

5. Rape charges may be dismissed as "unfounded" for many reasons—lack of evidence, failure to pursue the case, the D.A.'s unwillingness to prosecute, the woman's decision to drop her charge, and so on. These rapes may never appear in the statistics.

6. The charge is changed by police or courts to another criminal category easier to prove. Or if the rapist also murdered his victim, the charge is "murder" and the rape is not counted (according to police officers we interviewed). Both police and courts try to avoid charging rape.

7. The defendant may get off with a lighter charge or may agree to plead guilty to a lesser charge if the rape charge is dropped. Many cases are negotiated and settled out of court.

8. Many police statistics themselves are unreliable and incomplete. FBI totals are compiled from figures filtering in from city, town, county, and rural police departments in every state. Some departments fabricate figures to satisfy the FBI and keep up an active image for public or private funding. Even those starting to use computers provide few useful breakdowns, if any, on suspects, M.O.s, assault locations, characteristics of rapists, weapons used, etc.

New York Police Detective Al Simon, a policeman who understands many problems of rape from a woman's point of view, expressed the frustrations of women and enlightened police investigators when he pointed out:

A lot of officers, especially the oldtimers, believe that unless a woman comes in bruised, there's no

*rape. They also say, "Unless a woman's a virgin,
what's the big deal?" But I wonder if one of these
guys was suddenly jumped and forced to commit
sodomy at gunpoint, wouldn't he be pretty upset?
And wouldn't he submit? These women have no
reason to lie. Sometimes there's a love triangle,
where a woman yells rape to get even with a guy,
but you can screen those cases out easily enough.
But for God's sake, when the woman never saw the
guy before in her life, and she tells you that he
raped her in the park or in the hallway, and she
identifies him, what more corroboration should a
judge need? Why isn't this woman's word good
enough?*

Police Frustrations

Concerned police officers such as Detective Simon
are understandably enraged and frustrated when a rape
case on which they have worked long and hard is
thrown away by a prosecutor or discounted by a judge or
jury. Attorneys often blame police negligence for losing
rape cases, which indeed happens. But the opposite is
too often true as well.

A 1974 Chicago episode vividly illustrates the out-
rage of police officers who built a solid rape case and
then had the state's attorneys settle for minor charges.
Early one morning, two Chicago patrolmen suddenly
saw a girl running toward their squad car and waving
frantically. Choking back tears, the teen-ager said she
had been raped and the assailants were holding her
cousin in a nearby parked car. The policemen quickly
arrested the suspects and questioned the victims.

The two girls, thirteen and fifteen, had been waiting
for a bus late the night before, when a nineteen-year-old
boy one of them had seen at high school offered them a
ride. The youth stopped to pick up a friend, then some
liquor, assuring the girls each time that they would
immediately be taken home. Instead, the two youths

drove them to the lakefront. One girl jumped from the car, but the rear tire ran over her foot; the boys hit her and pushed her back inside. The victims were forced to remove their clothes by threats of being beaten and shot, and both were raped repeatedly for several hours. Finally, early the next morning, one rapist fell asleep, and the girl escaped and ran to the approaching police car.

The evidence seemed overwhelming. Medical examinations confirmed penetration and found other signs of sexual violence. Both offenders had long arrest records. The police officials agreed that rape charges should be brought. But the assistant state's attorney refused, contending that since one of the victims knew one of the offenders, if only casually, it was not rape. He said he would instead approve a charge of unlawful restraint.

A furious police officer demanded, "Do you mean I can rape any woman I know and be charged only with unlawful restraint? What would you do if that was your sister who was attacked?"

The lawyer replied, "I don't have a sister."

"Well, how about if it was your wife or girl friend?"

"I'm not married," said the attorney. "But if I was, I'd probably be emotionally upset and call it rape."

When the case was heard, another assistant state's attorney suggested to the arresting officer that he reduce the charge to unlawful restraint and a sentence of three years with probation. The patrolman balked. "Can't we get them some jail time?" he asked, and was told, no. Finally the prosecutor and the public defender agreed on a charge of contributing to the sexual delinquency of a child.

A Chicago police paper, *The Blue Light*, commented:

Through plea bargaining, the state's attorney would be assured of an easy conviction. The public defender would be assured the next thing to an acquittal, probation. The defendants, as the not-so-funny joke among policemen has it, would be

home before the arresting officer completed his
court disposition papers.

The arresting patrolman assumed that the accused
rapists would get at least some time in prison. The
prosecutor told him they would receive a year's misdemeanor probation with the first ninety days in the
House of Correction. Yet an hour later even that meager
sentence had been reduced—the state decided to settle
for a year's probation for both offenders with no jail
time.

Police are also thwarted by the refusal of parents
(especially fathers) to prosecute, by uncooperative victims, and by women who change their stories in court.
One officer told of his fairly common experience with
an obstructing father:

It is really tough on us. This is a good case. The girl
had time to observe the guy and she gave us a
complete physical description—he was naked so
she saw a tattoo. We have a suspect who fits the
description, and we think he probably did it. But
the father won't let her go through with it. If the
father won't cooperate, we can't do much.

Another policeman complained about problems with
witnesses: "Some women get messed up on the stand.
They get flustered by questions like, did he in fact in-
sert? Did he climax? What did he say? The women come
across sounding confused and contradictory." In a second officer's experience: "You have cases where the
woman screams for help, the police come and start
subduing the man—and then she yells, 'Don't hurt
him!' Or she charges rape and sings a different story on
the stand."

Police may also share the victim's rage at legal tactics
which tear the victim down as a person in order to make
her story sufficiently doubtful for an acquittal. A sympathetic Minneapolis cop pointed out:

We never even hear of 80 percent of the rape cases. So few call the police or even want to press charges. And I'll tell you why. When the girl gets to court it is as if she has to prove it was rape and not just sex. It is like she is on trial and not the man. The defense really makes it a terrible experience for the girl. The questions and accusations made about her can seem worse than any other experience.

In their book on counseling rape victims, *Rape: Victims of Crisis*, Boston nursing professor Dr. Ann Burgess and sociology professor Dr. Lynda Holmstrom mention serious police concern over convicting rapists: "Usually police are very much on the side of the victim. They are the one solid group of professionals who see case after case and see what happens to victims as they go through the legal process. Many actively want to get convictions on rape cases. . . ."

Negative Police Attitudes

We have already considered many negative and sexist police attitudes, but some further aspects and often overlooked subtleties should be stressed. Many police continue to believe that there are far more false rape reports than the small number which occasionally appear. Women generally feel there are few. As victims say, "Who would want to go through all that hassle out of spite?" The entire process is so long, complicated, and both physically and psychologically wearing that it is hard to imagine anyone other than a very disturbed or very determined woman making a false rape report and sticking with it. But the cultural bias, plus police cynicism from repeated disappointments with court procedures and with victims (who *do* often get flustered, forget details, remember others, or become frightened of pressing charges), make many officers extremely wary of "putting themselves on the line."

In *Freedom from Rape,* the Ann Arbor Women's Crisis Center tries to explain to women the social and psychological complexities involved in understanding what to expect from the police; their ideas are shared by many women:

> *Police officers, by and large, are male. Their views, like those of other men, have been shaped by the society in which they live. It is quite possible that if a policeman was raised in a typical American home, he developed a value system that typifies women as gentle, quiet, and sweet. He probably believes that women would do best to stay at home in the evening unless accompanied by a husband or proper escort. What happens if a woman reports she was raped while walking alone at night or after coming out of a bar alone? The policeman (consciously or unconsciously) makes a value judgment about "what kind" of a woman she is. If she is outspoken, independent, and/or "promiscuous" she is likely to be judged, "that kind," and therefore was probably "asking for it." The rape, in effect, is her just deserts. No real crime has been committed.*

A basic part of a policeman's job should be the proper treatment of victims—seeing that they are calmed and comforted; that they receive prompt and good medical treatment; that some relative or friend is summoned to help them; that they are given emotional as well as medical support; and that they are told of police, medical, and legal procedures in a clear and reassuring way (that they are, in essence, made to feel that the police and society care about what happened to them and will help them recover from the shock and anguish of such an assault). The police, after all, are social servants paid by the taxes of citizens who expect help when victimized by criminals. The police officer's *first* duty is to help and protect the innocent victim. His second duty is to find and arrest the suspect and prepare evidence for prosecution under the law. His third duty is to protect *all* women from becoming victims.

Too few police, however, seem to keep these responsibilities firmly in mind and convey a sense of concern and protection to sex victims. Their own "masculine" milieu abounds with dehumanizing stereotypes about women. Station house rape jokes are standard, revealing a deeply rooted (though perhaps unconscious) hostility to women. Officers laughingly define rape as "poor salesmanship." Policemen routinely repeat the old saw, "A girl can run faster with her skirts up than a man can with his pants down." Police phraseology can be extremely offensive. In interviews they often refer to the assailant as the "gentleman." Rape victims are asked, "What did the man say when he was making love to you?" Imagine the male victim sodomized in the movie *Deliverance* being asked that question. One self-defense teacher decided to practice some reverse psychology during the film. When the scene came on, she shouted at the horrified audience, "He likes it! He really wants it!" Men stared at her angrily, she told us, but a few women giggled; they knew what she meant.

Male police officials also use in their daily language the same expressions as other men, calling women *broads, cunts, chicks, bitches, whores, pieces of ass, tails, sluts,* in seemingly endless insulting terms. Just as words like "nigger," "wop," "kike," and "gook," dehumanize other oppressed castes, such sexist terms reinforce the belief that females are not really persons, certainly not "people" like men. The debasing and corrosive results of such expressions are not realized by the general public, but they are a significant cause— and expression—of the deep mistrust and alienation between the sexes. Such words and attitudes are also an integral part of the many reasons why so few women want to tell a man when they have been raped.

Reforming the Police

From the foregoing discussion, it is clear that many police reforms are urgent and long overdue if rape is ever to be brought under control in our society, if rapists are to be apprehended, and victims are to be adequately served. These include such basic changes as:

1. Having policewomen in all departments to interview and handle rape victims. Having questioning done by one officer, in private, with a friend or relative present if the victim wishes. Police interviews should focus more on suspects than on victims.

2. Taking victims to the hospital as soon as possible.

3. Providing better training for police officers in dealing humanely and effectively with all aspects of sex crimes.

4. Designing adequate forms for taking complaints, interviewing victims, and coordinating investigative information.

5. Giving victims and the community full information about police, medical, and legal procedures, including information about why questions must be asked and certain evidence collected. The communications gap remains wide and the police must work hard to close it.

6. Developing methods to prevent rape and help women defend themselves against attack.

7. Standardizing definitions and statistical gathering throughout the nation.

8. Establishing referral services for professional, nonpolice emotional support, such as with a public health or community family service agency.

9. Maintaining checks with complainants on the quality of police services and constantly striving to improve those services.

10. Improving police practices toward victims in minority or poverty areas.

11. Encouraging victims to prosecute but not coercing them in any way.

While some individuals and departments are becoming aware of such needs, it is essentially the continuing efforts of concerned women that are creating public concern about rape and pressuring officials into reforming themselves. Police are being visited with increasing regularity by crisis center volunteers and women's movement activists. Foremost in such work are the Rape Task Forces organized by the National Organization for Women (NOW). A pioneering kit is now available and being put into effect by most NOW chapters throughout the country. The kit features a detailed thirty-eight-point police questionnaire, with instructions, that is designed to elicit the most pertinent information from local police agencies, to educate women in the weaknesses of police approaches to rape, and to raise the consciousness of the police themselves. The NOW Rape Task Force Kit is extremely instructive and valuable for all citizens concerned about rape; no other group has developed such complete and sophisticated guidelines. (For more information, write Mary Ann Largen, National Organization for Women, 1957 East 73rd Street, Chicago, Illinois 60649.)

Foremost in police reform is the need to have the police regard the victim's physical and mental health as of primary importance. This means training the police in being sensitive, courteous, sympathetic, and non-judgmental; in asking clear and intelligent questions and recording answers accurately; and above all in showing concern about the victim's well-being. While police systems, techniques, methods, and procedures need improvement in many areas, no great or lasting changes in the overall situation will follow unless *attitudes* are changed at the same time. Until police come to view attacks on women and children as seriously as they view attacks on men and property—and until women are seen as equal human beings—real reform will remain an illusion, and forcible rape will continue its devastating acceleration.

4
THE MEDICAL COMPLEX: HEALERS OR OPPRESSORS?

Rape has been largely ignored as a public health problem. It should be considered as a medical–psychiatric emergency.
    —Dr. Edward Weiss, Washington, D.C. Medical Society

The rapist must have enjoyed you—you have such a nice tight vagina.
    —Private physician to a rape victim

The rape of women by men is not nearly as devastating an experience as the rape of men by men, because raping a woman is just an extension of the normal sex act.
    —Doctor in a metropolitan hospital

The young woman tried hard to control her trembling as the nurse helped her remove her torn, bloodstained jeans and shirt and climb onto the examining table. She even smiled wanly at the frowning doctor, but he seemed not to notice.

"Well, well, another wild weekend, eh?" he said, snapping on rubber gloves. It was more a comment than a question. "Now, young lady, just what did your boyfriend do to you?"

The student stared at him in bewilderment, her face pale. "Boyfriend? It was a—a man who—who came out of the dark. I never saw him before." Suddenly she stiffened and bit her lips in pain as the doctor roughly inserted a speculum. "Oh, please, that hurts!"

"Well, it wouldn't if you'd relax. My God, you girls go out at all hours of the night and you expect nothing to

105

happen." He shook his head impatiently. "Maybe you have to get raped a few times to learn how to behave."

Not all physicians treat rape victims with the callousness and condescension of this emergency room doctor in a large university town; but, tragically, all too many still regard rape victims as "provocative" and "getting what they deserve," and treat victims according to their own sexist prejudices. Dozens of women told us similar stories, experiences confirmed by rape crisis centers and women's groups all over the country.

A Boston woman graduate student described the insensitivity of the doctors who examined her. As she walked home one night from an evening seminar, two men forced her into a car, drove to a deserted part of town, and raped her. Terrified of being killed if she resisted, she pretended to cooperate. After the rape, the assailants left her near her apartment.

The next day she decided to see a doctor. "It wasn't easy," she recalled. "I felt terribly embarrassed and ashamed about what had happened. But I kept breaking down in tears, and I was afraid of VD or pregnancy. I didn't know any doctors, so I went to one I had heard was good and very nice. What I really wanted more than anything, I guess, was someone to reassure and sympathize with me, to understand the terror I had been through."

At first the doctor appeared kindly as the victim tearfully told her story. Then he asked if she had been a virgin, and when the young woman said no he began to seem wary. The student tried to explain that she was having her first affair and was not "promiscuous." The doctor examined her and then called in a colleague. The two men discussed "how untorn and unbruised I was down there, and how it didn't look as if I had fought at all." They berated the victim for being out alone at night and asked why she didn't marry her lover. Finally they dismissed her as needing no treatment, without advising her about the need for later VD and pregnancy tests.

The young woman felt devastated: "I left feeling

worse than I have ever felt in my life—shamed and unclean. I felt I was not believed and that the rape had been my fault. So for over ten years I never talked about it, but I didn't forget a thing. Looking back, I think I could more easily forgive those guys who raped me than those two doctors."

All too often, victims refuse to report because they fear such treatment. As a New York rape victim said: "I knew I'd probably be humiliated if I went to a hospital. I've heard a lot of victims talk about getting the same snickers and lewd questions from male hospital attendants as they get from police." A Michigan woman related how, although she was visibly upset from being raped, the male doctor shook her and yelled. "Shut up, you bitch!" Another woman, raped by four men, cried at her vaginal examination and the doctor scolded her for being "such a baby." A California housewife told us that when the doctor examined her, "He just jammed the speculum inside me—it hurt worse than the rape."

Most victims are taken to a particular public hospital which treats rape cases in their area. In a large city, several general hospitals may handle rape patients. Very often, however, public as well as private hospitals will refuse to treat victims of sex assaults. Hospitals and doctors fear becoming involved in time-consuming court cases, being attacked by defense attorneys for negligence and incomplete evidence, and being made to look foolish. In Washington's D.C. General Hospital, Dr. Eliza Taylor, Chief Medical Officer for Ambulatory Services, told us that it is often "like drilling teeth to get the doctors to court because most are part-time and have to leave other jobs and patients if they are called. A rape patient sometimes has to wait while the doctors battle over who will examine her." This situation is common elsewhere.

Many hospitals put their own self-protection ahead of humane service and professional responsibilities. In Chicago, for example, a city of eight million people, as late as 1974 there were still only six hospitals willing to care for rape patients. Dr. Frederick P. Zuspan, a University of Chicago professor and coordinator of a 1974 rape symposium, pointed out:

> *At Chicago Lying-In Hospital, we often have patients referred to us from other emergency rooms where they say they only render "emergency" care. One of the issues in the development of better health care delivery is treatment of patients in their local environments. Unless special expertise is needed, it seems unnecessary to send a rape victim for treatment into an area of the city foreign to her.*

Crisis Center women in different cities described to us similar experiences of apathy, ignorance, and hostility shown by medical personnel toward rape victims. Many doctors and male attendants, and even some nurses, are as contemptuous of these victims as policemen. Medical harassment runs the gamut, from the subtle insensitivity of "jovial" remarks to coldness and overt brutalization. Some doctors play judge and try to convince the victim that she doesn't have a case—she was "asking for it" by the way she acted and dressed. Doctors also fear becoming legally liable if they treat victims without reporting to the police. Many give treatment and medications without explanations to rape patients. Also, many women who are virgins or never had pelvic exams complain about the doctors' lack of sensitivity. People working with sex victims, as well as the victims themselves, point to one conclusion: as often as not, doctors and hospitals give inadequate medical help and actually increase the victim's psychological trauma.

Reformers often urge the use of women medical personnel whenever possible. Yet some women doctors and nurses, reflecting attitudes of the male-oriented medical hierarchy, show the same prejudices, callousness, and judgmental attitudes toward rape victims as men physicians. One Detroit victim went to a private woman gynecologist the day after being brutally assaulted in an alley. After waiting two hours to be seen, the doctor told her, "You girls ask for what you get." Then she asked the battered young woman, "What do you expect me to do for you?" The doctor merely tested the victim for gonorrhea and gave her a sedative, without informing her of the need for later pregnancy and VD tests. It was not until the gynecologist finally examined the woman that she observed: "My, he didn't treat you too kindly down there, did he?" The victim left crying and more upset than before.

A New York woman was attacked in her apartment elevator in the early evening, forced at gunpoint to the rooftop, sodomized, raped, and dragged to an equipment room where she was left locked up and naked. When she was found and taken to New York's Jamaica Hospital by two "very kind policemen," the hospital said it didn't handle rape cases and turned her away. At Queens General emergency room, the police rushed her through. The medical personnel were less sympathetic. The hospital took a semen test and gave her penicillin and morning-after pills. But the nurse dismissed the victim's bruises—important physical evidence—as trivial and not worth any attention.

Under the impact of feminist investigations and increasing publicity about such neglect, more hospitals are now opening their doors to rape victims and providing better care. What is *most* needed is not special medical care, but something more difficult to obtain— understanding and concern. As Dr. Zuspan stressed, "It is imperative that someone take time for discussion with the patient in a supportive, caring environment. Confrontation and lack of credibility seem to be the name of the game these days. The rape victim, like the drug addict, often encounters a health care team that tends to be hostile and unbelieving of the patient's history." Like the country's police departments, most American medical and mental health groups, public and private, are controlled and largely staffed by men who share the same sexual misconceptions as the general population. The result is the further victimization of female victims by the very people who should be expected to help them the most.

Where changes have occurred, they have often been caused by women's groups active on the scene. Miami, Florida, is one area where the high rape rate and the efforts of concerned feminists brought about great improvements in the existing institutional medical complex. In 1974, Jackson Memorial Hospital opened a Rape Crisis Center, with Dr. Dorothy Hicks as its director. Dr. Hicks is well aware of the prior maltreatment of rape victims by hospital personnel—maltreatment which is still routine rather than exceptional in city and county hospitals. Formerly, reported Dr. Hicks, the rape victim was seen by an intern who was:

> *rushed and often oblivious to the importance of collecting proper evidence in the event the woman wished to prosecute. The intern, like the police, had not been sensitized to the woman's extremely traumatic feelings. Very rarely did a rape victim see a gynecologist. It is a very sad fact that rape is the only crime in which the victim is treated like a criminal by the police, the hospital, and the courts.* (Emphasis added.)

At Jackson Hospital's new center, a victim is now met by a gynecologist, a nurse, and a social worker, and taken to a private examination room. She is tested thoroughly for VD and the possibility of pregnancy, and careful reports are filled out on her condition, evidence of penetration, and presence of semen. Follow-up counseling for the victim and her family is an essential part of the treatment. The victim can talk about her feelings in a comfortable "family room" at the hospital, and appointments are arranged for further treatment.

"It's not just the victim who needs to understand what

has happened to her," said Dr. Hicks, "but also her family and especially her husband. Many people see a rape victim as dirty and bad, and her husband often wonders what his wife did to provoke the attacker. I met a woman whose husband divorced her and then killed himself. An extreme case, but it's surprising how often misconceptions ruin people's lives." The center has created an "undeniable improvement" in victims' treatment by the hospital and police, according to Dr. Hicks, and more women are prosecuting and getting convictions "because we are so careful in collecting evidence."

The University of Chicago's Billings Hospital is one of the country's few medical facilities with a specific, well-defined program for treating rape victims. It includes the unusual feature of avoiding the denigrating term "alleged" rape by calling the program "Code R." Doctors and nurses, who commonly use this expression, have no right or need to call a rape "alleged," since this is a legal, not a medical term. Although medical evidence is used to establish whether rape has occurred, the fact of rape is entirely a question for the courts. The medical profession should use a totally nonjudgmental phrase, such as "sexual injury." "Alleged" rape gratuitously implies that the victim is shamming and labels her from the start. Nurses and doctors, however, frequently tell victims, "We'll see now whether or not you've been raped," as if it were a matter for medical determination. Rape patients, usually unaware that this is a matter for the courts alone, are helped along the path of self-accusation, guilt, and depression.

Philadelphia is another large metropolis with a special facility in the city hospital for handling rape victims. The Center for Rape Concern, directed by Dr. Joseph Peters, who initiated it, was opened in 1970 at Philadelphia General Hospital, and is now staffed by gynecologists, psychiatrists, psychologists, sociologists, and social workers who provide direct services to

victims, as well as undertaking research. Kathy Flana-
gan, head social worker on the center's team, summarized for us their major purpose as:

> . . . trying to understand the problems of the vic-
> tims in order to give useful services. Most victims
> are seen by the social worker two to five days after
> the report. Social workers make a home visit to
> interview victims, correct medical misinforma-
> tion, emphasize the importance of returning to the
> hospital for pregnancy and VD follow-ups, and
> they counsel victims and their families on a wide
> range of problems.

The Center for Rape Concern, which grew out of Dr.
Peters' pioneering work with sex offenders, is also making a long-range study of some 1,000 victims to learn the
social–psychological effects of rape on women and
children. Local institutions (including police, courts,
the district attorney's office, the medical community,
hospitals, and the community mental health centers)
are cooperating in this landmark effort. This Philadelphia Rape Victims Study was begun in 1972 with federal funds from the National Institute of Mental Health.
Research objectives include the medical and psychological effects of rape, the circumstances in which the rapes
occurred, and the reactions of police and courts.

In addition to the professionally staffed center, a local
feminist rape crisis group, Women Organized Against
Rape, sends volunteers to give aid, comfort, and support
to rape victims at Philadelphia General. Since they work
in a public hospital, WOAR tells members to be tactful
at all times: "We cannot afford arguments about medical
care in the emergency room itself. . . . You are working in a facility that handles many people and always
seems busy. The physical facilities are old but
functional—don't confuse exteriors with quality of care.
Learn to approach the staff, such as asking if the victim

would like a tranquilizer. They can be very helpful."
The completeness of the examination depends on the
doctor, and WOAR volunteers remind victims to point
out all bruises, lacerations, and other injuries.

The situation in Boston has also changed in the past
few years. Boston Hospital, where most area victims are
examined, set up an innovative crisis intervention and
counseling program in 1973, directed by Dr. Ann
Burgess and Dr. Lynda Holmstrom. Victims now receive
priority emergency room treatment by trained medical
and psychological professionals experienced in dealing
with sexual assault cases. Burgess and Holmstrom described their program in a study, *Rape: Victims of
Crisis* (1974), which offers effective methods useful to
all hospitals.

Washington's D.C. General Hospital has made some
improvements in response to victim complaints and
feminist pressure. Privacy is now provided for the medical examination and police interviewing. More
gynecologists examine victims instead of whatever doctor is available and willing. Assaulted children are seen
by resident physicians in a separate hospital section.
Washington is also a step ahead of most cities in that it
has a Public Health Nurse, Charlene Lanza, working
full-time with rape victims and their families. However,
more counselors are needed in D.C., but funding is slow.
Nurse Lanza gives supportive help to victims and coor-
dinates services among various agencies, such as D.C.
General, community mental health centers, VD clinics,
and neighborhood health centers. Says Nurse Lanza, a
pioneer specialist in counseling rape patients, "One
way or another I try to get to everyone, either by phone
or an office interview, as soon as possible after I have the
police report. I evaluate the individual's needs and offer
her help, acting as a resource person. I also explain the
VD and pregnancy tests, where she can get them, and try
to find out if she has any medical problems." The D.C.
Human Resources Department also has a mental health

unit for psychological counseling and referrals. (In Denver, Colorado, a similar service is provided by the Visiting Nurse Association.)

In Maryland's Prince George's County, a hospital rape crisis center opened in late 1974 as the result of a special county Rape Task Force investigation and the urging of local women's groups. Like D.C. General, Prince George's General Hospital began to have obstetricians and gynecologists examine rape victims rather than any doctor or intern who happened to be on duty. Private treatment and examination areas for rape victims were established, as well as psychiatric counseling and facilities for private police interviewing in the hospital. The hospital is also trying to change its priorities so that rape victims are not kept waiting for interminable periods. In many American hospitals, a wait of five or six hours is not uncommon.[1] "We're trying to tell the hospital and police that we want rape victims treated like gunshot victims," said Len Dolodny, a member of the county's Human Relations Commission. "Rape is a psychiatric emergency," emphasized Claire Bigelow of the county Women's Commission.

In New York's Erie County, another task force on rape was formed in 1974 following increasing sexual assaults. Dr. Vincent Capraro, a clinical professor of gynecology–obstetrics at the University of New York at Buffalo concluded that while the treatment of injuries was generally adequate in hospital emergency rooms, "the emotional aspects and the follow-up of rape victims and family leave much to be desired." In addition, the legal aspect required "meticulous attention to detail in collecting medical evidence." Adequate personnel were lacking in both Buffalo and Erie counties for such procedures. "We need people—interested, sympathetic, and specially trained people," said Dr. Capraro. He recommended that such personnel be available at all

---

[1] A victim may have to sit alone in a general waiting area and be further humiliated by stares and comments from passing personnel, and then crudely summoned with a call of, "Where's the rape?"

times: "They should not be mere technicians doing a job in mechanical fashion. They must understand the needs of individual rape victims and the concerns of parents. They must also understand the concern of the police officer who is there to collect evidence."

On the West Coast, Seattle groups also worked to establish model procedures for the medical handling of sex victims. In 1973, a Sexual Assault Center began operating at Harborview Medical Center, a University of Washington teaching hospital. Similar to the Philadelphia group, this unit brought together an interdisciplinary team of physician specialists in gynecology, pediatrics, and psychiatry, as well as psychologists, social workers, and paraprofessionals working directly with the patients.

Rape victims are given priority treatment, either by the pediatric resident (through age sixteen) or a gynecologist. Since the Sexual Assault Center was established, more women have come for treatment, reported their assault to police, and prosecuted. The program also aims at establishing similar services throughout the Seattle area; developing a model medical-counseling protocol; and educating health care personnel and the public about sex crimes.

The medico–psychological treatment of rape victims is complex, and the repercussions—positive, negative, and mixed—may be deep and long-lasting for both the victim and the community. While regular procedures have been developed in the more enlightened facilities, controversy continues over treatments and medications, such as the antipregnancy pill. Effective standardized medical protocols have been established in a few hospitals, but most are inadequate. Much more needs to be done in the psychological realm, where services remain sparse. The investigative–legal pressure to gather detailed physical evidence from the patient further complicates the need for immediate, sensitive, and humanly supportive health care. In all these areas, a dearth of knowledge and skills continues to be the rule rather than the exception; although, as indicated, a number of hospitals and individuals now use programs which can provide models and training for the rest.

Medical Procedures

When a woman, girl, or child is sexually attacked, she *always* needs immediate, sympathetic, and effective medical and psychological care. Victims of sexual assault are injured human beings for whom society should be fully responsible. The professionals in each local medical complex should promptly attend to the victim's personal injuries, as well as provide long-range attention and treatment. The quality of such care will often determine both the lifetime effects of this attack on the victim and whether or not others will come forward for treatment.

Since victims rarely know what medical treatment to expect from a hospital, few realize that something important may have been omitted. Women's groups are making a strong effort to provide information on medical essentials. *Attitudes* of treatment personnel are as important as medical proficiency. Doctors, nurses, and hospital attendants should all be trained and required to explain the need for each procedure carefully and *sympathetically* to the victim, and they should administer the treatment with concern for the victim's reactions. With such training, the benefits of the medical treatment are increased and the victim's emotional trauma is greatly reduced.

The police are responsible for rushing a victim to the proper medical facilities as soon as possible after the assault. This complex of doctors, nurses, psychological therapists, mental health counselors, and social workers has two major responsibilities: *to treat the victim's physical and emotional needs* and *to provide necessary physical evidence for the police investigation and the legal prosecution.* In many places, however, one or both of these priorities are not fulfilled, with double damage to the victim as patient and claimant.

The victim's personal treatment should always have *first* priority and should include:

1. A prompt and completely private physical examination by a doctor trained to handle the physical and emotional trauma of rape.

2. Immediate treatment of all physical injuries.

3. Immediate attention by a psychological professional or paraprofessional specially trained to respond to the emotional trauma of sexual assault.

4. Follow-up treatment for physical injuries, as well as the prevention of venereal disease and pregnancy, which require later testing.

5. Follow-up treatment and observation of the emotional effects of the assault on victims and families.

6. If necessary, a free therapeutic abortion.

The American College of Obstetricians and Gynecologists has issued general guidelines for treating rape cases, and all hospitals should heed them:

> The physician must protect the interests of the patient, of justice, and of himself. Every instance is a potential court case, and the physician should expect to be subpoenaed to justify his statements. Whether rape occurred is a legal matter for court decision and is not a medical diagnosis. Principal cautions to doctors are:
>
>   a. Get consent.
>   b. Get history in patient's words.
>   c. Record examination findings.
>   d. Get laboratory work.
>   e. Save clothing.
>   f. Make no diagnosis.
>   g. Protect against disease, pregnancy, and psychic trauma.

ACOG also advises doctors to notify the police of the case. We disagree. The victim should have the right to decide whether or not to report—largely because of the harassment of victims by police and legal authorities.

Treating Physical Injuries

In most rape cases, a pelvic examination is necessary and is done with a speculum (an instrument, coming in various sizes, that is inserted into the vagina and then opened slightly for viewing the cervix). Other procedures, however, are necessary in cases involving factors such as: severe vaginal bleeding requiring immediate treatment; an intact hymen; a too small victim (some hospitals have special small specula); intense pain and anxiety; a victim's adamant refusal to be treated. Great care is needed in this examination, since it can easily seem like a second rape, and it is essential to reassure the patient at all stages. The examiner must look for and record bruises, lacerations, or contusions to all parts of the genitalia—the perineum, hymen, vulva, vagina, cervix, and anus. Inexperienced doctors may overlook a woman's anal rape because she was not vaginally raped.

The victim's entire body is also checked for injury, and her blood pressure, temperature, pulse, and respiratory rate taken and recorded. In many cases, injuries are found on the head, face, throat, chest, abdomen, back, arms, and legs. All bruises, cuts, lacerations, and other injuries must be carefully treated and recorded. The victim's claim of invisible physical assault (such as being choked, held, thrown down, or poked with knives and other weapons) is also noted. Threats, felt or overt, and fears expressed by the patient are important to note. A few hospitals have the victim write down her own account of the assault. Details which the victim forgets or conceals from the police—often through embarrassment or shock—may be brought out by sympathetic medical personnel. All necessary medical facilities (such as surgical, orthopedic, and neurological personnel and equipment) should, of course, be readily available.

Preventing Venereal Diseases and Pregnancy

All rape victims are concerned about possible VD and pregnancy, and these worries should be handled expertly and sympathetically by emergency room doctors and nurses. It is *essential* to inform the victim that immediate tests for both VD and pregnancy only indicate if she was *already* infected or pregnant. *Tests for VD and pregnancy must be made later* to determine the effects of rape. Cultures for gonorrhea can be taken immediately, but should be repeated from one to several weeks later. If positive, a course of antibiotic therapy is given and the patient is again cultured for gonorrhea. A blood test for syphilis can be made three to four weeks after the assault, and tests should be repeated over a six- to eight-week range.

Penicillin can be given as an immediate preventative if the patient knows she is not allergic. Otherwise an antibiotic such as spectinomycin can be injected or tetracycline taken orally. The type of penicillin used should be aqueous procaine penicillin, because gonorrhea must be treated only with fast-absorbed penicillin. Probenecid, given orally, is also administered to increase the absorption of penicillin. Antibiotic therapy can itself induce vaginal, but nonvenereal, infections; these, however, are usually easily treated.

Pregnancy is often a greater anxiety for rape victims, but its incidence is much less frequent than VD. Some hospitals give estrogen (Diethylstilbestrol, or the "morning-after" pill) for five days to render the uterine wall nonreceptive to a fertilized ovum. DES, however, has potential dangers, as well as side effects such as severe nausea and vomiting, of which victims *must* be warned. Pregnancy tests must be done six weeks after the victim's last period. A menstrual extraction can instead be made four weeks after her last period to

prevent pregnancy. Many hospitals charge for all tests
and treatments, although some provide free services.
Victims should check carefully before having possibly
unnecessary tests (such as VD and pregnancy tests in
the emergency room). If there are charges, Medicaid
may pay for some. In several states, such as Massachusetts, a Victims of Violent Crimes Act legally
makes the state responsible for medical bills if the rape
is reported. Hospitals should inform victims of such
financial rights and alternatives.

Preventing or Treating Subsequent Trauma, such as Vaginal Infections

One unfortunate aspect of modern medicine is that
drugs, chemicals, and other medicines usually produce
side effects, which may have to be treated in their turn.
Any antibiotic therapy in women may disrupt colonies
of bacteria normally existing in the vagina and allow a
foreign strain to grow there. The result can be a vaginal
infection with accompanying symptoms of discomfort,
discharge, rash, and so on. Some women develop acute
vaginal infections after the rape which may become
chronic. Community hospitals and health services
should provide routine care for such problems.

Gathering Physical Evidence for Police and Legal Authorities

An essential part of any hospital's medical protocol
for rape cases is the gathering of physical evidence by
well-trained personnel. Such evidence is often crucial
both in tracking down the assailant and in a successful
court prosecution. In addition to carefully recording the
victim's physical injuries and general appearance and
condition (including her possible drug intoxication), a
thorough check must be made for evidence of semen.

This should be done routinely at the time of the pelvic examination, when a swab is inserted in the vaginal pool and smears are taken for laboratory examination. Smears should also be taken from the anus, the external genitalia, and the mouth (sodomy and fellatio are being increasingly forced on victims). The patient's body and clothes are thoroughly examined for foreign material, bloodstains, tears, etc., which may provide useful evidence. (In one case, a young girl claimed she had been raped at a beach party. Sand found in her vagina, along with evidence of force, helped to substantiate her claim.) Fingernail scrapings are analyzed, and her pubic hair is combed for further clues. Photographs may also be made by medical personnel. A standardized medical form is important for such examinations and record-keeping.

As explained earlier, because of evidential needs, victims should not wash, shower, or douche before their physical examination, and they should preserve all clothing worn at the time of the attack. The victim must also be questioned about intercourse prior to the rape, since sperm can remain active for many hours and even days (there is much disagreement about how long). These needs, like all investigative steps, should be explained clearly and tactfully to victims—which rarely is done. It is also rare that all the scientific tests known to forensic pathologists, toxicologists, and criminologists are used in rape cases. As one authority, Cyril H. Wecht, points out:

> *Much more is known scientifically in the detection and proof of rape than is usually and customarily utilized in most cases. One of the reasons for this seemingly paradoxical situation is that many inexperienced prosecutors and defense attorneys do not bother to research the medical literature to find out how they can best prepare and evaluate their case.*

Psychological Counseling

Many rape victims, women who work with them, and psychological professionals believe that the *longest-lasting effect* of rape is nearly always the psychological damage. Emotional help is also the most neglected area of treatment. The majority of medical, police, and legal personnel still deny that all rape victims need some emotional support and counseling. They view victims through unreal stereotypes, believing that only hysterical, obviously "disturbed," "neurotic," or "psychotic" victims need psychiatric attention. Rape, however, affects *every female* who is assaulted, because rape is a basic and often violent intrusion—an emotional as well as a physical violation.

A Maryland psychotherapist who has counseled many rape victims, Dr. Patricia Webbink, told us she found three major psychological effects. The first is *terror of physical brutality:*

> Whatever happened to her, whether she was attacked in her home or on the street or hitchhiking, the woman will suffer a generalized fear of physical vulnerability and being alone. Many victims are terrified to go out of their homes for weeks or even months after the assault. Others suffer prolonged problems in sleeping or being in the dark. These are all humanly common reactions to any similar personal crisis. But what is so little understood are the prolonged anguish and terror which often accompany rape.

The second major psychological effect is the victim's *generalized fear and anger.* The victim's natural anger is often directed inward in the form of guilt and feelings of worthlessness. She somehow feels responsible no matter how the rape happened—she shouldn't have been walking outside, or wearing "suggestive" clothing, or making remarks interpreted as suggestive to a man, or going out with a man who made her uneasy. Guilt in some form is nearly always present.

The third psychological effect, closely related to the others, is depression:

> Because a rape victim is repressing or denying her rage, fear, and feelings of helplessness, she may have crying spells, a frequent lack of energy, loss of appetite, fear of sex, constant feelings of fatigue and inertia, and other reactions which are a cover for her basic depression. Some victims black out completely and have to be hospitalized. Others suffer recurrent severe depressions and have sporadic hospitalizations. Some women's lives are ruined by their rape, while others are permanently handicapped but continue functioning as emotional cripples. A few lucky women escape permanent damage—but they are definitely in the small minority. And every woman retains some psychological scar, although it may eventually become encapsulated.

Every woman reacts in a different way, according to her makeup and the circumstances of the rape. Specific reactions depend on many factors: age, sexual experience, ability to take care of herself, general experience, emotional integration, and the sort of rape, as well as the attitudes of police, medical, and legal authorities, and of her family, friends, and community. If she has been fortunate enough to get genuine emotional support and understanding, she will have a strong chance of tolerating and transcending her dreadful experience.

Given the widespread availability of therapeutic services today, ranging from the Freudian analysts to the so-called "humanistic" therapists to community clinics and psychiatric social workers, one might expect the victim to find supportive counseling wherever she turns. Such is not the case. The theoretical bases of treatment differ widely, depending upon the school in which the therapist was trained; and not surprisingly, many therapies incorporate a malevolent antifeminism or sexism. And of course the therapist (man or woman) may, and probably will, reflect the sexism of the society at large. The experience of a single victim illustrates what happens to many women who seek help from traditional, and often misogynist, analysts.

The woman had been raped in an Arizona YWCA when she left her door unlocked. She had had no reason to fear any danger, for other rapes committed there had been hushed up. After her assault, she felt extremely upset and visited a psychiatrist. The analyst told her she had left her door unlocked because she wanted to be raped and have a baby. Women with "good coping functions," he maintained, don't get raped.

Until the recent development of crisis centers, feminist support groups, and special hospital facilities—still all too few—most victims received little or no understanding and empathy. As a result, many never talked to anyone about their rape. Some victims repressed the experience so deeply that they consciously "forgot" it. Only today can women speak out to other women and express their inner pain and rage. A Boston writer, Barbara Cohn, talked to sixty-two rape victims. Only two had reported the assault to the police. One had been in therapy for two years and never mentioned it to her analyst. Others had been raped many years before and never told anyone. Only a few had told close friends or boyfriends.

The emotional repression and denial of rape— common psychological defense mechanisms—have been widely documented. (*Repression* is the burying of painful and unacceptable feelings so they are not consciously felt; *denial* is the refusal to attribute felt emotions to their actual cause or to define them accurately.) Victims repress in different degrees. Some "forget" entirely, although their repressed emotions of anger, fear, and guilt may find neurotic outlets. In others, some later incident triggers recollection, such as vaginal bleeding from birth control pills, or being reminded she is not a virgin when she marries (by the doctor or her husband). In some, repression may last only a short time. If a woman does remember the rape, she may deny her natural feelings of rage. Dr. Webbink told us of one victim who gave all her money to the rapist because he was black and she, a white woman, felt sorry for him. Some women even deny that the rape affected them in any way.

Rape victims may deal with their psychological denials symbolically. Dr. Webbink described several examples:

One female artist who was raped by a black man subsequently began painting and sculpting black men, which she had never done before. Another woman began having meaningless affairs after her rape. A third victim had nightmares about being chased, yet consciously she felt no fear. Another became a rigid conformist, although she secretly felt this was an odious way to live.

Common isolation feelings may be intensified by the denial of the assault's reality and seriousness by family, lovers, friends, and social institutions. Dr. Joseph Peters, director of the Philadelphia Center for Rape Concern, found that referring victims to psychiatric or community mental health services was almost totally ineffective because 90 percent failed to report. This was mainly due to the massive denial of the rape soon after the initial trauma. As Dr. Peters described this syndrome:

The victim appears emotionally settled. The family is relieved to drop the charge. The police and courts, already overburdened and biased with a male viewpoint, are somewhat skeptical about the reliability of the victim's complaints and seem anxious to drop the matter. Finally, community mental health services and even private psychiatric facilities don't want to become involved.

New hospital rape facilities (such as those in Miami, Chicago, Philadelphia, Boston, and Seattle) stress the need for immediate and sustained psychological counseling as well as medical treatment. At Philadelphia, a home visit is attempted as soon as possible to deal with the victim's problems while anxiety and concern are at a peak and symptoms have not yet been denied or repressed.

Many researchers and mental health professionals emphasize the victim's need for "integration" and "adjustment" and the importance of the reactions of people close to her. While emotional support by people around and close to the victim are indeed important, it is not helpful to stress "adjustment" to a society which condones and in some ways encourages rape. Such therapists would increase the female's already conditioned dependence on society's reactions—if only the boyfriend or husband accepts the rape, they seem to say, all will be well; she will be "safe" once again. There is also generally an undercurrent of blame for the victim who should have been more "careful." These conventional, simplistic ideas underplay the very real physical and emotional trauma for the victim and increase her dependence on others—the very dependence that helped condition her to become a victim in the first place.

Reforming the Medical Complex

The attitudes and behavior of medical personnel involved in all aspects of sexually assaulted patients need drastic and widespread reform. Basic needs are as follows:

1. Victims should receive medical attention as soon as possible after the assault and high-priority hospital treatment.

2. Public and private hospitals should extend to sex victims the same services they extend to other patients.

3. Victims should be examined by gynecologists, preferably female, in private areas.

4. Hospital privacy should be provided for police interviewing.

5. All medical personnel handling rape victims should receive special training in sensitivity and medical-evidential procedures.

6. Victims should be fully informed, orally and in writing, about medical-evidential procedures and their options and needs for medical tests and follow-up treatment.

7. Hospitals should make certain that victims receive necessary VD and pregnancy checkups, as well as treatment.

8. All emergency room and follow-up care should be free for rape victims.

9. Mental health professionals and/or paraprofessionals should be immediately available for emotional support, and psychological follow-up counseling should be provided for both victims and families.

10. Medical treatment should not be conditioned on cooperation with the police, nor should minors need parental permission.

11. Full laboratory equipment and personnel should be readily available for analyzing physical data and specimens.

12. Careful and complete records should be kept of all medical-evidential procedures, and doctors should be prepared to testify in court.

The Miami/Dade County Rape Task force drafted a 1973 "Bill of Rights" for rape victims as a reminder that such women are citizens entitled to good service and human respect from their community's medical facilities. Victims are told:

—You are entitled to good quality medical care by doctors, nurses, and counselors.

—You are entitled to full information about your present condition, the treatment you may receive, the reaction your body may have to medications, hospital charges, and your own records.

—You have the right to be treated without discrimination and to dignified care.

—You have the right to privacy and confidentiality, for yourself and your personal records.

—You have the right to refuse (choose) treatment, to be told of the medical consequences of your action, and to leave the hospital when you wish.

—You have the right to refuse (choose) to have this event reported to the police.

—You have the right to complain about your personal or medical treatment.

—You have the right to continuity of care, including responses to your future related needs.

Every city, town, and county medical complex plays a key role in dealing with rape, its suffering victims, and both the personal and social aftermath of criminal sex attacks. Together with police and legal professionals, the medical and mental health personnel in each locale must change *themselves* before they can help change the problems. The task of doctors, nurses, and therapists is to heal the afflicted and to avoid increasing the injury. In the peculiarly complex and emotion-wrought crime of rape, *special care must be taken that would-be healers do not also become unwitting oppressors.*

5
COURTS AND THE LAW: JUDICIAL LAG

I am not here to do justice. I am here to play the game according to the rules.
>   —Oliver Wendell Holmes, Associate Justice,
>   U.S. Supreme Court

. . . as a litigant, I should dread a lawsuit beyond almost anything short of sickness and death.
>   —Judge Learned Hand, U.S. Court of Appeals

. . . the lawyer aims at victory, at winning in the fight, not at aiding the court to discover the facts. He does not want the trial court to reach a sound educated guess, if it is likely to be contrary to his client's interests. Our present trial method is thus the equivalent of throwing pepper in the eyes of a surgeon when he is performing an operation.
>   —Judge Jerome Frank, U.S. Court of Appeals

The cynical observations at the beginning of this chapter by judicial gentlemen long revered for their knowledge and interpretation of the law are trenchant comments on the American legal system. Most educated attorneys accept these judgments as a matter of course; only those of us outside the legal profession are surprised to discover that the law is a "game" in which the sole aim is to win, not to do justice.

Through the centuries, rape victims have had to learn this lesson the hard way, by personal experience of the court process and the administration of the law. Since both the process and the law are rooted in a patriarchal system, where women and children are the real or sym-

129

bolic property of the male ruling class, masses of women have fared disastrously in the courts. Unlike the victim of any other crime of violence, the rape victim must find her human rights under a mountain of legal mumbo-jumbo that serves in the end to benefit the criminals, who are, no matter how lowly or how perverse, members of the dominant class. Rape cases are the only cases that reverse the rights of the victim and the accused. The law goes to great lengths to protect the accused, who is "innocent until proved guilty." The rape victim, however, is almost invariably implicated in some wrong-doing—seduction, lying, mistaken identification, or "wanton" behavior—and she is forced to prove in public her own innocence beyond a reasonable doubt.

Most persons, especially women, have little or no experience of the court process, a fact that many lawyers and judges do not seem to acknowledge. This is especially unfortunate for the rape victim, whose enlightenment about the law comes when she is psychologically least prepared to confront our adversary legal system and its "game" of law. (An impressive number of young women are in law school today because they were introduced to the sexist nature of that system as rape victims.)

Many criminally assaulted women are shocked to discover that rape is generally considered by law to be a crime, not against them, as individuals, but against society, or the state. The California penal code, for example, describes rape as a crime against a person and "against public decency and good morals," categorizing it with gambling, horse racing, indecent exposure, and abortion.

As we have said, the laws governing rape and sex assaults, separately enacted by the fifty different states, reflect all the regional sexual attitudes, preferences, and prejudices of the various state legislatures. "Morality" thus varies from state to state, but in general what is sexual morality for the gander rarely applies equitably to the goose. Thus the interpretation and administration of the law by judges *and* juries reflects both the national patriarchal orientation and local parochial attitudes. The adversary "game" as played in Alaska will differ from that of Mississippi, and the judicial treatment of Chicano victims in New Mexico, or Indian women in Oklahoma, for example, is likely to have less to do with justice than with racial attitudes. As a lawyer from the Southwest told us: "Rape is a way of life with them—the Nigras and the Chicanos, I mean. Their women are fair game." This comment is particularly enlightening, for nearly a third of all reported forcible rapes take place in southern states, according to the U.S. Department of Justice.

Many states, perhaps most, still suffer such embarrassment over the sexual facts of life that their criminal codes are encrusted with Biblical euphemisms for sexual intercourse, the favorite being "carnal knowledge." (In some states carnal knowledge means sexual molestation or intercourse with or between minors.) It is a curious phenomenon to find state's attorneys who customarily use four letter words in conversation suddenly switching to "carnal knowledge" when discussing rape and sexual assaults. The antique language of the penal codes actually undermines what may charitably be supposed to be the law's intent to describe the crime. The word "knowledge" tends to upgrade and intellectualize a violent crime, while deemphasizing the criminal hostility associated with rape. Furthermore, for those programmed by Biblical ideology, "carnal knowledge" clearly implies that sex is sinful, abhorrent, dirty, and "of the flesh."

Because rape is pursued as a crime against the state, the rape victim, as in other criminal actions, appears in the trial only as a *witness* for the prosecution. She is the chief witness, to be sure, but she has no legal standing beyond that of any other witness.

Since the sex assault victim is not a litigant, though she usually is designated as the "prosecutrix" or "complainant"—which surely is more than a "witness"—she cannot choose the prosecuting attorney. This prosecutor, usually male, is arbitrarily assigned from the district attorney's office, and he may or may not have prior experience in sex assault cases. Very often the rape victim does not meet the prosecuting attorney until minutes before the trial. Thus many victims go into court—often for the first time in their lives—with only a ten-minute briefing to prepare them for the ordeal on the stand. (One Virginia commonwealth attorney told a victim: "In all my twenty years on the job, I've never seen a case like this that deserved more than three minutes' discussion anyway.")

Even if the victim can afford her own lawyer, this attorney has no legal standing and can act only in a supportive or advisory capacity, with no official courtroom power. Supplementary attorneys can be very helpful, both for the victim's morale, and the district attorney's case. But the number of victims able to hire such expensive professional help is extremely limited.

Technically, since the victim is merely a witness, she can be compelled to testify whether she wants to or not. In practice, however, reluctant witnesses, or those considered by the district attorney's office as unable to testify "productively" in court, are unlikely to be subpoenaed. In general, the D.A.'s office is interested only in winning the case. If the rape victim is thought to be a "poor" witness, the case may be dropped. In many states, such a case might wind up in the statistics as "unfounded"—an ambiguous "catchall" category —which easily gets translated into the so-called "false" charge.

The label "unfounded" has nothing to do with whether or not a rape actually occurred. Unfounded is police terminology, not a legal term. It means that, for various reasons, the police cannot or will not recommend prosecution. This may be due to many factors, such as the victim's delay in reporting the crime, a prior relation between the victim and offender, the use or threat of force without accompanying battery, or the destruction of essential physical evidence (the victim may have douched before reporting). Or perhaps the victim had been drinking; or refused to undergo a medical examination; or was simply too embarrassed, too fearful, or too emotionally upset to cooperate with the police investigation.

When a woman engages in what the police define as "questionable" behavior—hitchhiking, agreeing to sexual intercourse and then retracting, walking alone at night in poor neighborhoods, visiting bars, visiting a man in his quarters—they characteristically "unfound" the rape complaint because such charges are unlikely to lead to a conviction in court. The "unfounding" is thus based on prosecutorial difficulties, not on the "falsity" of the charges.

The rape victim's case is the only one of dozens of legal suits of all kinds in which the district attorney's staff is involved. These lawyers are usually overworked, underpaid, and unappreciated. In addition, the district attorney's representative, who is a kind of legal lifeline for the rape victim, often shares the prevailing misconceptions and prejudices about female sexuality. He will most likely, consciously or unconsciously, classify victims as "good" and "bad" girls or "those-who-ask-for-it." One Midwest attorney told us he could tell immediately by a "gal's manner" whether she had "round heels" and was an "easy lay," or whether she was (these are his *exact* words) "just some doll who found herself in an enamoured situation and because of her own physiological needs consented to a carnal relationship without mentally assenting." In this man's lexicon, older women who visit bars and talk to strangers should "know better," and are "asking for trouble."

The adversary system also protects sex criminals in a way that is legally proper but psychologically unfair. A Pennsylvania assistant D.A. told us (while pointing to an elderly, befuddled woman attorney who had come into his office to consult him): "It looks good in court to have a woman attorney defending a man accused of rape." After she had left, he confided, "She's made quite a career, done very well, defending rapists." The gladiatorial aspect of a woman (defense attorney) attacking another woman (victim) works to discredit the victim. Fortunately, women recently graduated from law school are having second thoughts about defending rapists. More and more are examining their consciences and asking to be excused from such service. "I couldn't be objective about it anyway," one of them told us. Young women attorneys, it appears, can be more objective about their own lack of objectivity than men.

Presumption of Innocence

The lawyer's battle cry of "innocent until proven guilty" is nowhere to be found in the U.S. Constitution; "presumption of innocence" is *not* a constitutional right. Like many other elements of our law, presumption of innocence derives from our adversary system of law, out of what is called "case law" as it has emerged at various times and states in judicial decisions by the higher courts, including a judgment by the U.S. Supreme Court (156 USS 432). But as sex assault victims have painfully discovered during the judicial process, presumption of innocence rarely extends to them.

The term "alleged" before the word "rape," for example, protects only the presumption of innocence of the accused, not the victim. During litigation, the crime with which a person is charged is referred to as an "alleged" crime because the crime itself has not yet been proven or disproven in the courts. In fact, omission of the term "alleged" when coupled with the name or other identification of the accused can result in a mistrial. Defendants identified in the press or other media by name can sue for libel if the "alleged" is omitted.

But if we shift the focus to the victim, who is also described variously as an "alleged" victim, the picture changes. Surely it is demoralizing for the assault victim, who has survived what may be one of the most grueling experiences of her life, to hear representatives of *other* institutional bureaucracies with which she must deal refer to the attack as "alleged." Doctors, nurses, hospital attendants, police clerks, and other minor officials often refer routinely to the crime as "alleged" in the course of their duties. Yet not one of these individuals has a legal obligation to judge whether or not rape actually has occurred. That is a job *only* for the courts. Outside the courtroom those attending a sex assault victim do not need to use the term rape at all, let alone the word "alleged."

The medical profession, for example, has no legal obligation or jurisdictional right to make a judgment. Yet the American College of Obstetricians and Gynecologists routinely instructs physicians to use the term "alleged" in connection with rape, even when there is only a theoretical discussion about it, with no identified victim or defendant.

Courts—Higher and Lower

Another legal aspect often not understood by victims facing their first court experience is that, after preliminary legal procedures, suits only begin with a trial jury. (In rare instances, if the accused waives his rights to a jury the case is heard and decided by a judge.) Victims also do not usually know that the law itself is fashioned by legislative statutes and the legal process in higher court decisions. The law of rape is largely a creation of judges in higher courts—those remote jurists sitting in the state court of appeals, the circuit courts, the state supreme courts, and on up through the hierarchy. In arguing cases, attorneys go back to case law, or what some legal critics like the late Judge Jerome Frank call "library law," supporting arguments with citations from similar cases decided elsewhere and at other times.

These decisions can be read in law libraries. The proceedings of the original trial, however, are not usually available in a library unless there has been a conviction and an appeal by the accused. (Victims are not allowed a second chance if there is no conviction.) It is difficult, and costly, and sometimes impossible to obtain court records of original criminal trials, if such records even exist. Theoretically, criminal court records are public documents—after all, the state is the prosecutor—and should be openly accessible. In practice, depending on the community, researchers are often looked upon with suspicion, especially if they do not belong to the legal fraternity, and trial transcripts are either unavailable or prohibitively expensive. Some courts even prohibit note taking during a trial without special permission; taking notes, a bailiff once informed us, does not show proper "respect" for the judge and court. (A similar prohibition exists in the public galleries of both houses of Congress, where note taking by the public is deemed "distracting" and "disturbing" to our paid public servants—our legislators.)

The Legal Procedure

Jurisdictions obviously differ in procedural details, but in general, when a woman reports a sexual assault she must make a number of statements for which she may later be held accountable, *under oath*, a fact of which she is often not made aware. Minor discrepancies and omissions in this first statement may be pounced upon later by defense attorneys, even though the early account was given by the victim in a disturbed or distraught state. This first statement, usually a cursory one, is given to the police at the scene of the crime. Some time later she must file a formal statement at police headquarters, repeating in detail what she recounted the first time. Still later, depending upon the extent of the police investigation, she may be required to reappear at headquarters to identify her assailant. If the attacker has not been caught, she will be shown mug shots (photographs); if a suspect has been apprehended, she will be required to identify her attacker out of a group of assorted criminals in what is variously known as a "lineup" or "stand-down."

Once the accused has been identified, he is arrested and charged with the crime and either held in jail or released on bail. Some time later, the victim must again appear at a preliminary hearing, along with the accused (unless he waives this right), before a local magistrate or judge, where she must again recount her story. The presiding official, whose legal function is to decide whether there is sufficient evidence for a trial, then either remands the case for another hearing before a grand jury where the victim once again repeats her story, or binds over the defendant and instructs the victim to wait until she is subpoenaed to testify at the trial itself.

The mills of the law, like those of the gods, grind exceedingly slow, but not often so fine. At this point there may be a new series of delays. Since the defense attorney's sole interest is to secure the acquittal of his client, or at least to see the charge reduced to something less than rape, more time will be demanded to conduct the defense and turn up derogatory material against the victim—witness. These legal delays are known as "continuances," and victims must continue to appear at the courthouse, prepared to testify, to learn about postponements. Some victims have appeared as much as twenty times as the court grants one continuance after another. Sometimes the actual trial will only be postponed once or twice.

The time lapse between the preliminary hearing and the trial itself may be between a few months and several years, some cases taking as long as four or five years to come to trial. The traumatic effect of these postponements, combined with the often fruitless and frustrating efforts to "find out what is happening," can plunge a victim into prolonged states of acute anxiety and sometimes severe depression. While waiting for the court trial, her attacker may be out on bail. His friends and relations will know that she has reported the assault and that he will have to stand trial. Victims have been harassed during this period by threatening, anonymous phone calls or letters. The rape victim particularly needs strong emotional support from friends and relatives at this period if she is to survive the greater ordeal that is ahead.

Many persons have never been inside a courtroom. Lawyers and judges are apt to forget that litigation is not a part of everyday life for most people. The chilling impersonality of the court with its routines and rituals is an awesome experience to one facing it for the first time. It is all the more so when it is a criminal trial and the crime is rape. One victim described it to us as "a game of Ping-Pong played over my head"; another as a "tournament of some sort where you don't know the rules —and nobody tells you."

Since the adversary system requires that the trial be public, spectator seats are filled with strangers—anyone may be admitted as long as there are seats. "Like an old-fashioned wedding," a friend of a victim observed recently, "his on one side, hers on the other." But unlike the wedding, the seats are not filled with friends and relatives. Sex trials are apt to draw those seedy individuals known as "courthouse bums," who seem to fill an otherwise empty life by "auditing" trials. One of these *voyeurs* pushed himself upon us when we came late into a trial involving a close friend. (It was one of those modern, in-the-round arena type of courtrooms, where the jury faces the judge, spectators sit on two sides, and a lectern and the attorneys occupy center stage.) "It's a rape," our *voyeur* whispered happily to us, relishing the word, and then proceeded to outline the details and point out the victim, the accused, and several witnesses; he would have recounted all the prior testimony had a court attendant not shut him up.

In general, the burden of proof in a rape trial is on the victim, and when all the fancy legal language is removed, the trial comes down to a question of who is telling the truth—she or he. Or more realistically, who does the jury—or the judge, in rare instances when the defendant waives a jury trial—*choose to believe.*

In the process of sorting out his word against hers, the law concerns itself with at least four major controversial issues which operate to one degree or another in most of the court cases across the country. (We are concerned here with the law as it governs the forcible rape of an adult; "statutory" rape of an underage victim will be so identified.) These are the four legal issues in which women victims have fared disastrously over the years: consent, corroboration, the "chastity" of the victim, and the past crimes of the defendant.

Consent

The issue of alleged consent by the victim is peculiar to the crime of rape. The highly polarized word "alleged" is not so frequently heard alongside consent, perhaps because it refers only to the victim. As a mere witness to a crime upon her person, she is not entitled to the same legal due-process protection and presumption of innocence allowed her attacker. There appears to be no other crime in which consent figures in the law as an issue. If a storekeeper turns over money or property to a thief, with or without a visible weapon, the law does not require the victim to prove he did not consent to being robbed. A man assaulted on a street corner, or in the privacy of his apartment, whether by friend or stranger, is not required to prove he did not consent to the attack.

The evolution of our legal process has thrust the consent issue into the center of the storm about rape. The legal obverse of consent is resistance, resistance sufficient to prove lack of consent. However, resistance, or nonconsent, is largely a subjective matter; and hundreds, if not thousands, of rapists have been allowed to go free by police, juries, and judges who have decided arbitrarily that the victim did not resist "enough."

How much resistance is "enough" is moot: every rape is different; every rapist is different; and most important, every victim has unique standards of behavior. These cannot be determined for her by others, yet every day jurors sit in judgment *not* on the accused criminal but on the victim: "Why didn't she do this or that . . .?" or whatever brilliant course of action reveals itself in hindsight.

Some women have effectively resisted rapists by talking their way out of a rape, conning the criminal with tales of disease, infection, menstruation, and other relevant or irrelevant maladies. (One attacker desisted when his victim pleaded she had contagious "cancer.") Others have stalled until they could escape. Some have surprised their assaulters with sudden moves and strange behavior. A minority have actually fought their way free. Many women have reported that their attackers did not expect any resistance. "Listen lady," said one criminal, "I've raped five women in the last ten days, and you're the first to give me an argument."

In general, the law expects a woman to prove that she did not consent by fighting the attack short of endangering her life. The presence of a weapon, revealed or hidden, however, complicates the situation. Can she be sure the assailant will not use it if she resists? Yet if she succumbs because of the weapon, and the criminal leaves no telltale injuries or bruises, how can she prove she resisted?

On the average women are physically smaller, lighter, and not as strong as the men who attack them. More important: they are socially conditioned from infancy not to resist anyone, male or female. In childhood girls are steered away from all forms of physical contact, whereas boys are encouraged in bodily contact sports. Boys are encouraged to defend themselves physically; girls are brought up to believe that "someone else" will defend them. In a culture where even verbal resistance to males provokes radical hostility and threats, a demand that women suddenly use physical resistance in a uniquely dangerous situation—let alone expect them to take the physical offensive—is preposterous.

As a Philadelphia Common Pleas judge says: "The definition of force is a male definition. . . . Women are conditioned in our society to passivity." Those self-appointed experts (and they include some attorneys, psychologists, and campus lecturers) who advise women to poke fingers in the eyes of attackers or kick groins, obviously have never experienced the hostility that even a mild objection to masculine behavior can evoke. Moreover, if the rapist's fantasy anticipates a struggle, the woman's reaction may only spur him to greater violence. The violent retaliatory tactics urged upon women totally unprepared to be violent would be ludicrous were they not so tragically inapplicable. The answer to the ubiquitous question, "What should I do if I'm attacked?" is not simple. *Each woman* must judge for *herself*, and must learn to trust her *own* intuition and to act according to her *own* best judgment. There are, alas, no rules.

The resistance-consent dichotomy permits many defendants to claim "consent" by their victims under circumstances that are nothing short of absurd. Why should a woman "consent" to intercourse with a complete stranger who has forced his way into her apartment? Why should a woman "consent" to intercourse in the most outlandish—not to mention uncomfortable —locations? One victim, raped at gunpoint by a complete stranger who forced her into an alley, commented astutely: "Who would consent to lying flat on her back for some stranger in an alley in the middle of January?" Despite the evidence, the jury acquitted. Four men in the District of Columbia not long ago claimed consent, although the young victim had leaped from a second-story window to escape, wearing only a raincoat, and had run immediately to a friend to report the attack. The jury acquitted the men of the rape but found them guilty of assault with a deadly weapon, a lesser charge.

Too often the rulings of higher courts have permitted the inference that insufficient resistance equals consent. In a 1960 case *(Farrar v. U.S.)*, the victim testified she had felt a knife at her throat, but that she had not actually seen it. The trial jury voted for conviction. But the appellate court reversed the decision and denied a rehearing, with these words: "The law may permit conviction of rape upon the basis of a concealed knife, but it does not permit conviction premised upon an invisible knife. The rape penalty does not rest upon imaginary fears."

Recently, however, courts have begun to look more realistically at the issue of consent. In 1973, the Wisconsin Supreme Court rejected the appeal of a convicted rapist who maintained that his victim, a young mother, had not "resisted to the utmost." The mother's concern not to involve her children sleeping nearby "in no way suggests consent or acquiescence," the court declared, and: "It was not the victim of the rape who was on trial; it was the defendant." Her fear for her children, her screams, her attempts to escape, her injuries were enough to establish utmost resistance. The man's conviction stood. But too much should not be made of such decisions, however promising they may seem on the surface. What is significant, and unpromising, is that the convicted man should have been able to appeal the conviction on the basis of the victim's alleged action or inaction.

Corroboration

Corroboration, in general, means any testimony or evidence provided by anyone other than the victim of a crime. In a rape case, corroboration may be supplied by the testimony of witnesses or through circumstantial evidence that will sustain the claims of the prosecution. The corroboration requirement as applied to rape victims is clearly discriminatory. In those states still requiring strict corroboration in rape cases, other crimes such as assault and robbery are not required to provide proof beyond the word of the victim; the victim's word is enough to prove that a crime occurred.

The majority of states, however, *thirty-nine at least,* have no such corroboration requirements in their law. Among the remaining eleven jurisdictions there is wide variation both as to the specific elements in the crime which require corroboration and as to the evidence considered adequate. Some of the corroboration states tend to be stricter in their requirements than others, among them (as of this writing) the District of Columbia, Nebraska and Georgia. New York, which for years had one of the strictest corroboration laws in the country, repealed these discriminatory requirements early in 1974, largely after loud clamor for reform by the women's movement; and Connecticut followed suit a few months later. Connecticut's Superior Court Judge Robert I. Berdon had ruled in March of that year that it was enough for a witness to have heard the rapist's voice to identify him, saying that the corroboration requirement reflected "an irrational belief in the dishonesty of a woman who has been sexually attacked."

What courts generally consider corroborative evidence was listed in *Allison* v. *U.S.* (1969) by the U.S. Court of Appeals for the District of Columbia:

1. The medical evidence and testimony.

2. Evidence of breaking and entering into the complainant's residence.

3. The victim's bruises, scratches, or other injuries.

4. The condition of the victim's clothing.

5. The promptness of complaints to friends, police, or relatives.

6. The emotional condition of the victim.

7. The lack of motive to falsify.

8. The presence of semen or blood on the clothing of the accused and the victim.

9. The conduct of the accused at the time of the arrest.

10. The opportunity of the accused to perpetrate the attack.

More than half of these requirements have to do with the *victim's condition and behavior*. The problem is that frequently *there is no corroborative evidence*. Criminals who use a gun, a knife, or other weapon, or who threaten to use weapons to force submission, do not have to bruise the victim, tear the clothing, or provide other evidence of force (items 1, 3, 4). A delay in reporting the crime may be traceable to fear, embarrassment, or simply ignorance of how to do it (item 5). Yet a lack of such corroborative evidence allows defendants to plead consent, even under patently outrageous nonconsensual circumstances.

The doctrine of corroboration as it pertains to rape did not exist in the common law; nor was it originally established by statute, in legislation. It is a creation of the judiciary, by its rulings and adherence to the precedents. It was eased into the court system by the unsubstantiated insinuations of one of the greatest legal sexists of all time, the late John Henry Wigmore, the author of a ten-volume standard legal text, *Evidence*. *Evidence* first came out in 1904–1905 during the Edwardian era. This text is a basic authoritative source in law on which all fledgling lawyers still cut their milk teeth.

While *Evidence* purports to explain the meaning of evidentiary matter in the law, even Wigmore himself finally admitted that one couldn't be sure about evidence; there were, he said, no "scientific" or "logical laws" for determining rationally the "net persuasive effect of a mixed mass of evidence." (Wigmore came to this conclusion in *Principles of Judicial Proof*, a thousand-page demonstration that there are no such principles.)

Though Wigmore admitted uncertainty about the

evidence in most matters, when it came to women, he wrote with powerful assurance. And though *portions* of the text have occasionally been revised (most recently in 1970 and 1972), on women and girl children *Evidence* has not budged an inch. Turn-of-the-century attitudes are perpetuated. Among these major legal myths about women are: that women fantasize rape because they desire it; that they are in general more prone to lying than men; that "unchaste" sexual behavior affects their ability to tell the truth; that women young and old of "excessive or perverted sexuality" are not to be trusted; that all rape complainants should undergo psychiatric examinations; that "respect and sympathy for the wronged female" tend to sway the jury to condemn the man; and that finally, the real victim in rape, too often, is "an innocent man." Over and above these myths, it is Wigmore who was basically responsible for establishing, in a legal context, the concept of rape primarily as a sexual offense, rather than a crime of violence calculated to humiliate, injure, and degrade the female.

These conclusions (still in recent editions) are documented by five case studies (all involving little girls) cited in an obscure 1915 textbook by a Dr. William Healy and in letters and monographs by psychiatrists, the most recent, dated 1933, by Dr. Karl Menninger. On the incarceration of the innocent man, Wigmore cites no cases at all, an incredible exception to the customary voluminous documentation and citations for every point.

Wigmore's worry about sexually precocious girl children is bolstered by a 1930 quote from a post-World War I German medical "expert," Dr. Otto Mönkemöler:

The most dangerous witness in prosecutions for morality offences are the youthful ones (often mere children) in whom the sex instinct holds the foremost place in their thoughts and feelings. This intensely erotic propensity often can be detected in

*the wanton facial expression, the sensuous mo-
tions, and the manner of speech. But on the other
hand one must not be deceived by a Madonnalike
countenance that such a girl can readily assume;
nor by the convincing upturn of her eyes, with
which she seeks to strengthen her credibility. To be
sure, the coarse sensuousness of her demeanor,
coupled with a pert and forward manner, usually
leaves no doubt about her type of thought. Even in
her early years can be seen in countenance and
demeanor the symptoms of the hussy type, which
in later years enable one at first glance to recognize
the hardened prostitute. With profuse falsities they
shamelessly speak of the coarsest sex matters.
Having come early into bad practices, they can
weave these into their testimony and decorate their
narratives with the most plausible details . . . it is
just such witnesses that often bring into their picture individuals who have never even been near
them and that throw suspicion recklessly on the
most worthy persons. . . . When the sex urge is
strongly developed, then if some man comes into
their vicinity, they may dally with a secret wish to
have some sex relation with him, and then his most
harmless conduct is transformed by these sex im-
aginative witnesses into acts which charge him as
a criminal. . . . In male youths, this peculiar sex
disposition plays a far smaller part.*

For his American source, Wigmore, still in current
editions, uses Dr. Karl Menninger to add to the paranoid
male image of the lying female. Menninger is quoted as
urging psychiatric examinations for "every girl who
enters a plausible but unproved story of rape . . . because fantasies of being raped are exceedingly common
in women, indeed one may almost say that they are
probably universal." (Italics added.) To back up his own
unproved fantasy, Menninger cites one case, that of a
"mentally abnormal spinster" who claimed to have

been repeatedly raped by a seventy-year-old man in his office and sent him to prison for a long sentence. (If Menninger changed his mind about any of this, it is not in the current edition of *Evidence.*)

But even Professor Wigmore had to admit, elsewhere and in the third edition of his great work, that the corroboration requirement was of questionable value:

> *The fact is that, in the light of modern psychology, this technical rule of corroboration seems but a crude and childish measure, if it be relied upon as an adequate means for determining the credibility of the complaining witness in such charges. The problem of estimating the veracity of feminine testimony in complaints against masculine offenders is baffling enough to the experienced psychologist. This statutory rule is unfortunate in that it tends to produce reliance upon a rule of thumb.*

If Wigmore himself casts doubts on the corroboration rule, apparently many judges do not know about it. In a survey recently, Carol Bohmer, an assistant law professor at Rutgers University, interviewed thirty-eight Philadelphia judges and asked them what kind of evidence they considered important in evaluating the credibility of the victim. Twenty-three said "circumstantial"; eleven said "medical"; four indicated something they described as "the demeanor of the complainant"; three said they "didn't know"; ten gave "no information." (The discrepancy in the figures is due to multiple responses by some judges.)

Of most interest is what the judges considered "circumstantial" evidence. This consisted, almost entirely, of judgments made about the conduct and condition of the victim and included such items as prior history of promiscuity, enticement, prior relationship, drinking in a bar, resistance, immediate outcry, time lapse between rape and complaint, torn clothing, bruises, whether the complaint was made without intervening circumstances, and cooperation in the identification of the rapist. Circumstantial evidence, according to Bohmer's survey, means that certain facts are *inferred* from circumstances rather than deduced from facts. These judges considered the speed with which the victim filed the complaint and the amount of cooperation she gave legal authorities for the prosecution as circumstantial. Thus a complainant who changes her mind about testifying raises doubts about her credibility; a witness who does not cooperate adequately in the judicial process must be lying. As Bohmer suggests:

> *The fact that the woman may simply have had enough of the legal system or that psychologically she is not strong enough to continue contact with the authorities does not occur to the judges. This is an attitude common to the rest of the legal profession, as evidenced by responses from both district and defense attorneys in other personal interviews.*

If the Philadelphia judges tended to apply Wigmore's corroborative rule of thumb, a few more enlightened men of the bench are attempting to move away from it. In the District of Columbia, early in 1974, Superior Court Judge Theodore R. Newman, Jr., directly challenged the corroboration requirement, using as a test the case of James E. Arnold, who was charged with two rapes. Before Arnold's trial, Newman went on record as saying that, contrary to D.C. law, corroborative evidence would not be required. Newman declared there was "no reason for corroboration other than blatant male chauvinistic sexism." In ruling on a pretrial prosecution motion, he announced: "The time has come for the law to stop being a sexist ass. I am going to give the D.C. Court of Appeals, most respectfully, an opportunity to reevaluate this situation and make a judgment." And at trial he intentionally omitted instructions to the jury on the need for corroboration. The jury convicted. The case was appealed and heard in May 1975, and the decision is pending.

Under a recent District court reorganization the appeals court can reverse an earlier appellate decision only by a full court hearing of its nine members. A full court hearing was requested but denied. Instead, arguments were heard by a panel of three judges, who are probably without power to reverse. The panel has now reversed itself and recommended a full court hearing. Late in 1975 we should know whether the court chooses to recognize the need for change or not.

Judge Newman concedes that the appeals court in Washington has in the past supported the corroboration requirement in the case of minors, but it has not yet ruled in a case similar to Arnold's involving an adult victim. Defense Attorney Frederick J. Sullivan defends the corroboration requirement on historical grounds: "It's always been the rule, one of the bedrocks of the law in the District." Sullivan believes that the issue "has been cloaked in the prevailing psychosis of the age" in which there is likely to be a passionate bias against an accused rapist, and that "a greater evidence requirement is needed to counteract such bias." Privately, Sullivan told us that corroboration is "just a simple rule of evidence. I predict that if the corroboration requirement goes, there will be fewer, not more, convictions in the District than at present."

Judge Newman's attitude toward rape obviously departs from traditional legal views, which tend to see rape as primarily a sex crime and corroboration as a "simple" rule of evidence. Not long before the Arnold case the judge had sentenced a rapist who pleaded guilty, to twelve years to life in prison. The defendant had been charged with sexual offenses against seventeen women. At the sentencing Newman said the defendant's crimes were "a repeated series of the most violent, degrading type . . . a graphic illustration of the fact that rape is not in fact a sex offense seeking normal sexual gratification. It is instead an assault and degradation of a female."

In this light, Judge Newman's views that corroboration requirements are sexist and discriminatory support the conclusions of the District's 1973 report of the Public Safety Committee Task Force on Rape, which was followed by a series of public hearings before the District City Council. The task force had pointed out that nearly 40 percent of the rape cases in the District not prosecuted during a twelve-month period had been dropped because of corroborative evidence problems.

A more recent District study, in 1974, by the Institute of Law and Social Research (described by *Washington Post* staff writer Eugene L. Meyer as a "think tank") said arrests for rape resulted in proportionally fewer prosecutions and convictions in the city's Superior Court system than any other major violent crime committed in the District in 1973. (Of the rape arrests in D.C., 57 percent went unprosecuted in 1973; the next lowest rate of prosecution for major crimes was in murder arrests, with 24 percent unprosecuted.) According to this study, rape was also the charge to which defendants were least likely to plea bargain "and for which juries were most likely to acquit."

This local study is interesting because it seems to reflect national trends. As we shall see, nationally rape is the one major crime with shockingly low prosecution and conviction rates; it is also one for which juries are most likely to acquit.

Most judges have been noticeably reluctant to comment publicly on the corroboration requirement. A personal survey of a number of high court judges in Washington, D.C., at the time of the District rape force hearings in the autumn of 1973, turned up polite refusals to discuss any aspect of rape law. U.S. District Court Judge John Helm Pratt expressed "sympathy" through his secretary in expressly vague terms.

David Bazelon, Chief Judge of the U.S. Court of Appeals, went on record as upholding corroboration. However, he acknowledged that it was rooted in a "tangled web of legitimate concerns, outdated beliefs, and deep-seated prejudices." It is to be hoped that Judge Bazelon, who has written critically of the psychiatric profession, will soon turn his attention to exploring the psychiatrists' monumental contribution *in the law* to the preservation of outdated prejudices and unproven speculations about women.

Chastity

In most jurisdictions, though there is evidence of slow change, it is a general rule that the so-called "unchastity" of the victim is admissible in court testimony as part of the evidence permitted to be presented to the jury. In the eyes of the law, apparently, an "unchaste" woman is one who, though unmarried, is not a virgin. The law thus inextricably links the consent issue to a woman's sex life, presuming that an "unchaste" woman will consent more readily to intercourse than a "chaste" one. In some states, "unchastity" also gets linked to credibility, the nonvirgin being presumed by the law to fabricate or bring false charges.

A number of states—California, Florida, Michigan, and Iowa among them—have recently amended their "unchastity" requirements, again in response to continuing demands from beleaguered women. California's law, passed in 1974, says that a victim can be questioned about her sexual conduct only if a judge finds it useful as a "measure of her credibility," and then only after a special hearing by the trial judge with the jury absent. The law also specifies that evidence about a woman's sex life which is heard in chambers cannot be used as a measure of her consent or resistance. In April 1975, the New York State Assembly moved in similar directions and passed a bill (140–2) limiting the admissibility of evidence about the victim's sex life. The bill became operative in September 1975.

Many women feel that the issue of their sexual activities has nothing whatever to do with whether they have been raped or not, and that the singling out of the victim for a special hearing is inherently prejudicial, especially since the prior sexual acts of the defendant are nowhere examined in court.

In general, prior specific acts of intercourse between the complainant and the accused are admissible in evidence; and the new California law still permits this. The legal reasoning is that the accused is unlikely to use force to obtain that which he had previously obtained without force, and that a woman who had consented once is more likely to consent again. This reasoning clearly smacks of a male orientation: once-available, always-available. Apparently, the law does not permit a woman to change her mind. In this it seems to reflect popular sexual mores, which dictate that a woman who agrees to intercourse and then withdraws is a "tease" and therefore "deserves what she gets"—which may be rape.

The question of the admissibility of evidence about the victim's prior sex life has been argued by legal writers for more than a century. The classic opinion, which has prevailed until very recently, was summed up in an 1838 New York case, *People v. Abbot:*

> *And will you not more readily infer assent in the practiced Messalina, in loose attire, than in the reserved and virtuous Lucretia? . . . Shall I be answered that both are equally under the protection of the law? That I admit, and so are the common prostitute and the concubine. If either have, in truth, been feloniously ravished the punishment is the same, but the proof is quite different.*

A sharp distinction should be made for the jury, the judge said, between someone who "has already submitted herself to the lewd embraces of another" and the "coy and modest female severely chaste and instinctively shuddering at the thought of impurity."

Wigmore recognized that there was a certain injustice to the woman in the unchaste admissibility dictum, putting her at the mercy of a possible villain, but he found it balanced by "the evil of putting an innocent man's liberty at the mercy of an unscrupulous and revengeful mistress." Clearly, when Wigmore asks, "Which state of facts is the commoner and the one most needing our protection?" he opts for the man, though he cites no cases to support his decision.

This overanxious father-cock attitude toward the defendant runs all through case law, and historically it has been implicit in the judicial contortions of judges who have sought to assist the accused man in court. For example, in 1945, a Kentucky judge ruled, in *Grigsby* v. *Commonwealth*, that a woman's prior "immorality" with other men was admissible: it would "strongly militate against the probability that she did not consent in the case under consideration." But in the same opinion the court refused to admit evidence of wrongdoing of the accused: it would be "unfair" to him since the "majority of men and women of average intelligence—the class from which most juries are selected—are untrained in logical thinking and are prone to draw illogical conclusions."

Some critics, among them law student Ann Williams of Washington, D.C., suggest that the evidentiary female "chastity" provisions are unconstitutional, violating the woman's rights of privacy and equal protection under the law. In a personal communication, Williams cites a group of recent Supreme Court decisions showing that a preponderant number protect the complainant from "unjustified governmental intrusion" into areas of privacy in matters pertaining to procreation, marriage, the family, and sex. Unless the alleged "immoral or indecent" behavior can be shown, with facts rather than assumptions, to have some direct bearing on the defendant's guilt or innocence, it may be unconstitutional. Since the woman's sex life alone is singled out for examination, whereas evidence of the defendant's prior sexual conduct cannot be introduced to show the likelihood that he committed the offense with which he is charged, it is discriminatory on the basis of sex.

Williams claims that the rule regarding the unchastity of the prosecuting witness is not applied in cases of sodomy involving male victims. In such cases, the male's prior sexual activities are not discussed, since a male's sex life has never been presumed to affect either his likelihood of consent, or his credibility. Nebraska has been particularly careful to institutionalize this double standard. In *State* v. *Narcisse* (1971) there was no attempt by the defense attorney to introduce the male sodomy victim's prior sex life or sexual reputation. But in another Nebraska sodomy case, where the victim was a woman (*Frank* v. *State,* 1949) the court spelled it out: ". . . in cases where a woman charges a man with a sex offense, immorality has a direct connection with veracity . . . and direct evidence of the general reputation of the prosecutrix for sexual morality may be shown by defendant. . . ."

Williams suggests that such discrimination is subject to scrutiny under the Equal Protection Clause:

> The rule regarding admissibility of evidence of unchastity of a rape victim is, at best, an anachronism, and its continued application is unconstitutional. . . . It acts as a powerful deterrent in discouraging the reporting of rapes, and operates to reduce the rate of convictions for those that are reported. It should be struck down without delay and replaced by the standard rule of evidence which operates in other cases.

This standard rule is defined in legal encyclopedias such as *Corpus Juris Secundum* as follows: "Evidence as to character is irrelevant and not admissible where the existence or nonexistence of the particular trait proposed to be shown would have no tendency to render probable or improbable the particular act in controversy."

Although we have heard many policemen and lawyers insist that prostitutes *theoretically* can be victims of rape, they also admit that in practice such women rarely get the protection of the law. For obvious reasons, few prostitutes report rape in the first place, but those that do find that police and attorneys are reluctant to bring their cases to trial since women's "chastity" weighs so heavily, and negatively, upon the minds of the American public.

In the rare cases where a prostitute has gone into court, convictions are rare, probably rarer than in other cases; and higher courts can usually be counted on to reverse the decision if it has gone against the defendant. But the Texas appeals court, in an unusual largess of spirit in September 1973, in *Haynes* v. *State* upheld a rape conviction, saying that even if the victim had been proven to be a prostitute, she still had freedom of choice, and that she had the right to consent or not, according to her own will: "The evidence shows that the prosecutrix and appellant were on bad terms, and nothing in the record suggests that on this occasion any financial arrangements were made to obtain her consent, or that she otherwise consented . . ."

The case then was decided on the issue of consent and not on evidence that the accused forced the woman. While the decision *seems* to impart equal injustice, it also seems to give legal approval to prostitution as a legitimate business enterprise. Could the Texas court have recognized the action as rape had the woman made a "financial arrangement" for sexual services?

Since Wigmore's *Evidence* continues to quote antiquated sources in support of the deleterious effects of "unchastity" on women, and since lawyers and judges continue to read and quote Wigmore, we offer a sample. It is from an 1895 Missouri court ruling (*State v. Sibley*):

> *It is a matter of common knowledge that the bad character of a man for chastity does not even in the remotest degree affect his character for truth, when based upon that alone, while it does that of a woman. . . . It is no compliment to a woman to measure her character for truth by the same standard that you do that of a man's, predicated upon character for chastity. What destroys the standing of the one in all walks of life has no effect whatever on the standing for truth of the other. Thus in Bank v. Stryker . . . it is said, "Adultery has been committed openly by distinguished and otherwise honorable members [of the bar] as in Great Britain as in our own country, yet the offending party has not been supposed to destroy the force of the obligation which they feel from the oath of office."*

Rarely has a defense of the double standard in the law been so clearly—and so prejudicially—stated.

A continuation of the double standard exists in the law today. Some juries are specifically instructed by judges in sex assault cases to exercise extreme "caution" in considering the testimony of the complainant. What the jury is never told is that in these states the cautionary provision is provided for by law, or that the law continues to demand caution from jurors only in cases involving women and children (see Chapter 6).

As vicious as the double standard is in the law, it is probably even more pernicious in its subconscious operation in the minds of the public at large. Defense attorneys have routinely benefited from this fact, deliberately introducing questions which they know are not permitted merely to plant suspicion against the victim in the minds of judge and jury. Even if the prosecutor is on his toes and quickly voices objection, sustained by the judge, the damage is done, the victim is made suspect; her "morality" rather than the accused's behavior becomes a central issue. As University of Michigan law professor Yale Komisar has said: "The very least that can be done is that this sort of argumentative cross-examination implying lack of chastity on the part of the victim should not go on. It simply should not be allowed. There should be legitimate questions. Period."

Past Crimes of the Defendant

It is a well settled rule of evidence (which again works for the criminal rather than the victim) that testimony about another sex crime committed by the accused at a different time and against another person, having no connection with the crime charged, is generally not admissible.

This means that the jury knows nothing about prior sex charges against the accused, while the victim's prior sexual history is offered to those whose job it is to determine the guilt of the defendant, not the complainant. A rapist may claim consent as a defense, even under seemingly outrageous circumstances, but the jury is not allowed to know about other cases in which he may have figured where he similarly claimed "consent." Surely it is relevant for the jury to know that women other than the complainant in a given case have independently reported being raped by the accused, and that in these other charges the accused has also claimed consent.

Some jurisdictions—Michigan, for example—have what is called a "similar acts" statute under which evidence of prior offenses by the accused are admissible to show a characteristic plan or scheme, motive, or identity. Michigan had seldom applied this law to sodomy and similar crimes since they rarely had similar motive or scheme. However, in 1973, the appeals court upheld the conviction of an armed sex criminal who had forced oral sex on two women victims of his armed robberies, allowing testimony on prior offenses since they were identical. But the Louisiana Supreme Court, in the same year, reversed a previous stand that allowed testimony on similar acts by the defendant when closely related by time, method, and neighborhood. In its reversal, the Louisiana high court held the evidence of another rape by the defendant in a different building of the same university campus four days prior to the case under consideration was *not* relevant.

The concept of the similar acts law, including acts for which the accused was not necessarily successfully convicted, is particularly useful where the defense claims mistaken identity. Arguing for wider application of the similar acts statute, a Michigan prosecuting attorney, Patricia Boyle told us:

> We're talking about offenses so similar to the offense charged that it is more likely than not that this individual is the one who committed the crime. . . . Similar acts has to do with similarity between the events of the crime. . . . It's important because rape is a peculiarly recidivist crime; rapists are characteristically persons who operate with what appears to be a preconceived plan. When it works, they repeat the plan over and over again. The data show that one rapist repeatedly commits the same crime in the same general locality with the same method of operation.

Marital Exemption in Rape

Since no state in the country allows a wife to charge her husband with rape, it follows that forced sexual intercourse in marriage is not a crime. This concept stemmed originally from the British law known as "implied consent" in marriage, where by "matrimonial consent and contract the wife hath given up herself in this kind unto her husband, which she cannot retract." The quote is from Sir Matthew Hale, a seventeenth-century British jurist who today is still probably the most frequently quoted legal "expert" on rape, his classic formula having been incorporated into most of the state rape laws in the country (the classic formula being the one about how "easy" it is to charge rape and how difficult it is to defend against the charge). None of the legal writers and judicial experts who regularly quote Hale even mention that he died three hundred years ago, and that his ideas on the law derived from feudal times.

While the courts have held that a husband is "legally incapable" of raping his own wife, a number of decisions have upheld the husband's conviction of rape of his own wife by assisting another man. Both Texas and North Carolina appellate courts in 1973 upheld the conviction of husbands who helped another man rape their wives, even though in the Texas case the "other man" had been acquitted of rape.

One legal expert, Camille E. LeGrand, writing in the May 1973, *California Law Review*, suggests that the consent standard is the "primary conceptual barrier" to designating forcible intercourse between husband and wife as rape. This is because a woman theoretically consents to all sexual intercourse with her husband as long as she remains married. Thus, although a woman may suffer as much, or more, humiliation, fear, and pain from a forcible sexual assault by her husband as from someone else, he enjoys legal sanction; she cannot charge him with rape. Other barriers to defining husband–wife assault as rape, LeGrand asserts, are "largely administrative" involving problems of proof and evidence, and perhaps "malicious" prosecution.

In the kind of double talk for which legal writers are famous, especially when it comes to analyzing the law as it affects females, California law professor Rollin M. Perkins in his classic 1969 legal textbook, *Criminal Law*, argues that the irrevocable consent to intercourse which a woman once gave in marriage is "definitely out of date, and was never needed . . . the true reason why the husband, who has sexual intercourse with his wife

against her will, is not guilty of rape is that such intercourse is *not unlawful* . . . unlawful is used as 'not
authorized by law.' " (Italics added.)

Perkins explains that only sexual intercourse between a husband and wife is sanctioned by law; all other
sexual intercourse is unlawful. Since "unlawfulness"
cannot exist in sexual intercourse between wife and
husband, if you follow this line of reasoning, a woman
cannot be raped by her husband. After this excursion
into never-never land, Perkins gives the nod to reality,
admitting that many jurisdictions do not punish "a secret act of fornication," an observation which surely
must rate as the legal understatement of the century.

The key factor of the use of force in sexual intercourse
is not mentioned by the professor; either it is irrelevant
or it is sanctioned through the magic word "lawful."
Nor does he discuss the wife's "will" against which the
husband employs force; presumably the law does not
recognize that women possess a will to be against.

Marriage apparently thus legally wipes out a
woman's human rights in sexual intercourse; if she is
under age, her husband cannot be charged with "statutory rape" nor with "carnal knowledge" of a child, since
these terms only apply *outside* the marriage bed. The
men who made the law clearly were thinking of their
own well-being. The marital exemption in the rape provisions echoes the ancient masculine prerogatives of
droit de seigneur and the frolicsome adultery of "distinguished members of the bar" in Great Britain; all the
rights in sexual intercourse belong, by law, to the male.
The need for reform is obvious; how to persuade the fifty
legislatures which are still mostly men to give up their
special privilege is another question.

Punishment and Penalties

In the hierarchy of crime, rape ranks second only to
murder. Historically, it has always received extreme
forms of punishment—long prison sentences, life im-

prisonment, death, and in some places and times, castration. Severe punishment, however, has never stopped rape; indeed, it is becoming increasingly evident that harsh penalties work largely to deter juries from convicting and victims from reporting. Jury studies, such as Harry Kalven and Hans Zeisel's classic The American Jury, show that even when jurors are convinced of the accused's complicity or guilt, they refuse to convict because they consider the penalties excessive. Victims are aware of this and often do not report the crime, and they urge others not to report because convictions are so difficult to secure. The combination of jury refusal to convict and victims' discouragement about reporting favors the criminal and probably contributes to the overall increase of criminal sexual assaults. Certainly the frequently outrageous risks taken by rapists in states with severe penalties seem to indicate that fear of punishment does not operate as a deterrent.

One study of the nondeterrent effect of harsher penalties was made in the late 1960s in Philadelphia, following the particularly brutal "Palm Sunday rapes," in which three men viciously raped, robbed, and beat an eighty-year-old widow, her forty-four-year-old daughter, and her fourteen-year-old granddaughter. In retribution the Pennsylvania legislature instituted maximum penalties for rape and attempted rape, setting a minimum of fifteen years to life imprisonment for rape involving bodily injury to victims. The study showed that the number of reported and attempted rapes the following year was the same as before the new laws; the proportion of rapes to attempted rapes increased slightly, and the injuries to victims remained the same. As the Journal of Criminal Law said: "Pennsylvania's new deterrent strategy against rape was a failure. . . ."

The castration, or removal of the testes, of convicted offenders is a punishment frequently suggested either by angry women and men looking for "revenge" or by criminologists who see it as some kind of "rehabilitative" procedure. It has been used, on a voluntary basis, though without definitive success, in a number of European areas such as Germany and the Scandinavian countries. Aside from American doctors' collective revulsion at the practice, the main objection to castration is that it does not reach the core of the problem—the rapist's antisocial drive to assault women. While castration may reduce sexual impulses (though this is by no means fully established), whether as punishment or rehabilitation, it focuses *only* on the sexual aspect of the crime, and perpetuates the myth that rape is the result of uncontrollable physical urges on the part of men instead of a manifestation of violence and hostility against women.

Harsh penalties for rape were first imposed by male legislators in this country, most of whom probably sincerely believed that such measures would deter rapists and protect women. But given a patriarchal society, rape was, and is, seen also as an invasion of a property right, the exclusive "possession" of a female. Thus the so-called "violation" of a woman by any man other than her exclusive "owner"—father, husband, brother, or other male relative—must be punished severely in order to protect that exclusive property right. One medical man, Colorado University's Dr. John MacDonald, who has made a specialty of writing books on various major crimes, estimates that the average time served by federal and state prisoners "released during 1960 was longer for rapists than for men convicted of manslaughter, robbery, aggravated assaults, or indeed, any offense other than murder."

The most severe penalty for rape is, of course, death. Many states considered rape such a heinous offense that death alone could atone for the crime and presumably prevent others from committing the same offense. In the South, where men are traditionally hysterical about rape and the chastity of women, there also were practitioners of the so-called lynch law, said by its advocates to be a necessary protection against black rapists. The need for this extralegal death penalty was epitomized in a speech by the late U.S. Senator Ben Tillman of South Carolina, who once told the Senate that as a former governor of his state, though he had taken the oath of office to support the law and enforce it, he would "lead a mob to lynch any man, black or white, who had ravished a woman, black or white." Tillman explained: "When stern and sad-faced white men put to death a creature in human form who has deflowered a white woman . . . they have avenged the greatest wrong, the blackest crime in all the categories of crimes . . . and they have done it not so much as an act of retribution in behalf of the victim but as a duty and as a warning as to what many may expect who shall repeat the offense." He went on to say that a rapist was worse than a beast and so had forfeited his legal rights. The rapist, said Tillman:

> . . . [was] outside the pale of the law, human and divine. He has sinned against the Holy Ghost. He has invaded the holy of holies. He has struck civilization a blow . . . our brains reel under the staggering blow and hot blood surges to the heart. Civilization peels off us, any and all of us who are men, and we revert to the original savage type whose impulses under such circumstances has always been to "kill! kill! kill!"

Tillman made this impassioned plea early in this century and one could dismiss it as Victorian lunacy were it not for the fact that it echoes contemporary attitudes. The typical immediate reaction of many men when they learn that "their" females have been raped is: "I'm going to kill the bastard!"—a motivation clearly directed more toward male ego gratification than concern for the victim. Stories of men setting out—outside the law—to avenge themselves on rapists are common. One victim told us that her lover insisted on nightly patrols with a gun and carving knife in the area where she had first been accosted, forcing her to accompany him to identify her assailant. "He didn't give a damn about how terrified I was," she said.

The death penalty for rape operated in a number of states until 1967, when litigation was begun in an effort to persuade the United States Supreme Court that the death penalty for any crime was unconstitutional, in particular that it violated the Eighth Amendment forbidding "cruel and unusual punishment." In 1972, the Court handed down its decision, in *Furman* v. *Georgia*, and it was, in a sense, inconclusive. The Court ruled that the capital punishment laws, as written and administered in the cases before it—two of which involved rape—constituted cruel and unusual punishment. The Court did not say it was unconstitutional to execute felons, but only that all such state laws, as written, were unconstitutional because they were so haphazardly imposed.

The consequences of this five to four decision remain unclear. The five justices disagreed on the reasons for their decision and, by implication, on its scope as a precedent for the future. All nine justices filed full separate opinions; none joined in the opinion of any other.

Since the Furman decision, some thirty-four states have reinstituted the death penalty, making it mandatory for certain crimes or setting up "guidelines" for the selection (usually by juries) of those who are to die. The constitutionality of these post-Furman statutes is now being challenged before the Supreme Court. North Carolina, which has one of the strongest capital punishment laws since the Supreme Court ruling, mandates death for anyone convicted of first-degree murder, rape, arson, or first-degree burglary (entering after dark with intent to commit a felony). The North Carolina legislature has revoked the death penalty for rape where life is not threatened, but did not make application of the law retroactive. Massachusetts mandates death for rape–murder; Georgia demands death for rape; and in Florida, the rape of a child under eleven warrants capital punishment.

Aside from questions of constitutionality, there is ample evidence that the death penalty in the United States operates in a discriminatory fashion against the nonwhite, the poor, the illiterate, and the disadvantaged. In the Furman decision, where all three petitioners were black, only Justices William O. Douglas and Thurgood Marshall acknowledged possible racial discrimination in the imposition of the death penalty. But in "Race, Judicial Discretion and the Death Penalty," a recent exhaustive study of race and capital punishment, Professor Marvin E. Wolfgang, a noted criminologist at the University of Pennsylvania, concludes that juries *and* judges sentence significantly more blacks than whites to death. Of some 3,000 people executed for all crimes since 1930, 54.6 percent have been black or members of other racial minority groups. Of the 455 executed for rape alone, nearly 90 percent have been nonwhite. Since 1930, 405 of the 455 executed for rape have been black; two were from other minorities. The Bureau of Prisons statistics show that all the executions for rape took place in southern and border states or in the District of Columbia. Virginia, for example, has had an exceptional history of discriminatory executions of black criminals. Between 1908 (when the electric chair was installed in the Virginia State Penitentiary) and 1965, 56 men were executed for rape, attempted rape, and rape and robbery. *All of them were black.* Only 12 of these men ever had a full appellate review.

That so large a percentage of executed rapists was nonwhite suggests that arbitrary or erroneous legal proceedings have occurred, a thesis developed by Yale professor Charles L. Black, Jr., in his book *Capital Punishment: The Inevitability of Caprice and Mistake.* In addition to arbitrariness or error there is inherent in any life-or-death trial a sensationalism that reaches a peak of social uselessness when the crime is rape. Moreover, the drive toward "normalization" of the penalties for sex crimes—or the scaling down of punishments to bring them more into line with those for other crimes of violence, such as assault and battery —raises fundamental questions about the imposition of the death penalty for rape. Although it is often alleged that many jurors consider rape a "low-caste" crime and therefore are reluctant to stigmatize defendants with conviction, their reluctance probably has more to do with the unjust severity of the punishment than with social stigma.

Regardless of the injustices of the law and its penalties, the fact remains that the conviction rate for sex assaults is inexcusably low. According to Justice Department figures in 1974, only 51 percent of the reported rapes resulted in arrests. Of those arrested for forcible rape, 60 percent were prosecuted. Of those prosecuted, close to half (49 percent) had their cases acquitted or dismissed because of prosecutorial problems. This 49-percent acquittal–dismissal rate is substantially higher than the acquittal–dismissal rate of adults prosecuted for *all* crimes—which is only 29 percent.

Thus these FBI records indicate that in only 15 percent of the cases could the victims rest assured that their attackers would be convicted. Eighty-five percent of victims reporting had to live with the knowledge that their attackers were free—*neither arrested nor convicted*.

Taking a conservative figure and assuming that the rape rate is minimally five times that of the reported cases, the following figures emerge: *only 3 percent of the rapists will be convicted, and 97 percent will escape either arrest or conviction.*

No matter where the responsibility for these figures lodges—and the fault lies in many places—the fact that 97 percent of our rapists go free—uncharged or unconvicted—is a national scandal.

6
MISOGYNY AND LEGAL REFORM

Most women want their lovers to be . . . aggressive and dominating. Some consciously want to be forced. . . . The struggle also saves face for the girl who fears she would be considered "loose" if she yielded without due maidenly resistance; it also relieves the guilt feeling that might exist if she could not tell herself that "he made me do it." Many of the wrestling matches in parked cars come within this category.
—University of New Mexico law professor, Henry P. Weihofen,
in the Journal of Public Law, 1959

The mentality which makes it possible to explain rape as a "wrestling match" seems to permeate the legal system, if statements from bar and bench are any guide. It also explains why legal reform has been so slow in coming. These attitudes are summed up in the article on victims of criminal violence from which this chapter's opening quotation is taken.

Professor Weihofen repeats the familiar accusation: "It is *fairly certain* that many innocent men have gone to prison on the plausible tale of some innocent looking girl. . . ." (italics added). But like Wigmore and others before him, he offers no substantiation for the many-men-condemned-unjustly theory. Guilt-ridden women cry rape, Weihofen confidently asserts, "who are caught in the act of fornication . . . or who are seeking compensation, marriage, or revenge." Women may indeed "cry rape" under such circumstances; but there is no proof that given such motivation, these cases *ever* reach the courts. They usually are weeded out long before.

Anyway, Weihofen continues, women are such addle-headed incompetents that they probably do not know themselves whether they have "consented" or not. Presumably this is the reason we need legal authorities like Wigmore and Weihofen to tell us what we really want. And Wigmore's text, you will remember, relies among others on another misogynist of the 1930s, Dr. Otto Mönkemöller, who conjured up disaster due to wanton, erotic females.

Weihofen repostulates in 1959 what is essentially warmed-over Mönkemöller:

> *Our law gallantly presumes that the woman in a rape or seduction case was truly a victim, but psychological investigations show that, even of women who complain, it is not unusual that a significant number actually consented, and another appreciable number engaged in reckless and even flagrantly provocative conduct. A representative case is that of a young woman who meets a strange man in a bar, makes the rounds of other bars with him, gets into his car, and ends up being raped, if that is the proper term. Even young girls and mere children, in an astonishing number of cases, are victims more in law than in fact. In incest cases, the relationship has often been going on for months or even years, a situation which could hardly exist without compliance on the female's part.*

No evidence is cited—always unusual in legal writing—for the "significant" or "appreciable" numbers of women who allegedly consent or provoke. In the law women are judged on the basis of what men have decided is the conventional, "proper" behavior for females—not on an evidentiary basis of the facts in the case. Drinking with strangers is tantamount to "asking" for rape, and victims of incest must have consented.

Too many lawyers share these attitudes, often making

strict mental demarcations between those women considered to be "real" victims and those they believe consented to intercourse but then changed their minds. Women are not permitted to change their minds about sexual matters, it seems; attorneys we talked to subscribe to the belief that a woman who is ambivalent about intercourse "deserves what she gets" in some cases, even if she suffers physical violence. "It is not really rape," one attorney explained. "She led him on. . . . She was a tease. You can't get a guy excited and then pull back, that's asking for it."

That sexual intercourse is something a man *does* to a woman rather than a mutually shared experience is a notion deeply imbedded in our culture. As another University of New Mexico law professor, Leo Kanowitz, says:

> *The notion is still very much abroad that the act of intercourse necessarily represents an assault by the male upon the female. This attitude is reflected, among other ways, in the secondary meaning of the epithet that contains the tabooed four-letter word, followed by the word "you." No notion of pleasurable sexual intercourse is intended when that phrase is used. Instead, a threat of physical injury is implicit in the expletive. . . . The idea of sexual intercourse as synonymous with the infliction of physical injury by the male upon the female may, subconsciously at least, be shared by much of mankind.*

Or, as offered to us by a less literate mind, an assistant district attorney in Pittsburgh, Pennsylvania: "It isn't really rape when a female consents to sex relations and then later wishes she hadn't. Besides, with all this sex permissiveness, and females giving such easy consent to carnal relationships, there's no need for rape." The prevailing mystique which finds forcible sexual intercourse a "relationship" is of course of masculine origin; the convenient corollary to this is the women-*want*-their-lovers-to-be-aggressive-and-dominating theory, both attitudes shared by many legally trained minds. One lawyer calls rape "assault with a friendly weapon."

A recent unpublished preliminary study by a pair of legal researchers in a large metropolis revealed some interesting differences between defense attorneys and those on the prosecutorial staff of the district attorney. Some sixteen lawyers were interviewed. Defense attorneys believed most rapes were between a male and a female who knew each other and had spent time together. One lawyer called forcible intercourse between such a pair "a date-rape." All defense attorneys tossed off rape as "just another case"; district attorneys displayed a kind of crusading spirit, what one of the researchers called a "get-the-fiendish-criminal-off-the-streets" philosophy, perhaps as a result of seeing too many television shows. The district attorneys tended to emphasize the dangerousness of rapists and would report an attack on their wives or someone close to them. Attorneys for the defense tended to be against reporting. One said he would not want his wife to report, unless there was violence: "I think I'd just dismiss it as one of the unfortunate ills of our society. I wouldn't want her to go through the hospital mill, wise-guy detective questioning, and to undergo the badgering of the defense counsel." Apparently even lawyers recognize their courtroom attacks on victims as "badgering."

All the attorneys seemed to feel that "certain segments of society are not as offended by rape as others" and that middle-class white girls were more upset by the attack than ghetto blacks. The victim's reluctance to testify was not automatically attributed to a false charge. Many believed rather it revealed disenchantment with the court system. Many attorneys said they did not feel rape was traumatic to the victims unless there was physical violence or damage; defense attorneys were prepared to use any method within the law to defend their client. Since they did not see rape as psychologically harmful to the victim, harsh cross-examination and "reputation" evidence would not be hurtful. Prosecuting attorneys tended to treat victims having difficulty in adjusting or frightened at testifying with more sympathy than those who were outwardly calm and ready to testify, again assuming, like the defense lawyers, that calm victims had not been traumatized, or had been "asking for it."

Many lawyers, female as well as male, seem totally incapable of sympathizing with rape victims, let alone empathizing with them. The prevailing attitude is that rape-is-just-another-case (it isn't really so bad) or that older women especially "want it." This attitude was tragically summed up recently by a Virginia court-appointed defender, Blair D. Howard. Howard acted on behalf of a criminal who pleaded guilty to the brutal rape of a forty-seven-year-old mother of four, a woman happily married for twenty-six years, who has suffered permanent damage as a result of the attack. Said Fairfax County lawyer Howard after the conviction of his client: "It's not the kind of aggravated case of a young girl who is going to be permanently scarred. Here was a forty-seven-year-old woman with four children who—to put in a crude way—she might be glad to have it happen. . . ."

Attitudes of Judges

Since judges usually have been lawyers first, it should come as no surprise that they share prevailing prejudices and myths about rape victims. The famed "stony-faced" judge is probably a literary creation, for in the courtrooms we have visited, few judges show neutrality; responses to the testimony were conveyed not only verbally or by tone of voice, but by facial expressions and gestures.

Case law, or what lawyers study in law school, is contained in the law books; it is the result of recorded decisions of the upper courts. In criminal trials, there often is no record, unless the case is appealed, and the route taken by a judge in making decisions can only be witnessed by courtroom observers. But it is of vital importance to the outcome. How does a judge respond to objections by the two attorneys, does he overrule or sustain the prosecutor as often as the defense attorney? Does he question the legal "conduct" of the prosecutor more than the defense? Does he display racist or sexist attitudes? And, finally, is he actually listening?

We watched a judge in a brutal rape trial preoccupied with attacking the prosecuting attorney (though *not* the victim in this case) pursuing a course of sarcasm and ridicule: "You've got a tight case. If you blow it, it'll be your own fault. . . . Give your witness [the rape victim] a chance to answer, she's not up there to satisfy *your* impatience. . . ." And finally, exasperated, he shouted: "Mr. ——, I don't know where you learned the law, sir, but it's obvious you never learned any manners!"

Old court hands later told us, "Those two have tangled before." The reputed disaffection, if not enmity, between the bench and the district attorney's office often emerges in the courtroom at the expense of both the rape victim and the accused, a phenomenon not dissimilar in tone, at least, to what we have seen between physicians and lawyers.

In another court we observed a white judge sitting before a predominantly black jury trying four young blacks accused of gang raping a young black girl. Throughout the testimony the judge sneered and taunted the defendants—whose obsequious and groveling comportment and obviously well-coached testimony raised questions about their honesty—sending the jury again and again into convulsions of laughter, turning what should have been a deadly serious matter into a legal joke. The judge's past record showed that this probably was not his intention; still, in other jurisdictions and other circumstances, the judge's comedic thrusts might have paved the way for an appeal. Given another judge whose attitudes are sexist instead of perhaps racist, the rape victim stands little or no chance.

Such judicial behavior belies the classic description of the bench described in a Maryland case, *State v. Babb:* "The assumed proposition that judges are men of discernment, learned and experienced in the law and capable of evaluating the materiality of evidence, lies at the very core of our judicial system."

Learning and discernment, however, apparently vanish in matters of sex: One observer, reporting in *Law and Contemporary Problems* on some 1,500 delinquency petition hearings in 1960, says that one metropolitan juvenile court judge consistently refused to punish any form of sexual behavior on the part of the boys, even the most bizarre, except by probationary status. This "man of learning and discernment" categorically blamed the girls—they were "prostitutes" and the "cause" of the boys' behavior—in all cases of coition between an adolescent couple. Another judge, a religious fundamentalist, also observed by the same writer, was vindictive against boys; the girls were invariably seen as "victimized" by the boy.

One remarkable case on the records in Missouri dramatically illustrates judicial attitudes. While this case dates from the 1920s, it is, unfortunately, typical of attitudes still prevailing in some parts of the country. Worse, it remains as a citation in the legal literature, serving as a model for young lawyers. The case was marked by an involved "legal" discussion as to whether the fifteen-year-old victim should be whipped by the sheriff or her mother in order to force her to testify at trial. She was already in reform school, and the girl's life as an alleged prostitute had affected her "credibility" as a witness, the court said, invoking the ancient masculine assumption that a female's sexuality governs her cerebral processes.

In reviewing the case the Missouri Supreme Court quoted Shakespeare and the Bible in a passionate denunciation of females who are not virgins:

> *A lecherous woman is a social menace; she is more dangerous than TNT; more deadly than the "pestilence that walketh in darkness or the destruction that wasteth at noonday. . . . For the lips of a strange woman drop as an honeycomb, and her mouth is smoother than oil; but her end is bitter as wormwood, sharp as a two-edged sword, her feet go down to death, her steps take hold on hell." . . . this wretched girl was young in years but old in sin and shame. A number of callow youths . . . fell under her seductive influence . . . the boys were immature and doubtless more sinned against than sinning. They did not defile the girl. She was a mere "cistern for foul toads to knot and gender in."*

The choice of *Othello* as a source of condemnation of nonvirgins is ironic, since the Moor's jealous ravings in Act IV are directed at the spotlessly submissive Desdemona, whose major mistakes in life seem to have involved trusting men. But *Othello* is typical in another sense; it portrays the worldwide masculine obsession with "exclusive" sexual possession of a female. This attitude views female sexuality as a commodity; if that commodity is touched by another man, it becomes "damaged" and the worth of the exclusive "owner" is also jeopardized. Or, as the *Yale Law Journal* pointed out some twenty-five years ago: "An unwise disposition of a girl's sexual 'treasure,' it is thought, harms both her and the social structure which anticipates certain patterned uses. Hence, the law of statutory rape must intervene to prevent what is predicted will be an unwise disposition."[1] The quotation refers to statutory rape; it is equally applicable to the rape of an adult.

[1] *Yale Law Journal*, vol. 62, pp. 55, 72 (1952).

Judges also share in the prevailing male mystique about so-called "normal" male–female sexuality and seem to see sexual intercourse under *all* circumstances as something a male *does* to a female. This concept was again eloquently expressed (in May 1975) by New York Supreme Court Justice Edward J. Greenfield in acquitting a thirty-eight-year-old television moderator named Martin Evans of rape and sodomy. Using words to describe the accused man's actions as "sexual conquest" and men "having *their* way with women," the judge wrote a ten-page decision (Evans had waived his right to a jury trial) saying that the line between rape and seduction was a thin one, and that Evans's case fell under the latter heading. Said the judge:

> We recognize that there are some patterns of male aggression which do not deserve the extreme penalty, in which the male objective was achieved through charm, guilt, protestation of love, promises and even deceit—where force was not employed to overcome reluctance and where consent, however reluctant, may be spelled out. This we label seduction. (Emphasis added.)

While we would not quarrel with the judge's reluctance to impose the "extreme penalty," the rest of the statement is reminiscent of the Weihofen-Mönkemöller-Wigmore doctrine of masculine prerogatives and feminine submission. Judge Greenfield, in fact, told other male sexual predators they need not fear the law: "Bachelors and other men on the make, fear not. It is still not illegal to feed a girl a line. Every man is entitled to the attempt and he need not take no as a final answer. He can attempt to persuade and cajole . . . make promises that may not be kept . . . every man is free to be a gentleman or a cad . . ."; only "if violence, force and threat" are used would they transform a "heel into a criminal." There is an undercurrent of judicial admiration for the con-man seducer who played "psychologi-

cal games with girls' heads"—surely a curious note for
an allegedly "unbiased" judicial bench.

Judicial consideration of sexual attacks often brings
out other unsuspected passions. In 1969 San Francisco
Superior Court Judge Bernard B. Glickfeld called a rape
victim "a horse's ass" and ordered her to leave his
chambers; back in the courtroom he said to a police
officer who had accompanied the woman "I don't want
police inspectors sitting here in court holding some
alleged victim's hand, and I am using that term
figuratively. . . ." The case involved the gang rape,
kidnapping, and robbery of a twenty-two-year-old hotel
cashier. The judge followed his "discerning" pro-
nouncements by dismissing some of the charges against
one of the defendants, William A. Morris, sentencing
him to fifty-two *weekends* in jail and allowing him to
continue working at his job while on probation. In 1971,
the state Supreme Court publicly censured Judge Glickfeld but kept him on *his* job. A few months later, Morris
was jailed for shooting a policeman during a burglary.
One of his accomplices had been a codefendant in the
rape case.

Another aspect of legal and judicial attitudes toward
rape is the disproportionately high percentage of criminals who receive probation. Criminal statistics from
California, New York, and Michigan bear this out. For
example, in 1967, nearly 60 percent of the convicted
rapists in California were given probation, whereas only
a little more than 33 percent of those convicted of robbery received probation.

An example of judicial leniency toward rapists is
documented by *State* v. *Chaney*, which went all the way
to the Alaska Supreme Court before a court acknowledged the severity of the crime. The victim had been
raped four times by two men, beaten, forced to perform
fellatio, robbed of all her money, and threatened with
reprisals if she reported to police. The facts, and the
brutality, were not disputed. What was at issue was the

"severity" of the sentence—two concurrent one-year terms, with the trial judge urging *immediate parole.*

Until the case reached the Supreme Court of Alaska, judges apparently agreed with the attitude expressed by the military spokesman who acted for the accused G.I.: "It happens many times each night in Anchorage," as if the extraordinary prevalence of rape in the community was a vindication of his client. Chaney, he said, was the "unlucky" G.I. who raped a woman who "told."

The high court did not agree; it ordered a stiffer sentence and commented on the defendant's lack of remorse. The trial court, it said, had treated him as only "technically guilty and minimally blameworthy." Still, even the Supreme Court regarded the victim's voluntary acceptance of a ride in the defendant's car as a "mitigating circumstance," meriting consideration in reducing the sentence.

In a pioneer effort to explore legal attitudes toward rape victims, Rutgers University assistant law professor Carol Bohmer conducted a personal interview study early in the 1970s of thirty-nine municipal and common pleas judges in Philadelphia. Bohmer was formerly research attorney for the Center for Rape Concern, part of the Philadelphia General Hospital, which sees between 600 and 800 rape victims each year brought there by police. Bohmer found that judicial attitudes "are far less impartial than is frequently supposed." The judges' comments confirmed allegations of the "courtroom victimization" of rape victims. Further inquiry into judicial attitudes was clearly needed, she concluded in *Judicature*, the official journal of the American Judicature Society.

Judges categorized victims much like the attorneys in the preliminary study quoted earlier: "genuine" victims; those who had "asked" for it, or engaged in "consensual" intercourse; and those who filed charges out of "female vindictiveness." According to attorney Bohmer, judges were sympathetic with the "genuine" victim (a stranger leaping out of the shadows in a dark alley) and reacted punitively toward defendants. As one judge said: "The effect on the average girl is devastating. She will never get over it, the indignities, the knowledge on the part of her associates; rarely do they ever adjust to a full, happy life."

Judges see situations such as the one where a woman meets a man in a bar, lets him drive her home, and then charges rape as clearly "consensual." The judges described this category as "friendly rape," "felonious gallantry," "assault with failure to please," and "breach of contract." In such cases the judges believed that the woman either got what she wanted, or "deserved" it, and this, in their opinion, could not be defined as rape. "Female vindictiveness" included situations in which the judges thought the woman lied to "get even" with a man; either the intercourse was consensual or it did not occur at all.

The judges had great concern for child victims, regarding them often as pawns in the adult world, incapable frequently of knowing fact from fiction. Most of the judges thought the courtroom experience traumatic for the child, but felt there was no way to eliminate the trauma without sacrificing the adversary procedure, which would result in a violation of the defendant's constitutional rights. Bohmer's interviews with the judges indicated that judicial concern for children did not extend to racial minorities or to Third World women. Judges alluded to the chaotic life-styles and attitudes of "ghetto dwellers" (by which they meant blacks) and said black women tended to be vindictive in their accusations. One judge said: "With the Negro community, you really have to redefine the term rape. You never know about them." Some judges referred to blacks as "colored," "Nigra," or "Negro."

Professor Bohmer's study was made through personal interviews and courtroom observation, and the sample was small. But it indicates nonetheless that judicial predispositions toward women and minorities mean judges cannot be relied upon to counterbalance the biases of lawyers, jurors, or policemen. In short, judges are not the impartial or unbiased arbiters we have been taught to revere. They affect proceedings directly by their rulings, and indirectly by their attitudes toward trial participants. How a judge conducts a trial, and the kinds of evidence he admits and weighs in assessing a case, can mean the difference between the victim's future emotional stability and her psychological deterioration.

As attorney Patricia Boyle of the Detroit prosecutor's staff says:

> *How judges respond or don't respond to public myths and opinions is very important. The judiciary has been pretty much removed from public scrutiny for a very long time and has not had pressure brought to bear on it. I think the creation of public opinion, even without a specific issue being before the court, is enough to influence and perhaps cause a judge to consider a particular issue or attitude.*

Moreover, the lack of women at the judicial level is a disgrace, and the habit of bypassing women for judgeships is long standing. Forty years after the appointment of the first woman to the federal circuit court, still only one woman sits there as judge; New York State's Court of Appeals, the highest state court, has not had a woman judge since its inception in 1948. As New York attorney Doris Sassower told the National Conference of Bar Presidents in Chicago in 1969: "At last count there were not many more than 8,000 women lawyers, and out of roughly 10,000 judges in the United States, fewer than 200 were women, the majority of whom were concentrated in the lower courts." Sassower later added that by 1970 black judges outnumbered women judges, both in absolute number and in proportion to the population. Moreover, black men had achieved that which is still denied women, a Supreme Court seat. "One might conclude," said Sassower, "that sexism is more deeply rooted than racism."

Sexism in the legal profession is only a hairsbreadth away from misogyny. Few have expressed it so colorfully as a lawyer from Michigan (who will not be identified here). Apparently he believes in the supersanctity of bench and bar and thinks judges should operate without scrutiny from the "outside," even from law professors and attorneys like Bohmer. Here is what he wrote:

> *I note your article in Judicature. . . . I also note with great disapprobation and disgust the rancid, fetid and feculent efforts of Women's Libbers and other fascists to change the burden of proof in rape cases to the defendant, who usually has it in practice anyhow. While the prospect of any such change in the law provokes me to vomit, I have a counter proposal to make, which you may convey to the Center for Rape Concern, whatever the hell that is: When a female has induced the prosecutorial authority to institute a charge of rape against a man, and that man is acquitted, without further delay the prosecutrix shall be carried in a cart to the nearest public square and there disembowelled alive, and then hanged by the feet and left to rot in the sun.*

So much for legal objectivity.

Attitudes of Juries

Men accused of rape rarely waive their right to a trial by jury; juries and the rapist's attorneys often share the prevailing sexist attitudes toward rape and rape victims. Despite the oft-repeated assertion that human sympathy goes "naturally" to the victim, the theory has no basis in fact. Wigmore's *Evidence* says:

The "unchaste" mentality finds incidental but direct expression in the narration of imaginary sex incidents of which the narrator is the heroine or the victim . . . the real victim, however, too often in such cases is the innocent man; for the respect and sympathy naturally felt by any tribunal for a wronged female helps to give easy credit to such a plausible tale.

This is speculation, a theory unproven in fact. Today probably the opposite is true; the public in general, and juries in particular, are in fact often hostile toward victims, especially if they "disapprove" of their conduct.

In theory, too, the jury is there only to ascertain the "facts" and to apply these facts to the rules of law laid down by the judge and thus arrive at a verdict. In most or many cases, what really happens is that juries often do not understand the judge's instructions, let alone the law as he reveals it to them (often for the first time in their lives), or they consciously or unconsciously ignore the law and simply bring in a verdict for the party they favor. In the consideration of rape and other sex crimes, jurors—female as well as male—tend to vote according to their personal hidden sexual beliefs, his against hers. As a woman juror in the Midwest put it: "After all, he's got a family. If we convict him, what'll happen to them? Besides, she's young; she'll get over it."

Thus in a case involving a personable teen-ager who attacked two elderly women, the jury acquitted. Despite positive identification by the sixty-six-year-old victim and her eighty-year-old neighbor whom the adolescent tied up before attempting to rape the first woman, the jury brought in a verdict of not guilty. And the judge commented: "Here's a nice-looking young boy who just didn't look like a rapist in the eyes of the jury. He looked like your average paperboy. Juries are going to watch out for a young kid in cases like this." A few months later the would-be rapist appeared before the same judge for robbery and drew a stiff sentence.

Another California jury acquitted a defendant who produced several witnesses who swore he was elsewhere. Among them was a good-looking girl who testified he had been in bed with her at the time of the attack. The nineteen-year-old victim had been pulled out of her car in a parking lot by a stranger who pinned her to the pavement with a coat over her head. The attack was witnessed by another man, who went away at the rapist's request. One of the jurors, an elderly woman, said: "I just couldn't believe that boy whose girl friend was as pretty as the one who came into court to testify would have even wanted to rape such a plain-looking girl." Besides, said this juror, he must have been with the witness who claimed he'd been in bed with her at the time because "no girl would come into a public courtroom and disgrace herself like that, admitting she was sleeping with a man she isn't even married to, unless she really was!"

As a Los Angeles County Trials Division head attorney Aaron Stovitz said: "Jurors are usually twelve hung-up people who won't convict in a rape case if they can avoid it. . . . Legal theory is not legal reality. A woman who hopes to win a rape case better have plenty of corroboration . . . no matter what the law in her state says."

Corroboration, which is required by the District of Columbia, was not enough apparently, in the case of the sensational 1972 trial of seventeen-year-old Santionta Butler, accused of sodomizing and raping two George Washington University students on the college campus earlier that year. Butler had confessed to the crimes, a fact revealed to the jury by the judge *after the trial* in a burst of anger at the jury's acquittal of the defendant (a legal technicality prevented the confession from being admitted into evidence). Three months later, in a long and rambling deposition marked by Butler's highly selective recall, the teen-ager repudiated his confession, claiming that an assistant U.S. attorney, Herbert Hoffman, and a detective, Frederick A. Cain, had "coerced" him into making it in the first place. Butler also claimed in his repudiation that the two women had enticed him into fellatio and sexual intercourse, the first in a campus toilet, and the second, only about fifteen minutes after the first episode, in the back of the university auditorium. (Butler's retraction came scarcely ten days after he had been arrested a second time and charged with grand larceny, unlawful entry, and assault on a police officer at Catholic University.)

The jurors in the first trial clearly judged the case by factors other than the data presented in the courtroom, and the verdict highlighted black backlash in the District, where, according to a well-known Washington attorney, there had not been a conviction in "a black-on-white rape case where consent was entered as defense since 1967." The two victims in the George Washington case were white; Butler and the jury—eight women and four men—were black. Jurors voiced no criticism of the defendant, who, the victims claimed, was a stranger to them and had used a concealed weapon, but concentrated censure on the victims. The jurors told the press, after the trial, "The girls hadn't resisted enough. . . . There were too many opportunities for the girls to get away. . . . They should have made an effort to scream. . . . I couldn't imagine the girls not protecting themselves any better than was presented. . . ."

The 1966 study *The American Jury* by Harry Kalven and Hans Zeisel confirms that juries tend to decide rape cases not on the behavior of the accused, but *by applying their own standards of conduct to the victim.* Studying 3,576 criminal jury trials of all sorts over a number of years, the authors compared the outcome of the cases as decided by the jury with the judgment of the trial judge had he been sitting on the case without a jury. Juries clearly have been more difficult to persuade than judges. The rape cases were divided into aggravated

rape (with extrinsic violence, multiple assailants, or
prior acquaintanceship between defendants and victims) and simple rape (all other cases).

Convictions for simple nonaggravated rape were extraordinarily rare. Where the judge would have convicted in twenty-two out of forty-two cases, the jury
convicted in three.

> *Further, the percentage of disagreement with the
> judge on the major charge [in simple rape] is virtu-
> ally 100 percent. The figures could not be more
> emphatic. . . . The jury chooses to redefine the
> crime of rape in terms of its notions of assumptions
> of risk. . . . It is thus saying not that the defendant
> has done nothing, but rather that what he has done
> does not deserve [the] opprobrium of rape.*

In aggravated cases, the jury acquitted when the judge
would have convicted in 12 percent of the cases. In
simple rape, the jury acquitted in 60 percent when the
judge would have convicted. In nine out of ten cases of
simple rape, when the jury was allowed to convict of a
lesser charge, they did so, indicating that they felt the
accused was guilty of some crime, but that rape was too
severe a charge.

Juries, according to Kalven and Zeisel, tend to apply a
doctrine of "contributory" behavior of the victim as a
defense for the accused. Contributory behavior can include such actions as hitchhiking, accompanying the
accused to his house or allowing him to come to hers,
joining him at a beer party, having had a former association with the defendant, or merely having given birth to
an illegitimate child in the past. If the woman had an
"unchaste" reputation, the jury sees no harm "in cor-
rupting the already corrupted." Typical is the case of a
fifteen-year-old victim: The rapist broke into her house
and raped her at knifepoint. At the trial she said she had
never seen him before; he claimed she had been dating
him and that he had given her money. What probably

swayed the jury was that the girl, unmarried, was pregnant at the time of the assault. ("I was made to look like a tramp in court; if I was pregnant by another man, why not him, too?" the victim said.) The judge, Henry Heading, said: "I certainly would have convicted if I had tried it without a jury, although the defense had some witnesses testify that she knew the man."

Or, as Michigan's Recorder Court Judge Robert J. Columbo says: "It's a very real thing for young men to be acquitted by sympathetic jurors who are mothers or fathers of sons the same age as the accused."

There is, therefore, a certain mystique connected with the selection of a jury, and individuals are apt to be categorized by prosecutors and defense attorneys on the basis of preconceived notions about human beings. The sexes as jurors are further categorized in the minds of many lawyers. As this attorney (male) puts it: "Men are tougher on the defendant. The prosecutor wants men jurors—the defense wants women." Another attorney, a woman, agrees that women are "hard" on women: "Women compare themselves with the victim. They listen to her story and they always decide, somewhere along the line, that she did something foolish that they wouldn't have done. . . . Younger women jurors are the worst of all."

Still, a change may be coming here, too. Women are learning to care more about each other and to identify with women victims in a sympathetic, nonpunitive fashion. In a recent Pennsylvania case, an *all woman* jury found the defendant guilty on all five counts, including rape, assault with intent to commit rape, and sodomy.

The Judge's Instructions to the Jury

One of the most sensitive areas of trial by jury is the charge. In most states the judge is required to issue specific instructions (or charges) to the jury, offering guidelines in the law to help them reach a verdict. As the late appellate judge Jerome Frank put it in *Courts on Trial*, quoting another judge, Curtis Bok: "Juries have the disadvantage . . . of being treated like children while the testimony is going on, but then being doused with a kettleful of law during the charge that would make a third-year law student blanch."

Not only are the judge's charges often difficult to follow, even by informed persons, but in rape cases these instructions are often prejudicial to the victim, serving to reinforce deeply rooted but unproven beliefs about the culpability, not of the criminal, but of the victim.

Further, what juries often do not know, and usually are not told by the presiding judge, is that he (more rarely, she) is required *by law* to issue such prejudicial instructions. For example, many states routinely require the judge to repeat a paraphrase of the dictum by seventeenth-century British Lord Chief Justice Matthew Hale that it is "easy" to charge rape, and "difficult" to defend against it. Lord Hale's shibboleth (which has probably been quoted more often by judges and lawyers and legal writers than any other in connection with rape) says: "Rape is an accusation easily to be made and hard to be proved, and harder to be defended by the party accused, though never so innocent."

Some states, having already instructed the jury on just how tricky the case before them really is, then go on to require the judge to warn the jury to be careful. California's jury instructions, only recently rescinded, said: "A charge such as that made against the defendant is one which is easily made, and once made, difficult to defend against, even if the person accused is innocent. Therefore, the law requires you examine the testimony of the female person named in the information *with caution*." (Italics added.)

The cautionary instruction is unique to rape; in no other crime do victims and witnesses hear the judge telling the jury to examine their testimony with caution.

Indeed, in any other crime, such as burglary or assault for example, any such "cautionary" instructions from the judge to the jury might result in a mistrial or a reversal.

In Pennsylvania the judge must charge the jury "to evaluate the testimony of a victim or complaining witness *with special care in view of the emotional involvement of the witness* and the difficulty of determining the truth with respect to alleged sexual activities carried out in private." (Italics added.) While the charge seems justified, at one level, it could also be applied to every other kind of criminal case dealing with a victim-witness. The fact is that only rape victims are singled out—by the law—for such cautionary instructions.

Many jurisdictions, among them Virginia and the District of Columbia, require the two opposing attorneys to submit to the judge suggested instructions for the jury (in the District of Columbia these are contained in something known as the Redbook). These are debated in chambers and the judge then decides on instructions he will transmit to the jury. Instructions thus can vary from case to case and judge to judge, depending upon the past, present, legal, and personal idiosyncrasies of the lawyers and judges involved. As in other criminal actions, instructions put the burden of proof upon the state, which means that the victim must "prove every essential element . . . beyond reasonable doubt." The wording of instructions specifically charging the jury to *acquit*, unless it believes the state has proved *all* elements beyond a reasonable doubt, often leaves loopholes in the minds of jurors (and spectators). In sex assault cases, juries often hear only the word "acquit" and delete the total meaning from their minds—making judgments based on what the penalty is rumored to be, and their "standards" of conduct for the victim, not the accused. Standards of conduct *for others*, especially if they are female, and victims of sexual assault, are likely to be punitive and vindictive. The prevailing misogyny which often masquerades as "morality" permeates the culture—and therefore those who are jurors.

Much has been written and spoken about racial injustices in the selection of juries; in many states it is possible still to operate with preponderantly white juries; black men accused of sex crimes are routinely sentenced to long prison terms—or death—by a jury clearly not composed of their peers. Juries in those southern or border states that have bypassed the United States Supreme Court ruling against capital punishment by making death mandatory for certain crimes (murder and rape among them) deal particularly harshly with blacks accused of raping white women. Racist jurors deal out ludicrous prison sentences to black defendants convicted of crimes against whites, including prison terms of hundreds if not thousands of years.

But women, too, have suffered from sexist and discriminatory jury selection, not only when they are charged with a crime but indefensibly when they are victims, witnesses for the state. Women constitute more than half the population of the country; any jury which does not find them selected for service (for the discrimination begins with jury *selection*), and in representative numbers, cannot in any way be considered a democratic jury. A number of states, especially in the South, have until very recently automatically exempted women from jury duty or required them to volunteer for service. In 1975, the United States Supreme Court struck down the last blanket exemption system in the country—Louisiana's—saying that the jury selection system must operate to allow women an *equal chance to be chosen.*

The Supreme Court Louisiana ruling *should* operate to allow female complainants a more equitable chance to be heard by their sexual peers. However, given the states' rights proponents' ingenious history of being able to circumvent Supreme Court decisions—in the death penalty, for example—it remains to be seen how an essentially sexist society deals at the all important local level with equitable jury selection for women.

One of the special problems in sex crimes juries is the requirement of unanimous agreement by all jurors for either conviction or acquittal. Frequently this results in hung juries, in which case the accused may be tried again, or permitted to plead guilty to a lesser crime carrying a lesser penalty. It may be time to reconsider the usefulness of the unanimity requirement in sex assault cases. As one law enforcement official (who prefers anonymity) says:

> The jury system with its unanimity requirements for sex crimes just results in recycling criminals. Sex offenders are known to have one of the highest rates of recidivism of all crimes. What's so sacred about unanimity? The jury system may be the best we've got, but I believe it would operate fairly and justly on a simple majority principle.

And a government attorney agrees:

> Even the U.S. Supreme Court makes its decisions on the basis of a simple majority. We could consider having a nine to three decision, or maybe ten to two, in sex crimes. That would at least prevent a lot of criminals getting back into circulation so fast.

Another problem with juries lies in the jury sentencing provision in criminal cases. In the Furman decision the whole question of jury sentencing came under review; two petitioners had been convicted of rape and one of murder, and the death sentence was imposed by the juries. The Court did not find jury sentencing of the death penalty unconstitutional. Indeed, Chief Justice Warren E. Burger said that the jury discretion expressed "the conscience of the community," maintaining a link between community values and the penal system.

"Community conscience" has often appeared in the past, where state laws mandated death for certain crimes but juries refused to convict because they believed that, *despite* the guilt of defendants, the death penalty was excessive. Some legislatures gave juries the power to recommend mercy or impose alternative sentences, usually subject to the review of the judge. (Judicial preferences often reflect prejudices, according to some minorities, who claim jury recommendations for mercy for black defendants are more frequently unheeded than similar recommendations for whites.)

The problem of jury sentencing remains an unsolved problem. But the 1967 President's Commission on Law Enforcement and Administration of Justice, Task Force Report, The Courts, points out that in Atlanta for some offenses recidivists got lighter sentences from juries than first offenders and "the transitory nature of jury service seems to preclude rational sentencing by juries."

Radical changes in the jury system (equitable representation by sex and age and nonunanimity decisions, for example) are anathema to traditionalists, who often take what seems like a "because-it-is-there" or "Mount Everest" approach to our legal procedures and customs. Given the endless stream of criticism written by learned legal scholars and jurists, pointing out the inadequacies and injustices in our legal system, radical changes may, in fact, be necessary.

Civil Suits: Next-to-the-Last Resort

Since criminal rapists are usually unlikely sources for recovery, civil suits usually are directed against a third party, such as the attacker's employers or the owners of the building or institution in which the assault occurred. But the course of civil action is open to a very few women; it takes money, time, and endurance. Very often victims who have gone through the ordeal of criminal trial, no matter what the outcome, haven't the strength to pursue another court battle.

Still, some civil suits have succeeded; in March 1974, a victim in the District of Columbia won a $33,000 damage suit in a federal court against George's Radio and Television Co., Inc., and the Pep Line Trucking Co., Inc. Her attacker had worked as a deliveryman for the trucking company. He had raped the woman during the "furtherance" of his job, insisting on cash instead of a check in payment for a delivery. He told her: "I'll either get the cash or take it out of your ass." He raped the woman at knifepoint, and also stabbed and beat her; she was totally disabled for nearly two months and has permanent scars as a result of the attack. The rapist pleaded guilty in the criminal trial and was in jail at the time of the civil suit. The six-member civil jury, five of whom were women, awarded the damages after a two-and-a-half-day trial. U.S. District Judge Barrington D. Parker, however, dismissed two other charges that the firms were negligent in hiring the man, and in keeping him on as an employee after he had been charged with a previous unrelated assault on another woman.

Another civil suit in Philadelphia in the same year brought $175,000 in damages from the owners of the apartment house in which the victim lived. She had been attacked by a building superintendent called in to repair plumbing in her apartment. The jury in this case agreed that the owner showed negligence in hiring a janitor with previous assault arrests on his record.

One of the biggest recent awards, $350,000, went to a British college student who was attacked and nearly beaten to death by a man who assaulted her in the washroom of the Greyhound Bus station in Miami. Greyhound was accused of "inexcusable negligence" for not providing guards at the bus station and permitting criminals to make the terminal "their second home."

Damages were also awarded the father of a sixteen-year-old victim at fashionable Gould Academy in Bethel, Maine. The girl had been criminally assaulted by an unidentified intruder who broke into her dormitory room while she was sleeping. In 1973, the Oxford County Superior Court awarded the father $10,000, supporting his claim that the night watchman for the school had been negligent in not investigating suspicious foot tracks in the snow around the dormitory. (Since the rapist was never identified, there was no criminal trial.) The judge set aside the jury verdict, allowing the school to appeal and then the plaintiff appealed to the Maine Supreme Court. Early in 1975 the high court upheld the jury verdict, saying it was the duty of the academy to protect its "young female residents and . . . to assume the dual role of teacher and family, providing its students not only with instruction . . . but also with the kind of environment that fosters their emotional and physical well-being."

Insurance salesman Benjamin Blum sued the owners of his apartment house and a furniture rental company for $20,000,000 claiming negligence in the 1971 rape–death of his wife. Mrs. Blum had been raped, stabbed, and strangled by parolee Robert E. Watson, furniture rental company employee working in the Blums' luxury apartment complex, the El Dorado Towers in White Oak, Maryland. Watson pleaded guilty and was sentenced to life imprisonment after a criminal trial in 1972.

Blum sued the furniture rental company for negligence in its hiring and supervisory practices because it had failed to investigate Watson before hiring him. The rapist had been convicted of armed robbery and was on parole when the company hired him, a fact apparently unknown to the company. Blum's suit for damages is believed to be the first case in Maryland centering on whether an employer is required to investigate prospective employees who are to deal with the public. A former rental company employee at the Blum trial testified that beer drinking on the job was common and that often Watson and he returned drunk and weaving to their warehouse. According to other testimony, employees of the apartment complex came into contact with the men when they were drunk. Blum's suit contended that they should have been ejected immediately from the property.

Blum's suit also accused the owners of the El Dorado of falsely advertising increased security measures when the number of patrolling guards actually had been reduced. There had been two rapes and ten other sexual assaults at the Towers during the previous year.

In 1975 a jury awarded Blum $13,000,000 in damages, some $11,000,000 of which was punitive, to be paid by the Investors Funding Corporation of New York, owners of the El Dorado. The remaining $2,000,000 was compensatory, to be paid jointly by the New York firm and Watson's employers, the furniture rental company.

Almost immediately Blum's settlement ran into trouble; the El Dorado's owners were bankrupt and Blum's attorneys were uncertain as to whether insurance firms holding policies for the bankrupt corporation were required to pay. The assets of the New York corporation had been frozen and were unavailable. The legal involutions and convolutions of the case, the lawyers said, were "incredible."

Among those who have not fared well in civil suits in connection with rape is a former college student at a large metropolitan university. She had been one of the two prosecutrixes in a recent sensational rape and sodomy case. One of the victims, whom we shall call Maria, was a minor, and her family sued the university and a university guard, alleging that the guard had failed to come to her aid, though present during the attack. Maria's family sued for $5,000,000, charging both the university and the guard with negligence. The guard countersued for $2,500,000, charging he was the victim of "false and malicious" statements.

In the autumn of 1974, lacking the financial and legal

support necessary to contend with a powerful university—a former D.C. police chief was brought in to sign a deposition that the guard had carried out his duty to the "best of his ability"—Maria acquiesced to legal and family pressure and settled out of court for $6,000. She told us: "My father couldn't face it; he was afraid it would ruin him financially."

Half of the $6,000 went to Maria's local attorney; $1,000 went to the university guard's attorney; and another $1,000 went to the New England lawyer who had referred the family to her lawyer. Instead of millions Maria's family received $1,000, one-sixth of the settlement.

Figuring significantly in the civil suit was Maria's attorney, who repeatedly had publicly impugned the "reliability" of rape victims in general, while privately asserting to us, in April 1973, his advocacy of civil action: "We think that this civil suit can open up a whole new field of law and can help lead to new rape laws giving civil liability in rape." Appearing on television some five months later, he said rape was a "natural extension of the sex act, caused generally, and documented in the psychiatric literature, by the provocative action of the victim. . . . Only lately has rape become an issue, due largely to the women's movement." The bill of rights had to be protected, the lawyer insisted, adding with gratuitous condescension: "Women always get very hysterical about this crime."

Perhaps this man was playing devil's advocate, but some who had contact with him elsewhere report his attitudes to be routinely sexist. If so, selecting him as an attorney in Maria's civil rape action was a little like using a fox to guard the chickens. Surely a man who espouses the "guilty woman" theory of rape is unfit to argue sympathetically for a woman suffering extreme mental and physical anguish as a result of an assault. Women contemplating civil action in connection with rape would do well to heed the first lesson: trust your intuition, seek lawyers who do not subscribe to sexist views about women. The second lesson might be to seek damages which are reasonable.

There have been successful civil actions in rape cases in New York, New Jersey, Illinois, and the District of Columbia; and other suits are pending in California and elsewhere. Business and institutional efforts to block civil suits are inevitable, because of the potential heavy financial burden to the responsible parties. If it can be proven in the court that the victim has been permanently scarred, either physically or psychologically, as a result of the attack, the institution or person held to be negligent might have to pay lifetime restitution. While the courts have ruled damages allowable for physical injury, mental anguish, humiliation, or embarrassment, or for support of a child resulting from the rape, "only such damages are proper as are reasonable and probable result of the act."

But even in civil damage suits the fundamentalist attitude toward woman's sexuality is part of the law. The less "virtuous" the woman, the less she may receive as damages, and even in the civil suit her so-called "chastity" is at issue. *American Jurisprudence*, one of the two major standard legal encyclopedias, says:

> . . . *when a plaintiff seeks damages for an injury to her feelings growing out of the indecency of the defendant's conduct, her character in regard to chastity is in issue, and her damages depend somewhat on the question whether she is a virtuous woman who would be greatly shocked at the peculiar nature of the assault, or a woman who is accustomed to yield herself to intercourse.*

This rule has been documented in court decisions in Florida, Maine, and Massachusetts.

The "character" of the plaintiff in damage suits, *Jurisprudence* explains, "may be shown only by evidence of general reputation, and not by proof of specific acts." (Section 119, 65 *American Jurisprudence* 2d.)

This means that even in civil actions a woman's sex life is subject to public scrutiny and question; a woman living with a man to whom she is not married is not entitled to the same kind of damages as a "properly chaste" female. A woman's "reputation" is what the neighbors "think" about her, and this evaluation is, as we have seen, subject to highly personal prejudices involving religious, racial, ethnic, and even economic "morality."

The fact is that women suffer serious injury, both psychological and physical, after a rape. If the attack can be shown to be in some way the result of negligence or act of omission by the responsible parties, victims ought to be able to collect adequate financial recovery, regardless of their so-called "reputation." Landlords, for example, have long been held liable for defective equipment, obstacles on their property or other negligence; court rulings also indicate they have a duty to protect their tenants from "foreseeable" criminal acts committed by third parties on their property. The requirement that women must submit sexual character references even in civil suits is discriminatory and must be ended.

The Last Resort

For some women the conventional legal process is too slow. They have taken matters into their own hands, forming armed self-protection units and, as a last resort, fighting and in several instances even killing their attackers.

Two women who elected this course are Inez Garcia and Joanne Little, both of whom killed their attackers. Garcia, a thirty-year-old woman, went out into the streets of Soledad, California, and shot the 300-pound, twenty-one-year-old man she said had held her down while another man raped her half an hour or so earlier. "I'm not sorry," she said. "I'm only sorry I missed Luis Castillo, the rapist. I meant to kill him, too. That's the only thing I'm sorry about." In October 1974, a jury of seven women and five men found Garcia guilty of second-degree murder. She was sentenced to from five years to life and sent to the California Institution for Women at Frontera. Garcia appealed and women's groups throughout the country rallied to her support, indignant and angry at the disposition of her case.

In August 1974, twenty-year-old Joanne Little killed her male white jailor in the Beaufort County, North Carolina jail where she was being held—the only woman there—on a breaking and entering appeal. The body of the jailor, sixty-two-year-old Clarence Alligood, was found in Little's cell, naked from the waist down except for socks, semen on his thigh (according to the medical report) and stabbed to death with an ice pick which he allegedly kept in his desk drawer. Joanne Little had vanished, but she later surrendered, admitting the killing of the white man but claiming self-defense because he reportedly tried to rape her.

Little was charged with first-degree murder, and bail was set at $115,000, a staggering sum for a poor, young, Southern black woman. Little's case quickly emerged as a *cause célèbre* for women's advocates and civil rightists. Between them they were able to raise bail-bond for Little's temporary release, with Southern bailors pledging their property as security and some $100,000 raised through the Atlanta Southern Poverty Center, headed by Julian Bond, the Georgia legislator. Bond calls the case "one of the most shocking and outrageous examples of injustice against women on record."

Little's case contains all the ingredients for a rallying cause, not the least of which is Ms. Little herself—an appealing and articulate young woman. Not only is she a member of three obvious minorities—female, black, and poor—but she represents the bitter plight of the "confined" woman, confinement in the sense of a woman at the sexual mercy of those in power over her. Women in prison and other institutions are particularly vulnerable, but women in jobs are also "confined" by the economic power of their employers; any woman who has been pawed by her boss (or her husband's boss, for that matter) knows what we mean.

Little's trial during the hot August of 1975 resulted in a quick acquittal, but not until her corps of attorneys, headed by Jerry Paul, had succeeded in getting the trial moved from Beaufort to the state capital at Raleigh. Presiding Superior Court Judge Hamilton H. Hobgood reduced the murder charge saying that premeditation had not been shown and Little stood trial for second-degree murder and voluntary manslaughter. The racially balanced jury made up of seven women and five men, took only 85 minutes and a single voice vote to acquit the 21-year-old defendant. Many of the jurors interviewed after the trial stated that they unanimously agreed, from the beginning of their deliberations, that the prosecution had failed to prove its case beyond reasonable doubt. Several jurors reported being especially impressed with the quietly persuasive arguments of Little's attorney and friend, Karen Galloway, the only woman, and the only black member of the defense team. Following Little's acquittal, Jerry Paul, a dedicated civil rights advocate who had sworn to the court that he would not only defend Little but put Southern justice, racism, sexism and prison conditions on trial as well, was sentenced by Judge Hobgood to two weeks in jail for contempt. Little meantime was freed on $15,000 bond on the appeal from the breaking and entering charge for which she had been held at the Beaufort jail when the killing occurred.

NOW's national rape task force chief, Mary Ann Largen, who worked closely with Little's attorneys in Raleigh, told us that the case "reaffirmed the dedication of NOW to continue to work to revise state rape laws . . . the court trial clearly demonstrates that the legal definition of rape, and the reality of rape, with all its violence and attendant sexual crimes such as oral and anal sodomy, were two distinctly different things. The Little trial further demonstrates the need to educate the judicial system itself to make it sensitive to all aspects of sex assaults, especially with regard to victim reaction and rights."

Little's reported reaction, quoted by UPI—"Maybe now there is a law that says a black woman has a right to defend herself"—does not go far enough; hopefully Little's acquittal will help *all* women, black *and* white, to defend themselves. And the case again points up the special sexual vulnerability of women at the hands of those who control them—whether in jails, hospitals, or any other institution, including places of business and government.

Deborah Kantaeng is another California woman who shot and killed one of her attackers the day after he reportedly raped her. The case is confused by the time lag, though many women are supporting the victim, saying, "Her fears and rage are the same whether it's an hour or a day later." But two Florida women who strangled a rapist who had been about to attack them further with an ice pick were acquitted of murder by a coroner's jury.

In Dallas, Texas, a group of women incensed by the October 1974 acquittal of a white assailant who had admitted beating, burning, and forcing his black victim to stick a car flare up her vagina, have formed their own protective group: Women Armed for Self-Protection, or WASP for the stinger-equipped insect. WASP's objectives are to become proficient in the use of weaponry and to encourage other women to do the same, supporting "immediate and drastic retaliation against all rapists" as a self-defense measure. They have turned reluctantly to armed self-protection. "I went from shaking at the sight of a gun," one member says, "to sleeping with a Magnum under my mattress. Personally I hate guns. I would rather live in a society without guns. As soon as policemen and truck drivers don't have guns, I will take the loaded .357 out from under my bed." Like other women, WASP members realize that women must become more aggressive in all ways, not just physically. Some armed women have had their guns taken away by

assailants, because as one WASP woman says: "That old
southern belle mentality will get you every time." Own-
ing a gun is no defense if the determination and training
to use it are lacking.

Legal Reform and Innovations

Changes in state laws are slow in coming, but a
number have begun to take action. A few states, Wisconsin among them, are organizing statewide coalitions
to get community support for change. Other states including Colorado have amended portions of their discriminatory penal codes, as we noted in Chapter 5. Only
one state, Michigan, has actually enacted sweeping
legislative reforms. The Michigan Criminal Sexual
Conduct law (the title alone is an improvement over
earlier descriptions) went into effect in April 1975. It
includes a number of innovations that other states
would do well to copy. In Michigan the burden of "nonconsent" is at last removed from the victim; resistance is
no longer required to prove force; and corroboration is
not required. There are four degrees of criminal sexual
conduct, graded by force, in descending order of severity. The first degree, for example, includes a situation
where the accused is armed or aided by a gang; it is
punishable by life imprisonment or any term of years.
The degree structure is expected to criminalize assaults
where the victim is not seriously physically injured,
assaults heretofore often ignored by police and attorneys. This law extends criminal sexual conduct to include attacks in which the victim is forced to commit
acts upon the body of the accused. Sexual penetration is
extended beyond penile–vaginal to include cunnilingus, fellatio, anal intercourse, and "any other intru-
sions" into any part of a person's body.

In Michigan now, the victim may not be cross-
examined about her "chastity" and sexual reputation
except in two specific instances: where there is evi-

dence of previous sexual activity with the accused or evidence of sexual activity showing the origin of disease or pregnancy. Such cross-examination is permitted *only* after the defense has submitted a motion and an offer of proof in writing within ten days after the arraignment and the judge has held a private hearing in chambers to determine if the inflammatory nature of such evidence outweighs its probative value. Similarly, if new information related to the two exceptions is discovered during the course of the trial, the victim may not be cross-examined without a prior private hearing with the judge.

Michigan now extends the definition of force and coercion to threats of *future* retaliation against the victim or other persons, as well as immediate threats of injury. Divorced or legally separated couples are protected from sexual assault by a spouse. Michigan is the only state in the union where a spouse in a legally separated couple can be charged with rape, though the marital exemption still stands. The law is sexually neutral, covering victims and offenders of both sexes equally. The statutory-rape age limit is set at thirteen; and at least thirteen and less than sixteen if the attacker is a relative or member of the same household or is in a "position of authority over the victim" using that authority to force submission. All except fourth-degree criminal sexual conduct are felonies with penalties ranging from fifteen years to life imprisonment. The fourth degree is a misdemeanor ("force or coercion used to accomplish sexual contact") punishable by not more than two years imprisonment or a maximum fine of $500. All four degrees have provisions for crimes committed on victims either mentally defective, mentally incapacitated, or physically helpless.

While the new Michigan law has not answered every reform need, it comes the closest to any existing model in the country today. It represents the work of hundreds of volunteers all over the state, work spearheaded by such forces as the Ann Arbor-based Michigan Women's Task Force on Rape, some 15,000 lobbying hours, and countless time and energy on the part of elected officials and state employees. But misogyny dies hard; at the eleventh hour (literally 5:15 A.M.), tired women in the gallery of the Michigan Senate heard and saw themselves once again singled out for the opposition leader's insults: "Girls, get some sleep and keep your legs crossed till September. We'll be back."

Barbara MacQueen, reporting for the task force, writes:

> *The new law is not a prosecutor's law, not a defendant's law, nor is it even a lawyer's law. . . . It belongs to the people of Michigan. If there is anything we have learned about the political process, it is that your opinions do count, and that many legislators are very responsive to voter pressure. Our political system can work, but only when we, as citizens, work. . . . This reform legislation succeeded because so many devoted the time.*

Rape is the only crime in which the action or nonaction of the victim has occupied more legal attention than the criminal's behavior. The new Michigan law at last shifts the focus to where it belongs, on the criminal, whom the law is supposed to regulate. Classification of that conduct by degrees of severity is a rational approach which other states might emulate. It does much toward "normalization" of the penalties for sex crime, bringing it into line with other criminal activities such as assault and battery. Radical feminists who argue that the new Michigan code does not go far enough—marital exemption and the statutory age limit at thirteen being two examples—should recognize that the entire law represents a stunning departure from medievalism and is probably the single most hopeful sign of progress toward legal justice in sex crimes.

Federal Legislation

At the national level, there was the Mathias–Heinz bill for setting up a National Center for the Prevention and Control of Rape with federal research and demonstration programs aimed, for the first time, at serious consideration of the victim along with the other aspects of sex assaults. This legislation was first introduced in 1973 by Maryland Senator Charles McC. Mathias, Jr. Later the bill was relegated to an amendment in the sprawling Health Revenue Sharing and Health Services Act. In the administration's blunderbuss efforts to wrestle with a failing economy, President Ford twice vetoed the whole package.

In July 1975 the Congress finally passed the health services bill over the second veto, cutting the Mathias rape center original authorization from $20 million to $7 million for the remainder of 1975, and $10 million for 1976. All authorizations are of course subject to later Congressional approval in appropriations bills.

The rape center is to operate within the National Institute of Mental Health. It is to study: (1) existing rape laws; (2) the relationship of traditional legal and social attitudes toward sexual roles and rape; (3) treatment of victims by law enforcement agencies, hospitals, and the courts; (4) root causes (social conditions, offender motivation, and effects on victim and her family); (5) sexual assaults in correctional institutions; (6) actual incidence of rape as compared with reported cases; and (7) the effectiveness of existing programs for rape control. The amendment calls for a central clearinghouse for compilation and dissemination of relevant materials and an advisory committee (the majority, women) to advise and consult on the center's work.

In a House subcommittee hearing early in 1975, at which only former HEW Secretary Caspar W. Weinberger was allowed to testify in person, Weinberger came out firmly against the rape center amendment.

Rape, he said was not primarily a health concern but more properly a subject for criminal justice and should not be "singled out from among the many forms of psychiatrically deviant behavior." Moreover, existing behavioral research under the National Institute of Mental Health could take care of investigating rape. Weinberger's opposition incorporates the universal negative attitudes about rape which ignore the victim, treat rape as a phenomenon isolated from our culture, and concentrate on the rapist's "deviance." Out of forty pages of testimony, the then Secretary dismissed rape in a single page.

7
THE RAPIST: PSYCHOPATH OR EVERYMAN?

Myth: Only "sick" or "insane" men rape women.
Fact: Most rapists are indistinguishable from "sane" men.
—University Women—YWCA Rape Relief,
Seattle, Washington

Who is the rapist?

What drives him to rape?

Can he be cured of the urge to rape?

These three questions are the root to achieving fundamental change in dealing with the widespread sexual attacks on women and children. Yet they continue to receive too little attention from criminologists and psychologists or from public officials who fail to fund significant research and rehabilitation for sex assailants.

Part of the problem of how to recognize and treat rapists lies in the variety of clinical definitions and procedures. Psychology and criminology are still infant disciplines, and professionals with similar credentials produce enormously different answers to these basic questions.

Many male psychologists view rape the way ordinary people tend to see it—as a potential in every male, although only acted on by the minority. The remark of a Philadelphia psychiatrist is typical: "Rape? I've seldom had a male patient who didn't have rape fantasies. The rapist is only acting out what other men dream about."

A New York analyst called rape "just an exaggerated form of the normal sex act." Even more startling is the comment of a man responsible for the care and cure of sex criminals, Dr. Ralph F. Garofalo, Deputy Director of the Center for the Diagnosis and Treatment of Dangerous Persons at Bridgewater, Massachusetts. Garofalo told a reporter, "I don't think there's a man worth his salt who hasn't seen some chick walking by and wanted to screw her." He later claimed he had been misquoted: he belonged to the generation which said "broad," not "chick."

We question whether these male fantasies of rape do resemble the assaults carried out by men. Many women admit to having fantasies of being raped, but detailed questioning reveals that their daydreams are quite different from the humiliation of actual rape. The element common to both male and female fantasies seems to be pleasure, not pain. But the central trauma for both rapist and victim in an actual rape is pain—psychological pain driving the rapist to rape, and physical and emotional pain that the victim suffers.

Even men are starting to understand this essential difference. One professional man analyzed his own changing feelings:

> I suspect that in most male fantasies, the woman yields willingly. There is an enormous difference between a fantasized sex act and the real thing. Men will admit a fantasized rape when in fact there is no—or very little—resemblance between the fantasy and the fact of a rape. Where once I would have said, and probably did, that I had fantasized rape, I would now deny it. The elements that exist in a rape as described by victims have never figured in my fantasy life.

The naive confusions expressed by unaware professionals and nonprofessionals tend to condone real rape and add to the general social atmosphere that some forms of rape—"social" rapes or the "she-really-wanted-it" variety—are morally acceptable. Many people are callous as well as ignorant about rape. New York State Assemblyman Joseph F. Lisa illustrated typical callousness when he commented, "Authors have written, and time has told us, that every woman resists to a certain degree, and the male must be the aggressor. When the defiled female says, 'That is the gentleman who raped me,' we need corroboration. If her jaw is broken, for example, that is proof of force. Otherwise, how do we know she was raped? The difference between rape and romance is a very thin line." Lisa's language—the "defiled" female and the "gentleman" rapist (what woman would ever call her assailant a "gentleman"?)—is clearly sexist.

Fortunately, the opposing opinion is held by some concerned men, such as Dr. Edward H. Weiss and his associates on the District of Columbia Mental Health Committee. These more enlightened physicians investigated rape in Washington and concluded: "Forensic psychiatric experts consider the rapist a potential murderer whose primary purpose is humiliating and physically assaulting a woman, the sexual act being secondary to the wish for violence against women." Dr. Charles R. Hayman, who spent years helping thousands of Washington, D.C., rape victims under the Department of Human Resources, commented, "In general, our observations support the hypothesis advanced by Amir [Menachem Amir in *Patterns of Forcible Rape,* 1971] and many others that rape is not so much an expression of sexual drive as of aggression and violence."

Other experts agree that rape is basically an expression of inner rage and violence, not the outcome of thwarted sexual desire. "Rape is not committed simply to gain sexual gratification," said Dr. Harry Kozol, Director of Psychiatry at the Bridgewater, Massachusetts, Center. "Some rapes appear to be part of a total pattern of hostility toward women." He pointed out that many offenders have ignored or rejected willing sexual partners to commit rape on unwilling victims. Many sex criminals are actually impotent, and must humiliate and violate their victims by perverse and artificial means. A 1965 study by the Kinsey Institute for Sex Research at Indiana University of 140 sex assailants of adult women (aged sixteen and over) showed that one-quarter to two-thirds were assaultive types. These sadistic men felt pronounced hostility toward women and obtained satisfaction only when sex was accompanied by physical violence or serious threats. They generally attacked strangers, often with weapons.

William Prendergast, a psychologist at New Jersey's Rahway State Prison, considers the rapist a sociopath: "His whole behavior is antisocial—but he's not necessarily 'sick' in the psychiatric sense. And it's not because he doesn't have available sex. He rapes simply because he feels tremendous contempt and hostility for women, and that is his way of expressing it." The ready availability of sex for many rapists has been widely confirmed. Three out of five rapists interviewed by the Kinsey Institute were married. Studies cited by Paul Gebhard (*Sexual Offenders*, 1965) and John M. Mac-Donald (*Rape: Offenders and Their Victims*, 1971) found 40 to 43 percent of the rapists were married. A sample of 389 New Jersey sex offenders showed nearly 44 percent were married (in Alfred B. Vuocolo, *The Repetitive Sex Offender*, 1969).

Feminists have long recognized the pathological core of rape. "Rapists are not 'just poor sex-starved bastards,'" said Denver activist Shirley McDermott. "Many of the men who rape women are married, have girl friends, and some even have apparently happy families with charming children and doting mothers. Rapists come from *every* life situation. Take the eighty-one-year-old woman who was raped in southwest Denver. As a sex object she is over the hill, but this old, frightened woman is in her prime as a humiliation object."

Psychologist Dr. Jo Ann Gardner, a founder of the Association for Women in Psychology, calls rape an act of political oppression: "Rapists perform for sexist males the same function that the Ku Klux Klan performed for racist whites—they keep women in their 'place' through fear. The threat of rape is used to keep women out of jobs. It keeps women passive and modest for fear they will be thought provocative." The experiences of most women bear out this conclusion. Millions of girls and women can echo the Chicago student who recalled, "When I was in high school, I had to walk by a construction crew on the way home. Every day they made obscene comments to me, and I dreaded walking home because they made me so furious and so frightened. . . . I cried all the way home."

Women feel themselves being viewed and treated as a depersonalized "thing" by men, a sex object regarded as "fair game," even if the "possession" exists only in the imagination. Men may think their rape fantasies are "harmless," yet their fantasies are bound to affect their outer attitudes and behavior, even if these stop far short of rape. In all situations—social, sexual, domestic, economic, and political—men tend to dominate and intimidate women through their physical strength and size, their control of social power, and ingrained customs and assumptions. Such assumptions may be wholly unconscious for both men and women. It is the *felt* reality of the entire culture which permeates, conditions, and binds women, even if the men in her immediate personal life are sensitive and caring. No female can completely escape this atmosphere. In thousands of subtle and crude ways, our society makes known to both sexes a presumed male dominance which intrudes, however deviously, into all intersexual relationships. Women, feeling helpless and sensing the omnipresent threat of male anger, brutality, and rape, tend to spend their lives placating real or imaginary attackers. They flee into passivity to avoid the

potential violence all around them, and in effect com-
pound the vicious circle of male-aggression/
female-victimization that continues to entrap us all.

A psychology professor at the University of New Mexico, Marc Irwin, has seen into this sexist double standard which helps perpetuate rape:

> *Though we* [men] *may reject committing rape, our
> attitudes about the act reveal much about us that is
> contradictory and troubling. These attitudes are
> indices of much more general feelings about
> women and about how we, as men, relate to them.
> I'm referring, firstly, to the widespread tacit ap-
> proval of existing rape laws. Our lack of initiative
> in removing such laws strongly suggests an unwill-
> ingness to accept women as free human beings
> (just like men). If this weren't the case, why would
> we put the rape victim on trial, and examine mi-
> croscopically her morals. The implication of doing
> so is clear: that a woman who has sex (any sex)
> must be a bad woman, and therefore is undeserv-
> ing of the protection of law and fair game for any
> man who wants her. That's a pretty bold statement
> of the double standard, which even in this sup-
> posedly liberated age is hanging on.*

Rape is one of humanity's oldest problems, as ancient
as war and conquest; it has existed as long as women
have been second-class citizens. Today's women are
starting to understand rape in its cultural totality.
Women who work with victims, such as those at Ann
Arbor's Crisis Center, define rape as:

> *. . . any form of genital contact which a woman
> has not initiated or explicitly agreed to, and which
> is imposed on her by a man using deception, social
> blackmail, threat, or physical violence. Rape is a
> different kind of crime. There is no economic mo-
> tive, and rape is not even primarily a sexual act:*

*the majority of rapists use some form of overt vio-
lence to force a woman into intercourse that is
sadistic at best, and at worst, fatal. . . .* In most
communities rape is uniquely an act of hostility
and contempt committed by men against women.
*There is no comparable crime perpetrated by
women against men.*

It is *essential* to understand these sociopsychological
dimensions of rape if we are to comprehend the rapists
themselves. Studies and treatment of sex offenders continue to be severely limited because they lack these
dimensions. In addition, current theories and definitions of rapists rest on a *very small sample* of the real
population of sex offenders—probably no more than a
few percent of the actual total (bearing in mind the lack
of reporting and convictions). This sample is further
limited by including for the most part men from lower
economic and educational social classes, as well as a
disproportionate number of racial minorities, who often
lack resources to evade police, legal, and mental health
authorities. While such minorities generally live in a
subculture of violence where rape is an accepted fact of
life, this subculture—or subcultures—cannot be considered isolated and distinct from our general culture.
Overall, violence, hostility toward females, and repressed anger are prevalent dynamics in American life.

We must keep these basic limitations of insight and
data in mind as we survey existing theories and
methods of treating rapists. Most theories and methods
are created and administered by men, who themselves
show the detrimental influences of social sexism. We
can see the extraordinarily narrow view of rape cur-
rently held by our male-controlled society in such evidence as our antiquated laws, the few resources allo-
cated for curbing rape, and the refusal of *all*
governments, state and federal, to recognize that rape
occurs in marriage. Much disagreement exists over
whether prostitution could be considered a form of

rape. Some women now believe that sexual exploitation of females—whether physical or economic—should be defined as rape.

Interviews with sex offenders reveal many of the same basic attitudes toward women that we find in our male-oriented culture—in media, literature, government, economy, educational systems, and every facet of social existence. The sex offenders who physically assault women are usually outwardly indistinguishable from other men. "There is no portrait of a rapist, no stereotype," says New York Police Officer Terry Enterlin of the Sex Crimes Analysis Unit, which tries to demystify the standard idea of the sinister rapist. "Some of them are clean-cut, some aren't. The days are gone forever where, like the movies, you could tell the rapist by his glittering eyes. Today they fit right into the neighborhood." A Chicago detective similarly observed: "Often the rapist wears a business suit. Women have been raped in the elevators of their office buildings during lunch hour, in their offices, and, until they started locking them, in the ladies' restrooms."

The ordinary, even innocent, appearance of many rapists was brought home to us when we listened to two young men, both committed psychotics at St. Elizabeths Hospital for the mentally ill in Washington, D.C., at a special police training session. The first was young, fair-haired, and soft-spoken, looking like the kind of boy any mother would want her daughter to date. "I really don't know why I raped her," he told us quietly. "I guess I'd been thinking about doing all those things a long time. Like when I'd watch women at night walking around in their bedrooms without any clothes on. I'd just stand there, masturbating and thinking all kinds of things. It sounds weird, I know, but I just felt like I had to do it." He shrugged apologetically. "I'd go out nearly every night to look in windows. I wasn't thinking about raping anybody then, at least not consciously. But sometimes I'd start imagining tying a girl up and doing things to her. So when I finally got the chance, it just seemed like I had to do all that to her. I guess I hurt her pretty bad."

The second, a young university student who had strangled a classmate, was almost angelic in appearance and speech. "I heard voices telling me to do it," he said gently, as though we would understand. "I loved her, but they told me to put my hands around her throat. She struggled a lot, but I kept squeezing and squeezing, like they told me. Then I lay down beside her and went to sleep. When I woke up—well, there she was. I don't know why, but I had to do it. I just had to." Many rapists express this sense of puzzlement over their acts, feeling they *have* to attack, even murder, women because they feel intense inner pressure—or, as in this second case, they hear the hallucinated voices of a psychosis.

The rapists' alienation from others and their depersonalization of women are evident in their own words. A good example is the troubled would-be rapist who telephoned his story to a San Francisco radio station during a broadcast about rape. He had never really thought about raping anyone until the day, at age seventeen, when he found himself alone with a nurse in a doctor's office. Then his hidden impulse abruptly surfaced. He grabbed the nurse from behind and held her against the wall. She was much smaller than this six-foot-four, 240-pound teen-ager, though she tried to resist. He slapped her hard in the face and she gave in, saying, "all right, just don't hurt me." It was then that reality shocked him into stopping. He realized, he said later, that it was not just a movie or television fiction, a heroic proving of his manhood. He had been on the verge of raping and dehumanizing another human being—and of making himself into an animal. The teen-ager was charged with attempted rape. "Because I was an upper-middle-class white, my case was handled very delicately. I was put in a private mental hospital first, then transferred to the state hospital. I spent a total of sixty days actually in custody."

Most assailants tend to fall into one of two groups:

those who commit a casual, generally unplanned rape on whomever they encounter when their compulsions are strong; and those who carefully plot out at least a part of their assaults, choosing the particular victim or type of victim ahead of time. The first group is illustrated by three convicted rapists at New Jersey's Rahway State Prison. Interviewed for a Public Radio program, all three expressed similar emotions of intense personal frustration and anger against the world and of bitter contempt and hostility for women in general.

Joe had been in the Air Force and committing rapes for two and a half years on the streets before he was caught. He described his sensations:

> *You'd be working and some of the pressures during a job or if a boss comes down on you would start to build on your mind and you don't realize it, but you want a release. And maybe toward four or five o'clock in the afternoon you start to get these feelings like you want to go out. But you don't really plan—most often the plan was a favorite town where I would go. I wouldn't know anybody there. None of the girls and women I did it to were girls I knew. The most planning was the town, just before dark so I could have plenty of time to get there and as the lights were going down, not too late. The pressure, it's always there. It's like you have a tank of water and you're an inch from the top and some pressure comes on, somebody pours the water into it, and it starts to overflow. Now you go out looking for a girl to rape. And if you accomplish this, you, like, take a cup or two out until the next time when some real pressure builds up. That's what I meant by a pressure coming on you, it's an addition to all the pressure of your whole life.*

Charley described similar feelings of an intense need to avenge himself somehow on women and, through them, on life:

Usually after spotting a person, I'd want to make an advance—not necessarily with rape in mind. Each attempt that I make and fail with this broad, usually it works in my mind to say, "Aaahh, the bitch ain't going to do nothing, she's going to push me away, I'm not a good-looking guy, I'm not this, I'm not that, and she's probably an old slut anyhow." You make all kinds of cop-outs to yourself, and you're giving yourself, I guess, consciously a good reason to rape her. And eventually it works up—like I said, you could plan what you'd do, whether you're going to make her go down on you or whether you're going to just rip her off and hurt her, or if you're going to cut her or if you're going to use your knife at all. And during it, it's the funny part about it—I can't remember any of my thoughts during the actual rape. Usually I left them in a heap, some of them beaten pretty badly. And after leaving them I was satisfied, yet I wasn't. Physically I was satisfied, mentally I wasn't. . . . The pressure didn't come off that easily.

The third rapist, Tom, also revealed feelings of rejection and anger against women, as well as tremendous self-contempt and guilt connected with his parents:

I always believed there was good and bad girls. This was a strong belief my father taught me. I had to find out the hard way that all women are alike. And I would see my father commit acts against kids, and my mother go out and hang in bars. They would come back and fight, and then make love and be happy again. Then I seen the home destroyed. But all the time I had them on a pedestal—they were always superparents to me, because I couldn't admit they had faults. To do that, I would destroy myself, I would have to admit I hated them, and I was just all screwed up.

Tom's fury against parental rejection is unmistakable, as is his anger toward his father. But to attack men is far riskier than to attack women. And so, like many rapists, Tom avenged his childhood impotency and oppression by assaulting women.

Blaming mothers and other female relatives for turning their sons into rapists is psychologists' greatest rationalization in dealing with sex criminals, part of the common social pattern of seeing women as causing men's problems. Either way, the woman cannot win: she is guilty if she is a victim (why did she dress that way or go walking there?) and she is guilty for being the mother—or wife or sister—of the rapist (who wouldn't become a rapist with a seductive, oppressive bitch of a mother like that?). In addition to victim and mother, there is also good old Mother Nature to blame for the "irrepressible urge" which turns into rape. Tom's "angel-devil" view of females also typifies the outlook of men who grow up in a sexist society; again implying that women are really to blame for their own rapes.

Hospitalized and imprisoned rapists also learn to describe their motivations in terms suspiciously like those used by male therapists. Charley admitted he "learned" in Rahway how his rape victims resembled his mother:

> There were my victims, ones that as I came here I learned resembled my mother when I was conceived. And up until that time I had viewed her as a good girl who went wrong, because I was born out of wedlock and that was one of my hang-ups and still is. But anything that resembled her, or my sisters who resembled her very much at that age, had to be bad, had to be put down. I had a general hatred for these types of people. Most of the time I didn't rape them, but if I seen them walking down the street I could not even know them but hate them enough to kill them if necessary. (Emphasis added.)

Examples of the second group of rapists—those who plan, often in cunning detail, part or all of their crimes—have been given in previous chapters: rapists who pose as repairmen and deliverymen, gasmen, postmen, and construction workers; rapists who claim to be looking for an address or a friend or have car trouble and need to use a phone; rapists who pretend their cars have broken down on highways; rapists who cruise around looking for hitchhiking victims; rapists who phone for typists and models to come to their "offices"; rapists who regularly search for potential victims in bars or dating situations to lure to their cars, apartments, or secluded spots and attack. These are usually stranger-on-stranger rapes, although some men may establish a dating pattern before assaulting their chosen victims. Police look for such telltale M.O.s in all rape cases, and in many such as these a giveaway pattern emerges which can lead them to the assailant.

One type of rapist studied by Dr. Murray L. Cohen and others at the Massachusetts Correctional Institution also showed a repetitive pattern. In "The Psychology of Rapists" Cohen reports this rapist is:

> . . . *always very sexually aroused and fully aware of what he is doing, although at times he feels as if he were performing under a compulsion. The victim is always a stranger but not one that he comes upon by accident. She is usually someone he has seen while on a streetcar or bus and follows her off when she leaves. It is not an impulsive act, however. This is a scene he has lived through many times in fantasy.*

A rapist who also deliberately sought certain types of victims was Eldridge Cleaver, the black revolutionary author of *Soul On Ice* and probably America's most famous rapist. Cleaver explored his inner motivations while serving jail sentences for rape and other crimes, established a warm friendship with his woman lawyer, and came to reject his earlier ideas. It is well known that Cleaver considered his rapes of white women as "insurrectionary" acts, but what is usually overlooked is that he callously "practiced" his modes of attack first on black women:

> To refine my technique and modus operandi, I started out by practicing on black girls in the ghetto—in the black ghetto where dark and vicious deeds appear not as aberrations or deviations from the norm, but as part of the sufficiency of the Evil of a day—and when I considered myself smooth enough, I crossed the tracks and sought out white prey.

This description gives the lie to Cleaver's own rationalization, for his assaults on women of his own race were hardly "insurrectionary." What we see is actually a very disturbed young man with deep hostilities toward *all* females who is masquerading as a revolutionary mystic. Black men, like white men, tend to view women as "property," and attacking white women can thus *seem* to be revenge upon white men.

Are such self-confessed rapists essentially different from the "ordinary" male at a Detroit rape conference who said: "I've talked to a lot of men. . . . It's because women got this attitude. Like they're walking down the street and they're too good to talk to you. . . . So maybe one of the guys will decide to do something about it"? As the San Francisco would-be rapist commented, "When I tell people of my experience, men and women react differently. Men want to know all the details. They say, 'You should have gone ahead and done it. Every chick wants you to do it.' When I tell a woman about my experience, she'll tell me hers. She says, 'Well, a man pulled me into his car,' and it's like trading stories." And are the violent men in prisons and mental hospitals basically different from the "normal" men who hire women to dance topless at stag parties, and then rape them?

Or from the men who laugh at movie and television

rape scenes, who buy every rape issue of detective magazines (which is nearly every issue) and masturbate while they read about unbelievable cruelties and perversions? Dr. Peter Rosen, who treats rape victims at the University of Chicago Hospital, said he found "the chief horror of watching A Clockwork Orange to be the audience cheering a rape scene." Such sadism is far from the isolated, "sensational" tale we might have once imagined. Rape in America has been going on everywhere for a very long time.

Judging from films and crime magazines—which feature a rapist and his victim on their covers more often than not—the sex offender is also seen as an envied daredevil by large numbers of males who know they will never have the "guts" to rape anyone themselves, but who live vicariously in the "exploits" of more "virile" and "daring" men. The ability to rape a woman is often presented by movies and novels as essential equipment of the detective or Western hero, equivalent to his gun and cold-blooded courage. The rape scene in contemporary films has become almost inevitable—with the audience presumably "lying back and enjoying it"—part of the virility-violence mystique by which a male comes to manhood (through raping someone himself) or purges himself of cowardice (by avenging the rape of a woman who in some way "belongs" to him).

Gang Rape: Fraternity of Criminals

Both individual and gang rapes are increasingly popular among supposedly "normal" boys and men. The term "gangbang" for a group rape has passed into the American idiom and is often used with ostensibly "humorous" connotations (though never in connection with a gangbang against another male). Nor are gang rapes limited to lower-class or ghetto youths or to hippie- or yippie-type motorcycle gangs. Youths of all ages and social classes have participated in planned group assaults on girls or older women, where each takes courage from the others to "prove" his "manhood."

Increasingly typical is the experience of a thirteen-year-old victim from a middle-class neighborhood:

> *I only knew one of the three boys. They were all from good families. One boy's father was a dentist, another some sort of high-up executive. I mean, they weren't low types or bums. One boy went to private school. So when they invited me to listen to records in one home, I didn't suspect anything. Maybe it was dumb of me, but I really didn't suspect. Only two of them were able to get their thing in me. I heard from the lawyer that one boy's father said his son wasn't guilty because he couldn't get his thing up. . . . The fathers were all there, defending their sons, saying how I had played hookey from school and was bad and everything. All of them got off. Afterward they went around school bragging about what they had done to me.*

To be attacked by a rapist in any situation is a horrifying and humiliating experience. In most cases, the victim's fear of being killed is uppermost in her mind and emotions. To be confronted by a gang of rapists is even worse—one of the most terrible experiences human beings can inflict on another person. The victim's realization of helplessness becomes total, for if she is very nearly powerless against a single rapist, she is almost always a complete prisoner of a group. Her fear of death, torture, mutilation, and pain at the hands of many men is doubled and redoubled. In the most devastating sense of the phrase, she is "thrown on the mercy" of her attackers—and often there is no mercy. Such a confrontation can be paralyzing. Group rape is the epitome of sexual sadism. It is a frightening commentary on the growth of sadism against women in our society that such gang attacks are increasing everywhere in America. In some large cities, gang rapes now number a third or even half of reported rapes.

One thing *is* known: man is the only animal that uses the herd to sexually assault the females of his species. Only the male of the human species bands together with fellow males for this particular form of fraternal criminality. Sociologists, wittingly or unwittingly, dignify mass attacks by calling them "group" rapes, but this merely disguises the essential criminality of the act. A "group" may come together for legitimate purposes; a "gang" gathers only for sinister design. Three or more males who join forces for criminal sexual assault are a gang.

Menachem Amir's scholarly investigation of Philadelphia rapists from 1958 and 1960 police files, one of the few such studies, reflects the national picture for gang and pair rape. Amir, an Israeli criminologist, was astonished at the absence of data; what existed was almost exclusively "psychoanalytically oriented" and therefore "speculative." Of the 646 rapes (single, pair, and gang) in his Philadelphia study, 43 *percent*, or 276, females were victims either of pair or gang rapes. Of 1,292 offenders, 71 *percent*, 912 in number, were involved in multiple rapes. Of these 1,292 offenders, 55 *percent*, or 712, participated in gang rapes; 16 *percent*, or 210, took part in pair rapes. These results were "amazing," said Amir, "if we remember the silence with which the literature on sexual offenses treats the problem of group rape."

Those participating in multiple rapes were young, concentrated in the ages between fourteen and nineteen; their victims were in the same age levels. In gang attacks, the victim was more likely to have been drinking; in pair rapes, the lead offender more often had taken alcohol. Most significant was the preparation factor: 97 percent of the gang rapes and 92 percent of the pair rapes were planned or partially planned. In single rapes, Amir found that 72 percent were planned or partially planned. The Philadelphia data also showed that gang participants had a significantly higher proportion of prior criminal records than single rapists— 60 percent and 40 percent respectively. Gang rapists also held a higher arrest record for sex offenses than single rapists—52 percent and 40 percent. Finally, multiple rape offenders had a higher arrest record for rape than single rapists—60 percent and 40 percent.

Gang rapists indulge themselves in the more extreme forms of physical force—pushing, slugging, kicking, roughness, beating, choking, and other brutalities. Amir also refers to something he calls "nonbrutal beating," defined as "slapping." It is difficult to imagine the slapping of a lone female by two or more males as anything but brutal. Another characteristic of group and pair sex assaults is confirmed by Amir's research—a high proportion of something he calls sexual "humiliation." Since humiliation is a basic ingredient of *any* sexual attack, the terminology leaves something to be desired. But what Amir is specifically referring to are forms of sexual assault beyond forced penile–vaginal intercourse: fellatio and cunnilingus (or oral–genital contact), sodomy and pederasty (or anal intercourse), and repeated penile–vaginal intercourse. Amir states that what he calls "sexual humiliation" is "psychologically as well as physically more damaging and humiliating than merely the unconsented intercourse." This is a fact attested to by *most* rape victims in our experience—whether victims of single or multiple rapists.

Some sociologists, among them West Coast professors Dr. Gilbert Geis and Dr. Duncan Chappell, suggest that the increase in gang rapes reflects a "growing masculine need to establish sexual identity and superiority through aggressive acts of humiliation against resisting female victims." They further suggest that in an era of sexual permissiveness, some men feel "deprived" and frustrated that they are not sharing in what they believe to be "free and easy" intersexual relationships. "Such 'relative deprivation,' its elements of anger and frustration triggered by a night of drinking," Geis and Chappell assert, "may set off a chain of events culminating in forced intercourse by a group of men with a victim from a bar or one picked up or kidnapped from a city street."

Gang rapes are particularly prevalent among juveniles; their victims are often deliberately chosen from among those who are known to be sexually "easy"—presumably with the thought that a female with a "bad" reputation is less likely to inform the police. Male fantasies continue to hold sway in gang rapes. Criminals often try to make dates with their victims after the attack and repeatedly demand assurance from women that they "really liked it, didn't you?" One rapist sent a message to his victim, a total stranger, through a friendly cop while being arraigned: "Tell Gloria the two chicks with her sure are cute." Another asked that his victim stand up alongside him in the court room because "you sure do turn me on, baby."

Dr. Geis also suggests that gang rapes involve a company of "men behaving in accord with well-established principles of collective behavior" with a leader who usually plans the act and often is the first to sexually attack the victim. Accomplices therefore get later "shares," and "suffer the definitional insult of dealing with already used and abused merchandise." Some psychiatrists add that the gang's involvement with the same "object" points up an underlying homosexuality, with something they call "eroticized adulation" of one boy for another a primary factor.

Probably the males' need to sustain their image in front of the group is important in instigating and carrying out the gang attack; gang members are responding not only to internal motives but to their view of the roles they must play with their fellows. Possibly a drive to defend themselves against sexual inadequacy, physical weaknesses, or so-called lack of masculinity results in a shared sexual attack. Their interaction with their victim may in fact be of less significance than the response of their fellows.

Probably most gang assaults are never reported. The usual embarrassment and fear suffered by *all* rape victims is very likely magnified for the women who suffer a gang assault. The difficulty of getting convictions even in what seem open-and-shut cases of single rape is well known. The victim of a gang rape may have been acquainted with one or more of the gang members; she may voluntarily have accompanied them to a place where she was attacked. Police often "unfound" such attacks because of prosecutorial difficulties. Also, victims of gangs often save their sanity by blocking out the whole experience; they can neither recall nor identify their assailants.

Horrors are tolerated by groups which would not be countenanced by individuals, as more than one survivor of Nazi Germany has pointed out. While the role of group "leaders" is accepted as fact, their specific role in these mass rapes has not been thoroughly studied. It seems likely that some "leaders" accept the role reluctantly, almost as if it were forced upon them, while others are clearly assertive and probably gain as much satisfaction from propelling the group into action as from the criminal sex assault itself. An example is the case of three boys who attacked a girl in Los Angeles after she had allegedly agreed to "do anything you want" to spare her boyfriend from being beaten. The "leader" of the trio felt a need to fulfill the role the other two had assigned to him: "I was scared when it began to happen," he said. "I wanted to leave but I didn't want to let the other guys know I was scared." A woman we know who was raped by three men "couldn't get over" the whispered apologies of one assailant: "He kept saying he didn't want to do it, but he had to or his friends would think there was something wrong with him. I couldn't understand it. I don't understand it now. Maybe he was just too afraid to stand out against the rest of them."

Such gang attacks are a frightening commentary on the emotional numbness and alienation of many males—that boys and men who may be in other respects outwardly "normal" and "decent" human beings feel the need to band together to attack a single female. The Vietnam War produced many horrible examples of American soldiers inflicting gang rape, often followed by murder, upon Vietnamese women. In such cases the psychological pressure of "follow the leader" was plain: "I didn't want to do it," G.I.'s have said, "but I had to. There wasn't anything I could do to get out of it."

Not only male "bonding" and sado-macho proofs of "manhood" are in evidence, but also the social dynamic active in all peer groups. Such group rape atrocities —tragically common in war—are now becoming increasingly common in our allegedly free and open society. Not until many men and boys can be moved to "stand out against the rest" can we hope to put an end to the barbarism of gang rape.

Psychopath or Everyman?

To return to our original question: Who, exactly, becomes a rapist? What are his psychology and motivations? Is he a perverted sex criminal, or a "normal" man who simply gave in to overwhelming temptation? Rapists come in every guise, social class, and relationship to victims: strangers, schoolmates, friends, neighbors, fathers, uncles, brothers, husbands, acquaintances, dates, fiancés, colleagues, bosses. As the New York Police Department cautions its investigators, "In a sex offense practically everyone is a suspect. Never try to avoid the investigation of an individual because of the fact that he is not the type, too religious, well educated, occupies a responsible job, has a beautiful wife, or a happy family." Yet what do these men have in common which makes them assault a female's body, seemingly oblivious of her feelings and often intent on hurting and debasing her in every possible way?

Most definitions fall into two categories, and the majority of criminal justice and mental health personnel hold fast to the idea that rapists are either: (1) the genuinely sick, so-called "social psychopath" or "sociopath" who is not mentally responsible for his acts; or (2) the male who is not mentally ill but rapes because of environmental conditioning or the special circumstances of the moment (such as a "seductive" women who then refuses to "come across").

Rapists in the first category, the *psychopathological rapists*, are committed to mental hospitals for treatment or to special prison facilities for the "criminally insane." In total number, they are definitely in the minority—both among rapists in general and among other "criminally insane" patients. This type of rapist is the one who figures prominently in popular imagination as the "sex fiend"—the masked, armed rapist who climbs in windows and lurks in alleys. His demented behavior may indeed be unbelievably fiendish. He is the one who often sadistically assaults his victims, who rapes and injures children, and who may murder.

Rapists in the second category, the *so-called "normal" rapists*, are most often never charged with rape, never brought to trial, or never convicted on rape charges. These rapists, as we have seen, include a wide spectrum of males, ranging from poor ghetto youths who grow up in an environment of racial prejudice, poverty, insecurity, violence, and "grabbing sex where you can," all the way up the social scale from middle-class to affluent upper-class white males who may be repeater rapists or may only give in once or twice to "temptation" or "intolerable teasing by a sexy female." This definition comes down to the belief that all women are in effect the property of all men. If some men see this type of rape as "regrettable," they do not view the rapist as really "sick"—his act was, alas, a mere lapse of the moment.

Similarly, psychological professionals tend to view the socially conditioned rapist as not mentally ill. Typical is the interpretation of Dr. Eugene Stammeyer, chief psychologist of St. Elizabeths Hospital for the mentally ill in Washington, D.C., who conducted an intensive study of forty-six committed rapists and shared his conclusions with us:

> *Rape is an act of physical violence and power which stems basically from a sense of impotence. It is generally based more on a social, cultural background than an emotional one. If a man grew up in a neighborhood where the way to get sex is to grab it, then he may commit rape but not feel emotionally alienated in any way. Psychiatrically sick rapists are different. They are downtrodden, bruised, lonely, frustrated men who feel like failures. Their sex behavior may start by looking in windows and masturbating and then progress to rape. The dynamics are complex, but I suspect that in the group I treated clinically an intense rivalry with a female sibling or sibling figure existed. In some cases the mother was both seductive and rejecting. The rapists at St. Elizabeth's attacked women out of a sense of impotence and frustration. But I wouldn't consider all rapists mentally ill.*

These theories are used to define the victim as well as the rapist. The victim of the "mad" rapist is seen as essentially "innocent," although she may have foolishly strayed into his path or not taken safety precautions or she may even suffer from an inner self-destructive compulsion which makes her "precipitate" the rape (a favorite theory of criminologist Amir). If the psychopath is also a sadist, the victim will present the wounds—or the corpse—establishing her innocence. A "sick" sex criminal will often have other peculiar habits, such as collecting hundreds of pieces of female underwear, which underline his "perversity." Some of these rapists actually ask for help in various ways: "Stop me before I rape (or murder) more," they write at the crime scene; or they may phone a psychiatrist, a hospital, or even a rape crisis center. Many recognize themselves as in the grip of an uncontrollable obsession. All of these rapists, being "crazy," will rape again and again, since they are incapable of controlling their own behavior in the long run (although they may have periods of successful resistance to their deep psychic urges).

The second group of rapists, however—the emotionally "normal" males—usually see their victims as causing the rape, a view often shared by the social professionals who treat them. The victim has "precipitated" the act by her behavior, way of dressing, walking or talking, and the places she frequents. The victim is really to blame because she put herself in the path of the rapist and "enticed" him. Washington, D.C.'s WMAL-TV commentator Paul Berry told us after talking to a number of Michigan sex offenders, "The rapists I interviewed painted every victim as a Jezebel. All indicated the woman had provoked him." This alleged provocation, as we have seen, can take nearly any form —including a woman's decision to sleep alone nude in her own home or wear an attractive nightgown. Too many psychologists and psychiatrists, social scientists, doctors, and other medical-mental health personnel, as well as law-enforcement officials share the "she-provoked-it" belief.

Diagnostic outlooks such as Dr. Stammeyer's stem from a profession filled with the same prejudices found in all our social institutions. Through all psychological literature and theorizing runs a strong theme of women as the underlying causative factor in sex crimes—as victim, mother, or sibling rival—whether the rapist is judged *psychotic* (dissociated from reality), neuropsychopathic (alienated from healthy human relationships but in touch with reality), or *socialized* to rape.

The lack of knowledge about diagnosis and treatment is revealed by the endless disagreements among psychologists and psychiatrists over classifications for rapists. The widely used term "sexual psychopath" is a legal label, not a clinical one, and its definition varies from state to state. Even when used, there is little consensus on the terms "sexual psychopath" or "psychopath," although they have been circulating for more than 150 years. William and Joan McCord, in *The Psychopath: An Essay on the Criminal Mind* (1964), point out that scientists have debated the definition of this disorder for nearly its entire history. Dr. Ralph Brancale, Director of the New Jersey State Diagnostic Center, has said that the term is psychiatrically meaningless: "It is quite obvious that this diagnostic label serves neither medical truth nor satisfies any useful or practical purpose. It has now been replaced by another label, 'sociopathic personality,' which is equally meaningless." A survey of prominent psychiatrists' definitions of "psychopathic personality" was made by Paul Tappan, author of *The Habitual Sex Offender* (1950) and *Crime, Justice and Correction* (1960). Tappan received a bewildering variety of responses and concluded that this term was "a most inadequate diagnostic tool for purposes of a legal finding and medical treatment of sex offenders."

Dr. Alfred B. Vuocolo, author of *The Repetitive Sex Offender* (1969), concluded:

A paradoxical situation exists in that although "psychopathic personality" or a facsimile thereof is considered the theoretic basis for the identification and separation for treatment of deviant sex offenders, there is the inherent implication that such individuals are psychiatrically untreatable. Many psychiatrists in the correctional field indi-

cate that the mentally disordered sex deviant is not
an easy subject to work with, and there is no recognized standard treatment.

The problem is compounded by the routine lumping
together of rapists with other types of so-called "sex
deviants," such as homosexuals, who still seem to cause
more concern among psychiatrists and legislators than
heterosexual rapists.

There are no established standard criteria to indicate
when a sex offender is rehabilitated and no longer
dangerous to the community. (As one prison official
said, "How can you rehabilitate people who have never
been 'habilitated'?") It is still clinically impossible for
institution specialists to predict the future behavior of
convicted rapists, yet they make such judgments all the
time. Dr. David A. Lanham, writing on "The Dangerous
Sex Offender" (in *Medical Annals of the District of
Columbia,* February 1974) points out:

> *Similarly, every day dangerous sex offenders walk
> out of prison by expiration of sentence. Very little
> seems to be made of this, perhaps because it is
> believed that they have "paid their debt to soci-
> ety," when in actuality there has been little or no
> real effort at rehabilitation and/or treatment of the
> underlying psychological disturbance. In that
> vein, it also should be clearly stated that many sex
> offenders are very disturbed individuals, ranging
> all the way from clearly psychotic persons through
> the whole diagnostic manual of mental disease
> (including organic conditions). . . . The prob-
> lems involved in aberrations of sex and aggression
> in human beings are more complex than the tech-
> nical and engineering problems of getting to the
> moon.*

Diagnostic centers suffer from the limited sample of
sex offenders they examine; the paucity of detailed and

sustained research; and the failure to consider such offenders in their total environment, including their relationships with women. Dr. Frederic Wertham, one of the country's leading authorities on violence, believes that "the largest number of these offenders belong to a group *between* crime and disease. If we treat them merely according to medicine or merely according to criminal law, we treat them as something they are not, and that can help neither them nor us." In general, it must be said that the cure of rapists in this country continues to exist in a Dark Age of ignorance, myth, and indifference. For the most part, rapists are invisible, unpunished, and untreated assailants. In study and treatment, very little is known or done.

Disagreement is rampant among those charged with rehabilitating rapists about the most basic questions. Are most dangerous rapists repeaters? Many experts say yes, others say no (on the weight of available evidence, we believe that they are). Do less serious sex offenses often intensify into rape? Again, opinion is split (although the probability of an ascending pattern seems clear to us). Can rape be predicted and ended? Theories of all sorts abound. Psychiatric definitions are controversial among psychological professionals, as well as very confusing to nonprofessionals. In the diagnostic terms used by many, it is not necessarily "sick" or "crazy" to rape and murder another human being—it depends on your thought processes and physical perceptions while you are doing the job. One of the strangest aspects of rape is that only the most brutal or bizarre rapists are considered by many mental health authorities to be mentally ill.

Only a relative handful of studies of rapists as yet exist. Dr. Manfred Guttmacher, a pioneer in the field (especially with his 1951 study, *Sex Offenses, The Problem, Causes and Prevention*), gave three categories which are often still followed: (1) the man who rapes as an explosive expression of pent-up sexual impulses, (2) the rapist who is a sadistic exaggeration of the masculine role, and (3) the aggressive criminal who is out to pillage and rob, with rape only one of his aggressive acts. In an opposite opinion, Dr. Benjamin Karpman, author of *The Sexual Offender and His Offenses* (1954), found *no* specific personality types.

Another psychologist, Dr. Sheldon B. Kopp, described *two* main patterns in the character structure of rapists he examined while on the staff of the New Jersey State Hospital in Trenton: "The first corresponds to Guttmacher's description of the aggressive criminal," he wrote in "The Character Structure of Sex Offenders" (*American Journal of Psychotherapy,* 1962, vol. 16):

> This antisocial psychopath is a cold, seemingly unfeeling man who has always taken what he wanted from others without apparent concern for the feelings of his victims or the consequences of his act. For him rape is just another instance of aggressive taking, except that in this case he steals sexual satisfaction rather than money or property. . . . The rape fits so well with his character structure and is so typical of his general behavior pattern that he can see nothing wrong with the act, and often goes on to rationalize that his victim probably enjoyed it. He wants no part of therapy unless he sees it as a means of manipulating his way out of incarceration.

Dr. Kopp found the second type of rapist to be markedly different:

> . . . This is the overly compliant patient who rarely asks for what he wants because he feels that he does not deserve satisfaction from others. He spends much of his time trying to please other people in order to earn their appreciation and affection, and often cannot accept anything which is freely offered without repaying it in some way. For such a man the act of rape represents a serious

*break in his character defense. Afterward he feels
quite guilty and is very much concerned about the
well-being of his victim. . . . This type of rapist is
usually quite anxious to begin therapy, though he
often views it as a painful process which will serve
as a kind of penance.*

For both types, Dr. Kopp concluded, "the act of rape
appears to represent a way of stealing love. They take by
force that which they feel they are not entitled to be
given freely." Dr. Kopp rejects Dr. Guttmacher's interpretation of one type of rapist as suffering from
"pent-up sexual impulses," an outdated but still commonplace myth, even among professionals. The disturbed character structures he presents are understandable in their apparently opposite motivations, overag-
gression or overcompliance; both grow out of profound
feelings of self-rejection, total worthlessness, and despair. Yet it is puzzling that Dr. Kopp refers to the
aggressive rapist as having a "psychopathic character"
while the second type is called an "overly compliant
character." Surely if psychopathic means anything, it
must be applied to *all* men who are driven to rape,
whatever the specific pattern of their pathology. Here
again, definitions and categories break down in the
light of common sense and female experience.

Dr. Frank V. Vanasek, former research psychologist at
Atascadero State Hospital, told us there was "no such
thing as *the* rapist—all different types of men become
sex offenders." Dr. Vanasek said the hospital had
legally established criteria called the Mentally Disordered Sexual Offender for men who have used force or
attacked children. Five classifications were established
for rapists: (1) The *psychotic,* where the sexual involvement is secondary and the main treatment is for
the psychosis. (2) The *psychopathic delinquent or
sociopath*—"he wants what he wants when he wants it,
with no regard for the rights of others." The category
includes men involved in armed robbery and narcotics,

with rape only a part of their crimes; they are among the most difficult to treat. (3) The *neurotic,* who often shows hysterical types of behavior including fetishism, rape, excitement related to sexual achievements. (4) Rapists needing a sexual *role identity.* Almost always there is a triggering reaction by a woman, some sort of rejection; for example, one man who couldn't achieve an erection for two nights in a row went out the next day and raped four women. (5) The *homosexual* who is trying to reject his homosexual tendencies and prove his heterosexuality by raping.

Such classifications are familiar for other types of mental patients. As Norman S. Goldner, an assistant sociology professor at Wayne State University in Michigan, concluded in "Rape as a Heinous but Understudied Offense" (*The Journal of Criminal Law, Criminology and Police Science,* 1972): *"No agreement has been reached on whether the motivation of rapists is different from that of other offenders in degree, kind, or pattern."* (Italics added.) Goldner points out that a University of Minnesota Medical School study of prisoners in Sing Sing Prison determined:

> *None of the sex offenders had a normal personality, while 70 percent had symptoms of schizophrenia. Another study of convicted sex offenders at the State of New Jersey Diagnostic Center concluded that high rates of disturbed behavior were "found among those convicted of forcible rape and exhibitory acts. . . . Underlying or overt hostility was particularly evident in those convicted of sexual assault, forcible rape, and incestuous relationship." Hammer and Glueck conducted a five-year study of the psychodynamic patterns of 200 sex offenders and found that other inmates were differentiated in the degree but not the kind of their mental processes.*

All of which seems to come down to the point that rapists are essentially no different from other emotionally disturbed men—they simply take out their inner disturbances in violent sexual directions.

A major reason for the failure of professional insights into rapists' motivations is the persistent Freudian frenzy, which for decades has immobilized so much psychiatric thinking in frigid patterns. This is evident in the theories—often presented as facts—in the still scanty professional literature on rapists. The five-year study of 200 sex offenders cited by Goldner concluded that rapists have less incapacitating "castration" feelings than other sex offenders. True to Freudian form, the researchers found the classic mère noire lurking in the rapist's subconscious: "The rapist, feeling rejected by his mother, feels he cannot be wanted or desired by any woman; hence he attempts to command a woman physically." Similar interpretations have been made by others. Dr. Benjamin Karpman opined, "In many cases, rape may be related unconsciously to early incestuous desires and the fury aroused by the Oedipus complex. . . . The victim may be a substitute for the criminal's mother who would naturally resist the attack by her son."

Some clinicians have even studied the wives and mothers of rapists—though apparently not the fathers—in their diligent efforts to find the responsible parties. Wives, not surprisingly, were found to be "masochistic, latently homosexual, and sexually unresponsive." The mothers had allegedly sexually overstimulated their sons during childhood, their "seductive behavior" alternating with cruelty and harshness. The femme noire, like the mère noire, is the universal psychic vampire supposedly sucking the lifeblood from every rapist's mind. Mothers are consistently "very cold and unforgiving" or "unloving and rejecting," "passive, moralistic, and religious" or "overprotective" or—the standard female stance—"seductive." The father may be described as equally harsh and rejecting, yet somehow his influence is never decisive in these clinical descriptions. The assumed Oedipal conflict (questioned by analysts from Karen Horney to Erich

Fromm), coupled with the sexual and aggressive "instincts" (totally unproven) and the male's immature ego development, are held to be the decisive factors.

What such analysts overlook is that if a mother is unloving, it may be because her own oppression has destroyed much of her capacity for love. If she takes out her anger on her children, it may be because society creates these hostilities and then offers her no avenues for release. If she is seductive with sons, it may be because her culture conditions her to be attractive to every male in order to survive. If she keeps her children dependent, it is because she is so dependent herself. To blame women for their own self-destructiveness is akin to blaming slaves for their own servitude. Women, like other victims, may take part in their own victimization; but their deepest motivation is fear and self-survival. Freudians who claim that women cause their own rapes persist in a circular reasoning that is false, vicious, and futile. As long as women remain the targets of displaced male hostilities, every male who feels rejected by parents and society may take out his self-contempt and fury upon the bodies of women and children. Only when women are no longer seen by men *and* women as the "weaker sex" will rape diminish as an outlet for the neurotic and psychotic emotional conflicts of males.

Feminist therapists increasingly view rape as germinated by our antifemale, violent society. Traditional analysts continue to interpret sex assaults as either the result of *individual* character disorders or of a *specific* environment. Both groups often agree on the underlying *hostility* which motivates rapists. What they disagree about is the fundamental cause of such hostility. Traditionalists tend to find the rapist's hatred for women rooted in his personality structure and family dynamics—most often a rejecting, "castrating," unloving mother or wife. Feminists put the major onus for such crimes on men and our sexist society. *It is a crucial difference.* If traditional theories were true, it would be extraordinary that women with the *same* personality traits or *same* specific environments do not resort to rape. Rape, in fact, is practically unknown as an outlet of American women, who are universally conditioned to passivity and dependence.

Consider the description of male rapists by Dr. Ralph F. Garofalo, deputy director of the Treatment Center for Sex Offenders at the Massachusetts Correctional Institution in Bridgewater, one of the country's few special therapy centers for sex criminals. Garofalo, whom we interviewed, and his associates divide rapists into three major categories: (1) *Rape-aggressive aim:* rapists motivated by hatred of a woman or women in their personal lives, which is then displaced onto stranger-victims (the alleged dynamics are typically Freudian). (2) *Rape-sexual aim:* rape clearly motivated by sexual wishes underlying repressed homosexuality (again, a sexist-Freudian interpretation is given). (3) *Rape-sex aggression defusion:* rape with a strong sadistic component necessary for sexual arousal; paranoid features predominate.

Garofalo's second classification is especially interesting in terms of sex-class evaluations. This type of rapist:

. . . *shows little or no antisocial behavior apart from the repetitive sexual offenses. He is, in fact, socially submissive and compliant. His friends and neighbors see him as a quiet, shy, "good boy," more lonely than most, but nonetheless quite normal. There is generally an absence of even a moderate amount of aggressive and assertive behavior. His approach to the tasks of life are tentative and have a phobic quality. This lack of assertiveness combines with a very negative self-esteem and a low level of aspiration, preventing him from making significant attainments in either educational or occupational areas. There is a stable employment history, but the level of work is far below his aptitude and potential abilities. Although intelligence varies across a wide range from dull normal*

to bright average and above among the rapists in
this group, in no instance is the potential realized.
Scholastic records show poor performance and
frequently withdrawal from school prior to gradu-
ation.

Simply change the sex and we have a classic description of *most women:* ". . . socially submissive and
compliant. . . an absence of even a moderate amount of
aggressive and assertive behavior . . . approach to the
tasks of life are tentative and have a phobic quality . . .
a very negative self-esteem and a low level of aspiration
. . . stable employment history, but the level of work is
far below [her] aptitude and potential abilities . . . in no
instance is the potential realized." This is a description
of the "ideal" female, the one our society works hard to
mold.

The lack of useful knowledge about rapists extends beyond psychological motivations—the difficult
"why" factor—and into specific parameters of "who,
where, when, and how," which detailed research
studies could go a long way toward understanding. Yet
here again compilations and comparisons are scanty.
Many sweeping statements about rapists rest on one
pioneering study published by Menachem Amir (see
page 221) in 1971, using material from 1958 and 1960
Philadelphia police files on 646 cases *(Patterns in Forcible Rape).* The limitations of this analysis are
obvious—the material is old, the sample comes from a
single city, and only a relative handful of cases were
studied. (Another limitation, of course, is Amir's often
sexist approach.) Other similarly limited studies include: Dr. John M. MacDonald's *Rape: Offenders and
Their Victims* (1971), which is based on 200 Denver
cases; "Rape in New York City: A Study of Material in
the Police Files and Its Meaning" by Duncan Chappell
and Susan Singer (1973); and an unpublished study of
rape in Denver, Colorado, by the Denver Anti-Crime
Council (1973). All four used police files for their data.

Characteristics of rapists and victims interpreted from
this and other data include the following:

1. *Relationship of offender and victim:* According to
all four studies, the majority of rapes are stranger-to-
stranger (Amir—52 percent; MacDonald—60 percent;
Chappell and Singer—78 percent; Denver Council—64
percent). A study of 278 reported rapes in Seattle,
Washington, in 1972 showed nearly two-thirds were
stranger-to-stranger. Dr. Joseph J. Peters in his survey of
149 victims, "The Philadelphia Rape Victim Study"
(1973), found that 80 percent of adult victims and 25
percent of adolescents had been raped by strangers and
that most children were raped by friends, relatives, or
acquaintances.

2. *Age of offender:* This is one of the few breakdowns
made by the FBI. The 1973 *Uniform Crime Report*
states that 61 percent of those arrested for forcible rape
were males under the age of twenty-five. Males sixteen
to twenty-four years old constituted the largest group of
arrests. More recent *Uniform Crime Reports* statistics
were similar. Amir, MacDonald, and Chappell and
Singer found most offenders to be between the ages of
fifteen and twenty-four.

3. *Age of victim:* No figures are given by the FBI. Amir
and MacDonald in their Philadelphia and Denver
studies found one-quarter of the rape victims to be fifteen to nineteen years old. Amir reported the next highest number in ages ten to fourteen, while MacDonald
found another quarter of Denver victims to be twenty to
twenty-four years old. Peters' smaller sample had 56
percent adults (eighteen years and older), 32 percent
adolescents, and 10 percent children (twelve years and
younger).

4. *Race:* The FBI's 1973 *Uniform Crime Report*
reported that 47 percent of those arrested for forcible
rape were black, 51 percent were white, and all other
races comprised the rest. Amir in Philadelphia found
that 82 percent of the 1,292 offenders were black and 30

percent of the 646 victims were also black. Among the 253 Denver rapists, MacDonald reported that 35 percent were white, 34 percent were Spanish-American, and 30 percent were black. The 200 victims included 126 whites, 42 Spanish-Americans, and 31 blacks. In Chappell and Singer's New York study, nearly 59 percent of the 484 rapists were black, more than a quarter were white, and the others were mainly Puerto Rican. The lack of New York police information on victims precluded analysis of their race and age.

5. *Previous record of offender:* Amir's study showed that 49 percent of the Philadelphia offenders had previous records, although most were for crimes against property. The Denver Council found 21 percent had previously been arrested for sex offenses. MacDonald cites three other studies: Of 77 rapists in the Colorado State Penitentiary, 85 percent had a previous arrest record and 12 percent had previously been convicted of forcible rape. A Canadian study found 95 percent of 30 convicted rapists had previous convictions. Another survey of 141 rapists in Denmark showed 77 percent with previous criminal records.

6. *Location:* Amir found that 82 percent of the Philadelphia offenders and victims lived in the same area, while in 62 percent of the cases offenders and victims lived in the vicinity of the crime. A study of 2,624 sex crimes in Chicago also found 82 percent of the offenders living within a few miles of the crime scene (O. Erlanson, "The scene of a sex crime as related to the residence of the offender," *Journal of Criminal Law,* 1940-41). Chappell and Singer found encounters and crime scenes most often in interior settings, but more than one-third of the attacks originated in streets and parks. Apartments are favorite locations in New York. MacDonald also found a high percentage of Denver victims seized on the streets and taken elsewhere to be raped. The victim's home or apartment was the next most dangerous meeting place. In Denver and Philadelphia 54 and 55 percent of the victims respectively were

raped in their own or the assailant's home. All agreed
that most rapes occur indoors.

7. *Time frame:* These and prior reports establish a
pattern showing the majority of rapes in the warmer
months between May and September, with the peak in
August. Studies made in New York, Philadelphia, Boston, and Los Angeles show a marked weekend trend.
Top risk hours (according to Amir, MacDonald, and
others) were from 8 P.M. to 4 A.M.

None of these sparse statistics are conclusive, although they do indicate some trends, especially the
continuing youthfulness of assailants; a high stranger-
to-stranger rate; and a disproportionate involvement of
blacks as both rapists and victims (which is not surprising in light of continued racial prejudice, low
socioeconomic status for minorities, and ghetto subcultures of violence in this country). Even less is known
about national or regional patterns, if any, of gang rapes,
M.O.s, weapons used, extent of force and injuries inflicted, and the educational and socioeconomic characteristics of assailants. Many more detailed local and
national studies are needed, as well as the *coordination*
of all efforts by a central body such as Senator McC.
Mathias's national clearinghouse for rape information
and programs. And on all levels, a feminist outlook is
essential.

Pornography and Sex Crimes

The difficulty of trying to define pornography is apparent to anyone who has investigated it—including
the United States Supreme Court. Critics run the risk of
being labeled puritanical and intolerant. But pornography, which has been studied at great lengths by many
men and very few women, is a rightful concern of *all*
women, if only because females figure so prominently
as the chief sexual objects and chosen victims in this
class of material.

The President's National Commission on the Causes and Prevention of Violence decided in 1969 that violence portrayed by the media can induce aggression. But a year later, the Commission on Obscenity and Pornography, with two women among the nineteen commissioners, gave pornography a clean bill of health, saying there was not "sufficient social justification . . . for the retention or enactment of broad legislation prohibiting the consensual distribution of sexual materials to adults." The commission concluded that its "empirical" investigation provided "no evidence that exposure to or use of explicit sexual material plays a significant role in the causation of social or individual harms." In simpler terms, the commission found no connection between sex crimes and pornography, a point of view which has been echoed by hosts of reputable psychiatrists, psychologists, and sociologists.

Among them was the late Dr. Robert Lindner, who declared he was convinced of the "absurdity of the idea that any form of reading matter . . . *can either provoke delinquency or criminal behavior or instruct toward such ends. . . .*" (Italics added.) Drs. Phyllis and Eberhard Kronhausen, educational psychologists specializing in family therapy and group guidance, studied pornography in the late 1950s and went a step beyond Lindner, claiming pornography actually was beneficial. As they wrote in *Pornography and the Law* (1953):

> *Instead of the comics, "lewd" magazines, or even hard core pornography causing sex murders and other criminal acts, it is far more likely that these "unholy" instruments may be more often than not a safety valve for the sexual deviate and potential sex offender. This is not only our own view, but that of many other experienced clinicians, especially those who have worked with more severely disturbed patients and delinquents.*

Dr. Asher R. Pacht, director of treatment for sex offenders at Wisconsin's Waupun Prison, concurs, saying
that research done at Waupun "clearly did not support
the contention that preadolescent and adolescent exposure to pornography contributes to later commitment of
sex offenses."

An opposite conclusion was reached, however, by
Gladys Denny Shultz, author of *How Many More Victims? Society and Sex Criminals* (1965). Herself a near-
rape victim, she interviewed seventy violent sex offenders at both Waupun Prison and California's Atascadero State Hospital for sex offenders and the criminally
insane. Her talks with these assailants confirmed the
view that perpetrators of sex-linked crimes invariably
had been extensive users of pornography, especially
during their young years. The emphasis on the deviant
norm—cruelty, perversion, bestiality in sex materials so
readily available—"made it harder for men with a sex
problem," one offender told her. Another man in his
mid-twenties, who had raped a sixteen-year-old girl,
had started using pornography before he was ten. During his teens, he was particularly impressed with a
sequence in which a woman was forced to have intercourse with a stallion. It was the pain that this act
caused the woman which fascinated him and lodged in
his mind through the years, he said.

Despite the assertion of the *status quo* apologists, we
agree with Shultz and others that a distinguishable relation exists between pornography and sex crimes, especially for offenders whose major exposure to sexual
material during adolescence is pornographic. Far from
having a beneficial effect, what we have seen in police
records is that pornography may indeed be linked to the
M.O. of sex criminals. The methods graphically portrayed in pornographic material usually involve violence and aberrant behavior in which females are both
willing and unwilling participants, with explicit descriptions of brutality and physical abuse of females.

Women, clearly, are the prime victims, at least in heterosexual material.

Offenders by and large are young men, barely out of adolescence. *Nearly half (47.2 percent) of arrested sex offenders are between the ages of seventeen and twenty-four,* according to the FBI's *Uniform Crime Reports.* Those between seventeen and twenty make up more than a quarter (25.7 percent) of all those apprehended. We know, of course, that during adolescence interest and investigation about sexual matters is immense; but the pornography shops and films and bars which have proliferated in our cities and towns are an open door for learning *all the wrong things.*

Single and gang rape of females is ubiquitous in heterosexual pornography. Popular features include sadism, cruelty, violence, phallus worship, nymphomania, bestiality, incest, group orgies and voyeurism, flagellation, beating, and other methods of inflicting barbarous pain, usually on females. Racism is also prevalent in the trash and smut world. The glorification and alleged perversities of supersexed minority women is a regular component—with Black, Chicana, Latin, and Oriental females lending themselves to unspeakable degradation and violence. Women are generally depicted as sexually insatiable, especially after being properly initiated by the dominant male or males.

The pattern rarely changes in the porno culture—after a few preliminary skirmishes, women invite or demand further violation, begging male masters to rape them into more submission, torture, and violence. In this fantasy land, females wallow in physical abuse and degradation. It is a pattern of horror which we have seen in our examination of sex cases translated again and again into actual assaults. Probably the single most used cry of rapist to victim is: "You bitch . . . slut . . . you know you want it! You, all want it!" and afterward, "There now, you really enjoyed it, didn't you? Why don't we do this again?"

It is useless to confront those intellectuals firmly

locked into Freudian devotion to the "female masoch-
ist," thanks largely to Dr. Helene Deutsch's massive
—and misleading—classic work *The Psychology of
Women*. Undoubtedly some women, like some men,
induce ill treatment, but masochism is at heart a learned
trait. Many women have dutifully come to believe and
accept it as they have so many other socially conditioned attitudes. This naturally makes the unnatural
work of the rapist and sadist that much easier.

A basic problem with the violence and sadism per-
vading the world of pornography is that often it is the
only sexual material to which adolescents have access.
It thus introduces them at a highly impressionable age
to a grossly distorted portrayal of women, spelling out
warped and dangerous concepts of the female's sexual
nature. Other critics of the pornography commission's
findings and the porno-is-good-for-you view include
psychiatrist Dr. Frederic Wertham, a leading authority
on sex crime and consultant at New York's Queens
Hospital Center; Dr. Hilde Mosse, professor of
psychiatry at New York Medical College and school
psychiatrist for the Bureau of Child Guidance of New
York City's Board of Education; Dr. Frank J. Vanasek,
former research psychologist at California's Atascadero
State Hospital; Cincinnati lawyer and "decency"
crusader Charles H. Keating, Jr., who resigned from the
pornography commission in protest; and anthropologist Margaret Mead.

Dr Wertham believes:

> . . . *sex combined with violence—the whole mind
> pollution with violence that is so prevalent in this
> country—is what causes problems. . . . The trend
> in pornographic literature is toward sadism, to-
> ward brutality. . . . This reinforces preexisting
> sadistic impulses and suggests enjoyment of
> sadism. . . . Sadistic pornography is definitely
> contagious. . . . Many men who commit violent
> acts not only read pornography, they collect*

*it. . . . There have been cases of sadistic murder
where it was proved in the courtroom that the murderer used sadistic pornography as a textbook.*

This psychiatrist studied Albert Fish, one of the worst
sex criminals in U.S. history, who murdered fifteen
children and molested or tortured a hundred more. Dr.
Wertham told author Gladys Shultz that he had spent
hours in Fish's cell, "eliciting the story of his life and
crimes. He had a vast collection of sadistic clippings. *I
learned things from it I hadn't known in all of my
medical reading. He acted them out with children.*"
(Italics added.) Dr. Wertham criticized the pornography
commission's studies as "irrelevant pseudo-science,"
and stressed the need for time to study the *whole*
person, not just responses to a few isolated questions.

Dr. Vanasek, whom we interviewed at Atascadero
State Hospital, had studied sex criminals and pornography and discounted a *causal* relationship between the
two. Nevertheless, he said that pornography is a
"poison" and children should be shielded from it during formative years: "You wouldn't let them drink
iodine; you teach them to leave such things alone. They
must be taught to stay away from harmful mental material," Dr. Vanasek said. "The deviant and sadistic material is sick. . . . If seen by a youngster in the formative,
adolescent period it can make it more difficult for him to
reach mature development." Further, this psychologist
believes that pornography can be used as a tool for early
diagnosing of sexual sickness: "Sado-masochistic material . . . furnishes the basis for scientific study of two
major factors, sexual and aggressive drives. Much of
what we have been seeing lately is concerned with
aggression, and the sexual aspects are only secondary."

Dr. Hilde Mosse stresses how mass media deliberately
play upon the teen-ager's sexual insecurities, creating:

*. . . mass hypochondriasis in order to create a
teen-age market. . . . Now there are teen-age*

porno comic strips. . . . Sex organs are drawn in abnormal size and the grotesque is typical. . . . There are of course erotic paintings of value, some are great art, but this is not what is shown to children and adolescents now. The stress is on ugliness, crudeness, distortion and sadism. . . . Tenderness, subtlety, romance do not exist. This gives youngsters peculiar ideas about what goes on between their parents and creates child-parent difficulties.

Lawyer and "decency" crusader Keating says the pornography commission chose to ignore several of its own studies which differed with the majority opinion. One such study involved 365 men, including prisoners, college students, and Roman Catholic seminarians, and the "data clearly suggest that exposure to pornography at early ages, under fourteen, plays a role in the development of sexually deviant life-style."

Anthropologist Margaret Mead emphasizes the dehumanizing effects of the pornography culture where people become things and audiences are exhorted to be callous and insensate, devoid of compassion and sensibility. Mead also provides a useful working definition of pornography: "Cross-culturally, it is words or acts of representations that are calculated to stimulate sex feelings *independent* of the presence of another *loved and chosen* human being." (Italics added.) Victims of sex crimes may be chosen; they are never loved.

Sex Offenders and the System

Every year some 60,000 to 70,000 sex offenders —sadistic rapists, child molesters, exhibitionists, and voyeurs—pass through the U.S. criminal justice system as it operates on federal, state, county, and municipal levels. Yet there are very few facilities in either prisons or hospitals designed and operated exclusively for the treatment of rapists and other violent sex assailants. As

LEAA analyst Cynthia Jackson points out, in a 1974
study, "Forcible Rape":

> *Although there are numerous institutions
> throughout the country operated by either correc-
> tions or mental health departments which have
> mandates to treat sex offenders, none can boast of
> successful treatment programs for rapists. Gener-
> ally, rapists are being warehoused in institutions
> where they are exposed infrequently to improvised
> treatment modalities; i.e., behavior modification,
> and group and individual therapy.*

Few states have any special rehabilitation programs
for sex offenders; most are sent routinely to prison,
except for the overtly psychotic criminals who may be
committed to state hospitals. A Michigan prison director of treatment, Dr. Barry Mintzes, observed, "Most sex
offender treatment seems to take place in hospitals, and
very little has been done in prisons." (Michigan is one of
the few exceptions.)

Psychiatric care for inmates of state penitentiaries is
largely nonexistent or extremely limited. It is common
knowledge that prisons usually dehumanize rather than
rehabilitate, that prisoners sexually assault each other,
and that a man is apt to reenter society with an even
deeper burning hatred and desire for revenge than when
he went to prison—and women and children, as the
most vulnerable members of our society, become frequent targets. Yet many citizens, and certainly
thousands of rape victims, would agree with a Virginia
prosecuting attorney, Robert Horan, that "at least while
the criminal is in prison he won't hurt any more
women." Lawyers like Horan know that "incarceration
is not a human solution, but at least nobody will be hurt
in the meantime. To me, that's worth all the psychiatric
experimentation in the world, because I deal with victims."

"Psychiatric experimentation" is an apt phrase for the present state of knowledge and treatment for sex offenders. Although researchers and media interviewers have until recently focused far more on sex offenders than their victims, the attention given to understanding and remedying the criminal dynamics of rapists is in most states and jurisdictions inadequate or nonexistent. On every level of the criminal justice system—from the police to the courts, prisons, mental hospitals, and social welfare agencies—realistic, humane, and sensible treatment of rapists is lacking. Our penal institutions, as is widely proclaimed but little heeded, breed the very crimes they exist to curb.

With the recent women's movement outcry about the rising rate of rape and other sexual assaults, a few cities and counties started to look seriously at the pressing problem of evaluating and treating sex criminals. A preliminary study in this neglected area was begun in 1973 in Denver, Colorado, under "Operation Rape Reduction." The Denver Anti-Crime Council formulated guidelines for a cooperative effort by the criminal justice system and community-based organizations. Their recommendations included "a strategy for evaluating and treating the offender. At the current time, the rape offender receives very little, if any, diagnosis or evaluation of his psychological problems; and thus courts are compelled to sentence the offender without the benefit of complete and adequate psychological reports. The rapist is generally sentenced to a term in the penitentiary. Typically, this merely defers rather than resolves the problem."

The Council pointed out the need for improved diagnostic capabilities, including a thorough examination of rapists, using the most advanced techniques and experienced professionals. With the resulting data and information, a model treatment program could be developed. This would probably include behavior modification techniques and the use of positive role modeling procedures. A research program was also recommended to keep current on practices here and abroad and to develop new treatment alternatives.

Some thirty states, plus the District of Columbia, now have sexual psychopath laws providing for the presentencing psychiatric evaluation of sex offenders to determine whether they will be committed by the court to indeterminate terms in psychiatric institutions; sent to prisons; or put on probation with outpatient mental health treatment. Only a few states have as yet set up special treatment centers for sexual psychopaths. Leaders in this still primitive area of research and treatment have been Wisconsin, Massachusetts, California, New Jersey, Michigan, Washington, Florida, Illinois, and the District of Columbia. (In 1968, however, Michigan repealed its sexual psychopath statute and commits many sex criminals to prisons instead of to state hospitals.)

The major limitations of offender programs have been noted: diagnostic theory and treatment practices are controversial and largely ineffective; prisons usually change men for the worse; and above all, the psychological climate of our *entire* society reinforces rape by all disturbed males, not just by an unfortunate minority. As Dr. Cynthia Cooke of Philadelphia General Hospital observed, "At present there is an undercurrent of approval for the rapist coinciding with smug assumptions of collusion on the part of the victim. The potential rapist can interpret these attitudes as a signal to proceed, since he can be relatively certain that the wrath of society will be directed toward the victim." Dr. Vincent Capraro of Buffalo, New York, pointed out, "These people are sick, but until we as physicians can treat and cure them, we are committing an injustice to society in helping to get them back on the streets. All they can do is commit more such crimes."

Where psychiatric treatment is available, three types are largely used: group therapy, individual therapy, and chemotherapy (often used in conjunction with individual and group counseling). As in the area of diagnosis, a wide and conflicting range of claims and counterclaims for such treatments have been made. Thus far, no single body of effective and verifiable treatment has been developed for rapists and similar sex criminals. (In parts of Europe, treatment includes psychotherapy, hormonal treatment, brain surgery, and castration, with inconclusive results.)

In general, group therapy is the most common method, allowing men to meet others with similar feelings of anxiety, anger, conflict, confusion, shame, guilt, inadequacy, hopelessness, isolation, and rejection. This is the primary treatment in the special program for sex offenders at the State Prison of Southern Michigan. Called SONAR ("Seeking Out New Approaches to Reality"), this program has two main goals: to help the offender understand some of the emotional conflicts underlying his behavior (which usually involves learning how his sexual behavior is a function of his total personality) and to help him learn more appropriate ways of handling interpersonal relationships. In mid-1974, treatment director Dr. Barry Mintzes reported, "We're rather proud of our program. Since it began three years ago, we have had 135 paroled, and thus far 120 have made successful adjustments."

Another innovative program for sex offenders was started in 1955 at Philadelphia General Hospital by Dr. Joseph Peters, who later set up a special program for victims. Prisoners on probation or parole are brought into group therapy by court recommendation. Psychiatrists and psychologists, aided by sociologists and social workers, have worked with thousands of men in this community outpatient clinic. Follow-up reports on sample cases indicate significant success in terms of lower rearrest rates, voluntary extension of therapy, and improved psychological adjustment. Rapists, however, are only a minority of this group.

We must also view rehabilitative claims cautiously, for we have as yet few ways of knowing the real success or failure of "adjustments" unless offenders are again

imprisoned. Therapists tend to overlook a major draw-
back in their programs: the groups they set up to help
offenders adjust to society cannot be models for the real
world because they lack the basic ingredients which
induce such crimes—the sexism and multiple pressures
toward violence of our pathological society. Also absent
are the women who are targets of this sexism and
violence. Thus offenders may learn to adjust to each
other without learning much about the underlying hostilities toward females in themselves and in the society
they will reenter.

One exception is the unusual experimental Sex Offender Rehabilitation Program at South Florida State
Hospital directed by a woman psychologist, Dr.
Geraldine Boozer. In this counseling program, rape victims and feminist women are brought into personal
discussion sessions with convicted rapists within a controlled therapeutic setting. Some of the women participants reported enthusiastically on their encounters,
saying, "You can really get through to some of these
guys. It's amazing how their attitudes can start to
change when you rap openly with them." Said Florida
activist Mary Dunetz, "These rapists don't relate to
women as people—only as objects. But they can relate
more to feminists who talk to them as people and don't
have the unreal expectations of other women. We need
projects like this in every state."

Conventional group therapy has been questioned for
other reasons. A Washington, D.C. psychiatrist, formerly at Washington's Psychiatric Institute, warned
against group therapy for sex offenders: "If someone has
antisocial behavior patterns, they don't work out in the
therapeutic community. They appear to be doing exactly what you want them to do. It's a standing joke
among professionals in these wards that the sociopath
runs the patient community and is probably running
you too." The tragedy of inadequate treatment has been
demonstrated repeatedly over the years in thousands of

cases. In early 1974, Washington's Psychiatric Institute came under public criticism for releasing a patient, a former sex offender who had molested young girls. Soon after, this young man assaulted a female student. He left her tied half-naked to a tree, where she died from overnight exposure in freezing weather.

Some sex offenders, like other emotionally troubled people, are starting to try to help themselves more. In 1973, Richard Bryan, a former compulsive exhibitionist, founded a Los Angeles organization called Sex Offenders Anonymous. Operating like Alcoholics Anonymous, this group won court approval to rehabilitate offenders ranging from rapists to voyeurs. Says Bryan:

> *Our aim is to shut off the modus operandi of the sex offenders. We make sure they aren't left alone all day seven days a week. It's like baby-sitting. If a man has a wife or girl friend, she has to do the watching, but if it's a single guy the other members do it. We have a permanent crisis line to organization headquarters. If a single member calls and says he is ready to go out and commit a crime, we go over to stop him.*

Ray Gailey, a supervisor of the Los Angeles County probation office, calls Sex Offenders Anonymous "the best help for offenders I have ever seen. It's much better than psychotherapy. There's no question at all about its effectiveness." Bryan's wife, Rosemary, helps with the distraught wives who come to the weekly meetings: "Once they understand it's a heavy problem that they also contribute to, they look at it from a different standpoint," she says. "The main thing is that we are giving people hope. They feel there is a way out." Bryan sees sex offenses as "psychological escape mechanisms. The anxiety or hostility builds up within a person and he goes out to commit a sex crime to relieve them. Our

method is to interrupt the pattern—to help him contain
the anxiety and hostility within himself and deal with
it. The method is very effective."

Reviewing the overall picture, any consideration of
rapists, child molesters, and other sex assailants which
is limited to convicted criminals and the committed
mentally ill dwells on a plane of unreality. The illusion
that only legally or clinically defined psychopaths,
neurotics, or psychotics rape and murder is partly perpetuated by pseudo-scientific studies with their tone of
factuality and inclusiveness. The fact is—as every
woman realizes who confronts her own life and the
experiences of other women—countless men force
themselves sexually upon women in ways not *legally*
classed as rape, but which have many elements of rape.

Historian Newton Garvey points out, in *Violence in
America*, that human violence:

> is much more closely connected with the idea of
> violation than with the idea of force. What is fun-
> damental about violence is that a person is vio-
> lated. And if one immediately senses the truth of
> that statement, it must be because a person has
> certain rights which are undeniably, indissolubly,
> connected with his being a person. One of these is a
> right to his body, to determine what his body does
> and what is done to his body—inalienable because
> without his body he would cease to be a person.
> Apart from a body, what is essential to one's being
> a person is dignity. . . . The right to one's body
> and the right to autonomy are undoubtedly the
> most fundamental natural rights of persons.
> (Emphasis added.)

We have seen that there is no such thing as *the*
rapist—rape being committed in many forms and guises
by males of every age, race, social and economic status,
intelligence and educational level, and physical and

personality characteristic. Yet certain emotional defects seem characteristic of all people who sexually assault others. A useful summary is given by Dr. Murray L. Cohen and Richard Boucher in "Misunderstandings About Sex Criminals" (*Sexual Behavior,* March 1972):

> *The sexual offender may be passive and inhibited or active and assertive, gentle or violent, religious or irreligious, masculine or effeminate. He may hate his mother, love his mother, or be ambivalent about her. He may have had a repressive sexual development or he may have been overstimulated. And we could go on with these polar opposites.* But what there is in common is a serious defect in interpersonal relationships, *an absence of mature, selfless concern for the victim of his obsession,* an inability to love *in a desexualized manner, a terrible sadness and sense of loneliness, a lack of sublimation, and a totally narcissistic,* self-centered orientation. (Emphasis added.)

These are *exactly* the immature, neurotic qualities which our competitive, violence-prone society inculcates in its members: ". . . a serious defect in interpersonal relations . . . an inability to love . . . a totally self-centered orientation. . . ." It is these characteristics which enter the deepest subconscious levels of both psychopath and "Everyman." Men are conditioned to be rapists; women are conditioned to be victims. In the most dehumanizing sense, it is a "perfect" pathological fit.

8

WOMEN AGAINST RAPE: CRISIS CENTERS, COUNSELING, AND INSTITUTIONAL CHANGE

Remember: You are not the wrongdoer. It is not a crime to have been raped. There is no disgrace in needing or seeking medical help or counseling.
        —Rape Counseling Center, Minneapolis, Minnesota

It is a center's primary job to provide the kind of deep human backdrop from which all personal and political changes emerge.
        —Women's Crisis Center, Ann Arbor, Michigan

"Listen, can you give me some information?" The woman's voice sounded middle-aged and hoarse, tremulous yet impatient.

"I'll certainly try. What information would you like?" The young volunteer at the rape crisis center tried to keep her own voice calm and friendly, though she felt nervous; it was only her second week on the phone.

"Information? Well, you must know—I mean, *you* know, the kind of information people need about diseases—about—about—" The voice faltered and fell silent.

The center worker tried to reach out through her tone

257

even more than her words. "It's all right," she said softly. "You can ask me anything. That's what I'm here for—to help you, if I can."

"God, I don't know what's the matter with me!" the woman burst out. "You've got to help me! Somebody's got to help! That man—I never saw him before, I swear to God I never did—pushed his way in my door this morning. I thought he was the gasman, like he said. Oh my God, it was awful! He—made me get undressed —but I couldn't scream because he had a knife. He said he'd—he'd cut me up if I tried anything. I thought sure he was going to kill me! There wasn't anything I could do. Then he—then he, you know, raped me. Thank God, he left right after. But what if he comes back? I'm scared to death to open the door. Do you think he's outside, waiting for me to come out?"

The volunteer tried to sound reassuring, though she felt a familiar tremor of fear. She, too, had been a rape victim. "No, I don't think he'll come back. But keep your door locked. If you want, we can send someone over to help you. Have you seen anyone since the attack?"

"No, like I told you, I'm scared to death even to look out the window. You're the first one I've called."

"Did you tell the police?"

"No—though I thought about it all day. But Henry—Henry's my husband, he's away until Friday—Henry would just die if he knew about this. I can't tell anyone! What am I going to do? Maybe I'm pregnant or something awful!" The woman seemed close to tears.

"Okay, now, don't worry, we're going to help you," said the crisis worker. "Two women will be coming over as soon as they can this afternoon. They'll get you to a doctor and help you with everything you need to do. Now just give me your name and address."

"Oh, yes, I'll do anything if only you can help me." Her voice sounded suddenly relieved. "It's been a nightmare—please hurry!"

This telephone conversation between victim and volunteer typifies the daily calls received by rape crisis centers now operating across the country. The call illustrates the basic anxieties of most victims: the fear of the assailant's return; of being alone; of venereal disease and pregnancy; of relatives and friends finding out; of reporting to the police; and of what may happen if she does report. Other worries are also common: of returning to work, of resuming relationships with men, even of simply walking down a street.

Until very recently, victims of sex crimes had nowhere to go to relieve their intense feelings of shock, guilt, terror, and rage; to discuss their dreads and anxieties with a sympathetic listener; or to find help in coping with the strange new problems engendered by a rape (how to get medical help, whether to report to the police, whether to prosecute an assailant, how to act in court, how to tell one's family and husband). Too many social institutions and personnel, as we have seen, are cold and unsympathetic; often they further traumatize the victim. Relatives and friends are frequently horrified, fearful, and disapproving of the victim, blaming her for the attack and the "shame" she has brought on her family. Lawyers and courts have been overwhelmingly judgmental and rejecting. There was literally no place for most victims to turn for help.

This situation has changed dramatically in many areas, thanks primarily to the reborn women's movement. Early in the 1970s, rape crisis centers began springing up in a few large cities and university centers where sex assaults were widespread. Initially, many centers were started by feminists and students who were rape victims themselves. Soon they were joined by other women activists from all walks of life. As women began meeting and exchanging experiences in consciousness-raising groups, they discovered that rape was not an isolated individual problem but a widespread—and growing—attack against women as a class.

In many groups, more than half of the women had suffered sexual assaults as children or adults (or both), but most had never before told anyone.

Women soon became bolder in speaking out, privately and publicly—sparked by such innovators as the New York Radical Feminists, who held a 1971 public "Speak-Out On Rape." Taboos against mentioning rape dissolved as brave women discussed their victimization in the press and on television and radio. While much of the media played up the bizarre and sensational aspects of rape—which unfortunately continues—solid information also filtered across the nation. Some reporters became serious supporters of the growing anti-rape movement, and local news outlets now often give constructive coverage in their communities.

A number of centers took the same name: Women Against Rape—WAR. These women truly felt themselves at war, in a battle for their lives and control of their own bodies and life-styles. Initially, the centers aimed at providing empathetic support for victims by hotline counseling or escort services to hospitals, police stations, and courts. The centers acted as buffers between victims and the sexist attitudes and behavior of public institutions. They gave women supportive alternatives, as well as a chance to develop self-determination. Many calls also came from women who had been sexually assaulted years before and now, for the first time, had found a sympathetic listener. In addition, self-defense and community crime prevention soon became important center programs.

In the past several years, many crisis centers have been able to move beyond basic services to offer a full range of group and individual counseling for victims and their families, including: medical, psychiatric, and legal referrals; self-defense workshops open to the public; sensitivity training for police, hospitals, and other groups; legal counseling; and a wide range of public information and legislative reform assistance. Churches, YWCAs, and other social organizations have started to join the new trend to provide services for sex victims. Today, rape crisis centers and task forces exist in every state in various stages of activity.

All crisis centers start out with one basic service—a telephone answering line staffed by volunteers who take calls from victims and sympathetically listen to their problems. Facts on local police, medical, and legal procedures are also gathered for the volunteers to give to victims. Many centers try to add an escort system to help victims through the difficult and often frightening treatment provided by police, hospitals, and courts. The more advanced centers have become active in court watching, in testifying for changes in legislation and institutional processes, and in demonstrating publicly for such changes. Educating the public about rape is also an important area of work.

Telephone counseling, which varies considerably in skill and sophistication from center to center, is also usually supplemented by emotional and psychological counseling offered to victims at the center itself. Some centers, especially those located in public hospitals and universities, are staffed by medical and psychological professionals as well as volunteers. Others use para-professionals. But many centers have to rely on the experiences and insights of their own members to offer emotional support and encouragement to victims, as well as specific advice on procedures and help in basics such as jobs, housing, child care, education. Consciousness-raising for victims on their general oppression as women is a large part of the more feminist centers.

Most centers encourage victims to become self-reliant as quickly as possible and to take an active part in the center's on-going work. Since few rape crisis centers are adequately funded, they depend on the volunteer help of new as well as old members for survival. The personnel turnover is constant and the drain heavy, since few workers are paid. Lack of money is the greatest handicap centers face in trying to provide adequate services.

Public or foundation support is rare. Most centers
scrape up meager operating funds through donations
from other women; sale of self-produced newspapers,
pamphlets, and books; and speaking and consulting
fees.

The training of volunteers varies considerably, according to a center's resources and philosophy. Many
use role-playing sessions, where an experienced worker
takes the part of the victim and "calls in" to the new
center member. Guidelines are placed near the telephone, and a veteran counselor is usually on hand for at
least the first few calls to help train the neophyte. Centers try to have more than one counselor on duty at a
time to give each other support and assistance. Many
use answering services at least part of the time, and calls
are referred to volunteers at their homes.

The rape victim quoted earlier was fortunate. She
lived in a city with an active rape crisis center whose
volunteers could give her immediate help and emotional support. Two women came to her home as prom-
ised and took her to the city general hospital, since she
did not want to see her own doctor. They stayed with
her though the medical examination and made certain
she was well treated and understood the procedures
and the need for return tests and checkups. They also
told her that the hospital would probably report her rape
to the police, although this did not mean she would
have to prosecute. By now the woman had calmed down
and was able to give the police a clear, detailed description of her assailant. Later she came to the crisis center
for psychological counseling. Her husband, contrary to
her fears, proved understanding and sympathetic.

Through all these strange and trying experiences, the
center women gave the victim constant emotional
warmth and concern. They encouraged her to express
her feelings and helped her to start dealing independently with her own problems. While the rapist was
never caught and the woman still lives with occasional
fear, she has resumed her normal way of life (although

she keeps the chain on her door at all times and is extremely suspicious of strangers). This victim has also volunteered for daytime telephone duty at the crisis center twice a week and has joined the local women's movement. Through this work and regular meetings with other victims, she has moved beyond "adjustment" to an active role in the struggle against rape.

Telephone counselors have developed many useful techniques, such as those summarized by Mary Ann Largen, Rape Task Force Coordinator of the National Organization for Women (NOW):

1. For the victim who has difficulty in communicating, the counselor can usually begin by asking her how she feels.

2. Simply listening and indicating that you understand are very important. The victim is, in essence, helping herself by trying to share her feelings of the moment.

3. Even if the caller says she is a relative or friend of the victim, remember it may be the victim herself. Some women cannot bring themselves to admit the assault immediately.

4. During the impact period, the victim is hypersensitive to any action or statement and often fears "pressure" from you even when she asks for advice.

5. Assure the victim she has not been singled out for attack, but that what happened to her has happened to thousands of other women.

6. Do not phrase questions so they inhibit the victim, such as, "Are you using a form of birth control?" Say instead, "Do you have any physical concerns right now?"

7. It helps the victim to be told that this experience will cause a disruption to her life for a while.

8. If she feels guilt because she failed to fight, tell her that fear inhibits most women or that survival is the most important thing—depending on the individual situation.

9. If she is alone, offer to call someone for her. If she does not want anyone called, assure her you will be available if she needs to call again.

One of the earliest and most successful rape crisis centers is California's Bay Area Women Against Rape (BAWAR) in Berkeley, founded in 1971. BAWAR members include students, working women, mothers, single, married and divorced women, and both rape victims and nonvictims. Many also belong to other feminist collectives, and BAWAR emphasizes the political and ideological aspects of rape. Spokeswoman Toby Perry Mickelson told us, "We discuss the definition of rape and oppression to prepare women for the phones and other BAWAR activities. Our training is done by women in the group. We do not support 'professional' approaches to dealing with rape."

Volunteers operate a twenty-four-hour switchboard and give immediate counseling, help in rap groups, or short-term problem-solving. They offer escort through the institutions, act as advocates, provide medical and legal information, and maintain lists of "alternative and straight" legal, medical, and emotional referrals. Some 100 to 150 calls come in monthly, half from victims and half from friends and families, the media, or people seeking information. Three-quarters of the victims phone soon after their assaults, mainly seeking advice, support, and sometimes places to stay. BAWAR community work includes organizing the University of California women at Berkeley to press for better campus facilities and training local police. "We are in constant demand for speaking engagements," reported Mickelson.

Another highly active group typifying the dedication and organizational talents of aroused feminists is the Women's Crisis Center of Ann Arbor, Michigan, which opened early in 1972. The center describes itself as a "nonprofit, free counseling service run for and by the women of the community. Trained peer telephone counselors are willing to talk with you about any problems you might have. The center has information about referrals, community resources, and women's community events, and organizes support groups for women." The Ann Arbor women told us: "Most of our members were not organization women, and thus our center is a place for women to learn these skills. The center provides twenty hours of empathy skill training, plus specialized training in rape counseling, problem pregnancy counseling, referral systems, and problem-solving."

Like other groups, the Crisis Center offers escort services for victims, as well as counseling, referrals, self-defense training, and community education programs. These Michigan women are also trying to maintain a rape emergency medical fund to pay the costs of a victim's medical exam, follow-up treatment, transportation, and abortion when needed. They want to have their own building, including a Safety Haven with living space for women and children fleeing from domestic violence. Through their Rape Education Committee, the members constantly research rape and survey victims in the Washtenaw County-Detroit area. The center's book, *How to Organize a Women's Crisis-Service Center,* is a valuable resource for all anti-rape groups.

Asked about community attitudes, the Ann Arbor women said that local support came slowly:

> *It took us two years to get any city government recognition of the problem. The police still can't get themselves together to coordinate with us. The reasons are partly bureaucracy, partly the fact that the police constantly lose their good cooperative staff because of lousy working conditions. Part of their negativism is also sheer male piggery.*

On the positive side, the center's free self-defense workshops and speeches given weekly to many different groups have created considerable community sup-

port. The center persuaded the mayor to set up a
Mayor's Task Force on Rape, which includes center
women; designed training programs on rape for Detroit
and Ann Arbor police recruits; and produced three vid-
eotapes which are shown all over Michigan. Funds for
such efforts come from donations; sale of publications;
speaker and workshop fees; and funds from city,
churches, and local foundations. But like almost all rape
centers, income is always inadequate to meet or expand
service needs.

On the East Coast, rape crisis centers in New York City
and Washington, D.C., also helped lead the way in fighting spreading sex crimes and educating their communities and public institutions. New York Women
Against Rape (NYWAR) is a grass-roots, self-supported
group of working women and students. In rape prevention, their work has gone beyond self-defense advice
given over the phone and in school talks. NYWAR
women, unlike many groups, go directly to areas where
recent attacks have occurred.

In one case, a young woman was raped by a sodomist
who was terrorizing other women in Brooklyn's East
Flatbush and Canarsie sections. NYWAR immediately
printed a leaflet with a police composite sketch and
written description of the assailant and his method of
operation, warnings on how to avoid him and protection precautions, and information on what to do if
raped. They distributed these leaflets to women shopping in the area. NYWAR members said they found "a
very concerned and appreciative public. Women asked
us questions about this rapist, and we told them as much
as we could. We consider this work extremely important." Stickers have also been placed around the city,
and stories about the center in magazines and newspapers and on radio and TV have helped advertise its
existence.

NYWAR workers cooperate with New York's Special
Rape Analysis Unit run by city policewomen, although
they are completely autonomous and do not hesitate to

criticize police tactics. These women also provide courtwatchers to accompany victims through their court proceedings and give legal advice and moral support. They found that going to rape trials made defense attorneys and judges much less cavalier in casting aspersions on the victim's sexual habits and mental stability. NYWAR has demonstrated against unfair court procedures, and they organize women to fill the courtroom whenever they learn of a serious miscarriage of justice in a sex case.

The Washington, D.C., Rape Crisis Center served as a catalyst for the formation of many other groups by producing an early handbook, *How to Start a Rape Crisis Center*. This manual offers guidelines and sample research forms on all aspects of rape, and has been widely read and used by other women throughout the nation. The center has suffered, like most centers, from a lack of funds and a high turnover of transient volunteers. Daytime staffing has been difficult, but the growing women's movement in Washington has strengthened the center's efforts as several organizations started rape task forces to change conditions in the metropolitan region's police, medical, and legal services. In addition, a well-supported women's center and hotline at the nearby University of Maryland offer a model of campus students and professionals working together in a college anti-rape team. By 1974 a Washington Feminist Alliance Against Rape sought to provide liaison for these different groups. In New York, the Women's Anti-Rape Coalition also acted as an umbrella group.

A recent trend is for women to set up crisis centers in their community hospitals, where answering services and professional medical and psychological personnel are always available to help rape victims. Sometimes the hospitals themselves take the initiative, but usually they are prodded by local women's groups. One of the country's earliest and best-supported groups is Philadelphia's Women Organized Against Rape (WOAR), which became active in mid-1973. A twenty-four-hour hotline was established in the emergency room of Philadelphia General Hospital, and several foundations, as well as the federal government, provided operating funds. Unlike many rape centers, WOAR acts within the existing social system, an approach containing advantages and disadvantages. Assets include more stable funding, personnel, and specific services. As WOAR's Jody Pinto put it, "We can't ignore the institutions. They're here to stay, and the basic methods they use are functional. The problem is the administrators' level of consciousness." But some women see disadvantages in the loss of operating independence and self-reliance; the use of nonfeminist professionals; and the danger of being co-opted by old-line, male-oriented institutions.

WOAR's guidelines on crisis intervention can be useful to all centers:

Not all calls have to end with a referral or answer. You can help just by being there to listen and empathize, by letting [the victim] know she is not alone and that her feelings are often realistic. Don't be afraid to take time to think about what to do. You can always ask to call back or for time to find the needed information. Your best tool with any caller is your own sense of caring and wanting to help, and she will feel this. It is as important to realize that you too have feelings and they can be drained. Be open about your feelings with colleagues; share experiences and failures. This will help you understand your reactions, find new ways of dealing with situations, and realize that often there are no answers and you did everything you could. Most of the time you will find yourself helping and growing.

Other pioneers among today's widespread rape crisis centers, now numbering more than a hundred, include: Chicago Women Against Rape (C-WAR); the Rape

Counseling Center established by the Neighborhood Involvement Program (NIP) of Minneapolis, Minnesota (a church founded and funded group); the Rhode Island Rape Crisis Center in Providence; the Roanoke Rape Crisis and Information Line in Roanoke, Virginia; the Boston Area Rape Crisis Center at the Cambridge Women's Center; the Rape Counseling Team (RCT) of the Boulder County, Colorado, Mental Health Center; the Rape Crisis Center of New Mexico at the University of New Mexico's Women's Center in Albuquerque; the Tallahassee Rape Crisis Service at Florida State University; Sacramento Women Against Rape (SWAR); and the Seattle, Washington, Rape Reduction Project, which includes the Rape Relief Program of the University of Washington YWCA and the Sexual Assault Center of Harborview Medical Center.[1]

Community responses vary greatly, from general indifference to active concern and support. In Providence, Rhode Island, for example, center coordinator Jan Gray reports the use of "excellent community resources." Says Gray:

The Attorney General's office is very helpful and provides a woman attorney to give legal advice to us and to victims without any involvement. We have professional counselors always available. We can pay them for a first visit with a victim. Planned Parenthood and Women's and Infants' Hospital provide excellent confidential medical treatment and we direct people to these facilities whenever possible. The community in general is very supportive.

Seattle claims to have the most comprehensive anti-rape program in the United States. Its publicly financed Rape Reduction Project offers a wide range of services

[1] A regularly updated list of centers is available in the *Women's Rights Almanac*, Nancy Gager, editor (Harper & Row, New York).

closely linked to the Seattle Police, the King County Prosecutor's Office, and Harborview Medical Center. The Project, a key part of the City's Plan for Criminal Justice, aims at increasing victim willingness to report and prosecute rape offenses. The two community operating agencies—the University YWCA Rape Relief Program and the Harborview Sexual Assault Center —focus on five main goals: medical and support services; information, referral and advocacy; third-party reporting of sex crimes when the victim does not want to go personally to the police; model procedures; and public information and education.

Roxanne Park of Rape Relief pointed out an important innovative aspect of their work:

> We are trying to get more Third World women involved as advocates so we can relate better to minority victims and encourage more minority women to report rapes. Right now, few do report assaults. We have employed a student as a Third World advocate to speak in local housing projects and community centers. She will also train other minority women as advocates.

Centers themselves differ widely on the need for participants to be aware feminists. At Albuquerque's Center, according to coordinator Gail-Dorine Vison:

> We do not consider feminism essential for a woman to be a good volunteer, but working for a Rape Crisis Center tends to turn women into feminists. Some volunteers are university students; others are Air Force housewives, secretaries, and businesswomen. Our basic philosophical agreement is that women have a right to their own bodies.

This agreement is actually a basic tenet of all feminist schools of thought, although women who follow this idea may shrink from the label of "feminist."

Some Centers, such as Sacramento Women Against Rape (SWAR), actively train their workers in feminist principles and techniques. As SWAR member Ruth Sample describes their specific instruction:

> Our counselors are required to have a feminist viewpoint of rape, and to facilitate this they must read "Politics of Rape," "Stop Rape," "Rape and Rape Laws: Sexism in Society and Law" (1973 California Law Review), Our Bodies, Ourselves, "Sex Codes of California," and the SWAR Crisis Counselor Handbook. Workshops are given on first-aid, self-help examination, and self-defense; and counselors do role-playing and attend orientation meetings. Counselors work as trainees with an experienced advocate, and at the end of this period are interviewed by a board and the findings are discussed with them.

The continuing growth of rape crisis centers in this country is an essential impetus for change in the rape situation. As we have seen, these centers take many forms and work according to different philosophies. All, however, offer—or try to offer—basic counseling, escort, self-defense, and public information services. Three general types of centers are now in operation: self-supporting centers of feminists to whom ideology and autonomy must underlie the social services they provide; feminist-oriented groups willing to work within established systems; and centers founded and run by professionals within hospitals, churches, and other established organizations. Considerable overlapping occurs among and within these groups, with feminists becoming more willing to work with the male-dominated social system, and establishment-supported groups becoming more feminist. In the still scattered and inadequate struggle against America's ubiquitous sex crimes, all direct-action centers and supportive groups and individuals are vitally needed.

Unfortunately, most federal and state funding sources

have been spending the bulk of their anti-rape budgets on study rather than action programs. While the Law Enforcement Assistance Administration (LEAA, part of the Justice Department) increased its sex crimes funding due to criticism generated by the women's movement, much is siphoned away from the crisis centers and into poor and often trivial research by nonfeminist agencies and private profit-making groups. With the surge of popular interest in rape, institutions have moved in to compete for the limited funds available for community services. Often the slim lifeline of rape crisis centers has been squeezed out, and the highly developed expertness of women's groups is frequently overlooked in favor of those with establishment credentials. The potential effectiveness of women's centers is severely limited by such competition for service funds and by the shortsightedness of those who administer these budgets.

A second major catalyst for change in recent years has been the activities of the National Organization for Women (NOW), whose membership is expanding in every state. Under the dynamic leadership of national coordinator Mary Ann Largen, NOW Rape Task Forces have leaped from 15 in early 1973 to more than 200 by 1975, working for local and national reform from Maine to Hawaii. These groups are increasingly spreading out from the large urban areas into isolated Northwestern regions and small, conservative communities in the deep South, rural as well as suburban.

NOW created the first major organizational effort to deal with rape problems from a national perspective. Task Force goals include just and humane treatment of victims, as well as basic institutional reforms and innovations in handling sex offenses. With the establishment of comprehensive grass-roots structures throughout the country, NOW members can provide cohesion and united strength to achieve aims both locally and nationally. NOW Task Forces have also taken a leading role in forming statewide coalitions among different groups, probably the greatest hope for faster, significant progress.

NOW groups are putting five major programs into effect:

1. *Crisis intervention:* NOW works to assure the availability of victim support services in all communities, as well as for institutional reform in procedures and responses to victims.

2. *Investigation:* NOW's National Rape Task Force has developed an investigative kit of detailed questionnaires and instructions for chapter use in assessing local police, hospital, and court systems. Similarly, a legislative kit helps the state task forces effect legislative reform.

3. *Legislation:* On the state level, NOW tries to eliminate inequities in rape laws through public education, lobbying, and coalition with other groups. On the federal level, NOW lobbies for Congressional recognition of rape's national impact; for increased funding of rape-related projects; and for reforms in federal programs and spending to meet the needs of women.

4. *Prevention/self-defense:* NOW evaluates current self-defense programs, reviews self-defense literature and films, and works to have self-defense courses included in schools and other community agencies.

5. *Public education:* All these goals are met in part through public education activities. Locally, NOW chapters hold special community programs on rape, speakers bureaus, workshops, and symposiums. Good media coverage of the issues is also sought, and task force members monitor this reporting.

In addition, by 1975 the National Rape Task Force was working with the FBI's Uniform Crime Reporting Division to draft a national sex offenses survey. This innovative research aims to provide new statistical data to help resolve some long unanswered questions about assailants and victims and to develop better prevention and control programs.

In the important and controversial area of self-defense, NOW National Rape Task Force member Alyce McAddam formed a Self-Defense Committee to help set up programs nationally. As McAddam summarizes the different functions of self-defense training:

> *It serves as a means for women to get in touch with their bodies. It provides women with an opportunity to gain strength and improve their general health. It increases their physical confidence, which, in turn, creates overall confidence in themselves. And, the obvious, it allows us to gain more control over our lives by having a range of options from which to choose when we are being hassled by someone.*

NOW also warns women against programs which may actually harm women by selling misleading advice. Many women are outraged by carnival-style performers ostensibly "educating the public," such as the sensational, self-appointed rape "expert" Fred Storaska. Storaska, who actually denigrates women, has made highly profitable tours of campuses and the TV circuit, produced a book and a high-priced film, set up a private official-sounding organization called the National Organization for Prevention of Rape and Assault, and applied for tax exemption for his "Fred Storaska Foundation." Women who have called NOPRA's advertised, toll-free number for assistance tell us of repeated frustrations in getting aid. Such enterprises are not only of questionable value to rape victims, but may influence naive women into following potentially dangerous or inapplicable advice, such as Storaska's instructions to "emanate humility"—and if that does not work, to gouge out eyeballs and squeeze testicles. *There are no*

blanket rules on how women should act under attack.
Some women have successfully fought or frightened off
rapists by pretending acquiescence or by assertive behavior. Others have only provoked their assailants into
more savage assaults and even murder. Some rapists are
sexually excited or enraged when victims resist.

Basic to the problem of women's self-defense is the
psychological and physical passivity inculcated in
most American females. Thus while self-confident
women (unskilled as well as skilled in physical techniques) may cope effectively with would-be attackers, other women—even some who have studied self-
defense—may collapse emotionally or freeze when attacked. Therefore assertiveness training and sound
self-defense courses should be not only available but
required at all school levels, and they should also be
open to older women. Feminist groups are trying to fill
the desperate lack in self-defense knowledge for
women, but as in all their efforts, they are too few and
have too little support to meet the present need.

With or without such training, however, all females
can take basic daily precautions to help prevent their
being sexually attacked. Increasing numbers of police
departments and other public groups are disseminating
such precautions, as are the women's centers and the
media.

The following precautions, summarized from many
sources, can serve as a checklist and regular safety re-
minders. Women may want to add their own particular
precautions, depending on locale and circumstances.

—Keep doors and windows locked with adequate
locks, especially a dead-bolt type.

—When leaving your apartment or house, even for a
few minutes, lock the doors. Leave on inside lights at
night, perhaps the TV or radio also. During vacations,
stop newspaper deliveries. Have a neighbor pick up
your mail and check your house periodically.

—Always have a chain on the door before opening at night or even during the day. If alone at night and expecting no one, consider carefully whether to answer the door at all.

—Make sure entranceways are well lit.

—Keep outdoor house lights on at night. Keep blinds, shades, or curtains completely closed.

—In apartments, make sure the intercom is working.

—Always keep your car doors locked. Check the back seat befoι e getting in.

—Avoid dangerous, isolated, ill-lighted areas, both on foot and in cars.

—Have your key ready for your door, and be alert. Be prepared to scream or run to a neighbor for help.

—If a door or window has been forced or broken in your absence, do not enter or call out. Leave silently, call the police from a neighbor's phone, and wait outside until they arrive.

—If attacked in an elevator, press the emergency button and as many floor buttons as possible.

—If attacked in a hallway, scream *fire!*

—Know the route home from work, school, and friends' houses. Note stores that stay open late, buildings with doormen, police and fire stations. Be aware of dangerous areas, alleys and unlighted parts of the street, and avoid them whenever possible.

—If you live alone in a high-crime area, use only your first initial, not full name, on your door, mailbox, and phone listing.

—Always ask service men, repairmen and deliverymen for identification before you open the door.

—Don't let a stranger use your phone. In an emergency, keep him outside and make the call for him.

—At work avoid deserted or poorly lighted stairwells. Check for suspicious persons around elevators.

—Wear clothing and shoes which allow free movement—no clogs. When in danger, yell FIRE rather than HELP or RAPE—it gets a better response.

—When walking in a strange or potentially danger-ous area, take one or more friends; "safety in numbers" is a wise adage for avoiding rape.

—Carry a whistle for quick use (a majority of women who ward off attackers use only noise).

—If a car starts following you, run in the opposite direction and scream.

—If you suspect you are being followed, look quickly for a safe place—any inhabited or lighted area. Run quickly, as fast as you can, yelling all the way. If you make it to a lighted house, act fast—ring the bell, bang on the door, even break a glass if you have to—your life may be at stake.

—If you can't escape, try to psych out your would-be rapist. Some women have talked their way out of rape. Stay as calm as possible and act as strong and unintimi-dated as you can. You can also try acting crazy, fainting, or claim a contagious disease.

—Actually fighting back can be dangerous unless you are well trained. A knee in the groin is not as easy or effective as often claimed. But if the man isn't armed, bigger, or a maniac, a struggle may work. Remember, a rapist always expects a passive victim, so any effort may surprise and unnerve him. Don't ever be reluctant to hurt him if you can. But screaming and running, if possible, are still two of the best defenses. An instant, unexpected blow may give you time to escape. The use of weapons also depends on your skill, experience, facility, and the rapist's power of disarming you or retaliating. It is impossible to give general advice on this. Each woman must make her own decision whether to submit or resist and perhaps endanger her life further.

—If you have children, warn them against riding with and opening doors to strangers or letting telephone callers know you are out. Acquaint them with the list on pages 62-63. Try to explain precautions calmly and clearly without frightening the child. If you have any reason to think that male friends—or even relatives

—might become sexual aggressors toward your children, don't *hesitate* to take action and seek help.

Whatever you do and whatever happens, always remember that your body belongs to you alone. You have a right to your own body, and a right to defend it in any way you can.

9
AN END TO RAPE?
TOWARD A MORE
HUMAN SOCIETY

There is no difference between being raped
and being run over by a truck
except that afterward men ask you if you
enjoyed it. . . .

There is no difference between being raped
and going head first through a windshield
except that afterward you are afraid
not of cars
but of half the human race.
> —Marge Piercy, Living in the Open

It is society that needs to be rehabilitated, not just the person
guilty of an actual physical sexual assault.
> —Women's Crisis Center, Ann Arbor, Michigan

In the six years since we first began to examine rape, its victims, assailants, and the groups responsible for dealing with both, we have found several fundamental facts:

1. Sex offenses constitute the fastest-growing crime of violence against people in this country, and nearly all victims are female. In some areas, rape has reached crisis proportions. While the vast majority of rapes are not reported to authorities, experts estimate that each year as many as half a million women and children are sexually assaulted.

2. The social institutions responsible for handling and reducing rape—police, hospitals, and courts—are

279

for the most part doing an inadequate job in treating rape victims and in arresting, prosecuting, and rehabilitating sex criminals. Some hopeful changes are occurring, thanks primarily to the growing women's movement and political feminists. But by and large, America's police, hospital personnel, and court systems exhibit a cultural, behavioral, and psychological sexism that condones and even encourages rape.

3. Any solution to rape is complex and must involve a multifaceted approach. Basic to all reforms is a change in attitudes toward the female half of the population and in the ways in which men, ordinary citizens as well as rapists, intimidate and oppress women. Rape is not an isolated phenomenon of "sick" males, but rather an inevitable part of the entire social matrix which denigrates women—psychologically, physically, economically, and politically—and which still tends to regard females as male "property." As long as our society is divided between men as the wielders of power and women as a largely powerless caste, sex offenses against females will continue to be a prerogative of the ruling class. Thus basic changes in the current situation rest upon basic changes in each individual and in society as a whole. Until America becomes humanistic toward all its citizens—and humanism by definition includes feminism, or the full equality of women—there can be no lasting or widespread change.

Our overall outlook is optimistic, since women's struggle for justice is making some inroads. Rape crisis centers are mushrooming across the country and have sparked significant reforms. Rape is no longer the tabooed subject it was even a few years ago. The mass media are helping to alter attitudes toward rape and its victims, even while the sex and violence they often market perpetuate dangerous mythology.

The rape victim, who for so long has been either ignored or treated as a sensational and scandalous outcast, is slowly being recognized as an individual who deserves the most sympathetic help society can offer. Feminists have from the beginning doggedly worked for the needs of rape victims, and these are beginning to be met. Victims' basic rights need support from all social agencies. These rights include:

—To be treated with dignity and respect during questioning.

—To be given free medical and psychological treatment by sympathetic, sensitive, and skilled personnel.

—To be informed about preventive medication and given a choice of medical alternatives, including a therapeutic abortion.

—To have access to emotional support resources, such as trained crisis center workers.

—To have rape defined as sex assaults on *any* part of the body (female or male) including oral and anal penetration.

—To be given responsible, expert, thorough, and sensitive police treatment and investigation.

—To be educated about legal procedures and her role as a witness for the state.

—To have personal privacy throughout all procedures and to have her prior sexual experience inadmissible in court.

—To be considered a credible witness equal to one in any other crime, with the corroboration requirement dropped.

—To have sexual relations with her spouse without violence or coercion (i.e., eliminate the husband/wife exclusion from rape laws).

—To financial compensation by state and/or federal agencies as has been recommended for victims of other crimes.

—To be advised about the possibility of pursuing a civil case.

In previous chapters we explored how the rights of rape victims are violated by the very social institutions set up to protect our women and child victims. It seems useful to review the major steps which these institutions should take to reduce both the incidence of rape and the trauma to victims. To reemphasize: there are no easy answers, no shortcuts to end this corrosive problem. The solutions are multileveled and interlocked. The essential key, we believe, is a change in attitudes.

Meanwhile, specific behavior can be changed more rapidly than institutions. Behavioral changes themselves produce attitudinal changes as people learn new methods of responding to old problems. The widening of suffrage and economic opportunities open to women and racial minorities have amply demonstrated this. When police, hospitals, courts, legislatures, and ordinary citizens accept the fact that *rape can happen to anyone and can be committed by almost all men* and that they themselves are part of the social context which encourages or discourages rape, only then will part of the battle be won.

Regarding the *police,* who are primarily charged with controlling crime and apprehending criminals, we have seen how their prejudicial attitudes toward women often impede investigative functions. Sensitivity training, as well as better techniques, are essential to increase police efficiency and to change their negative impact upon rape victims. As police attitudes and behavior change, more victims will come forward to report assaults. This change is vital if sexual crimes are ever to be controlled and reduced.

In the *medical and psychological* area, much improvement in support services is necessary if victims are to be healed in both body and mind. All health personnel—doctors, nurses, psychologists, psychiatrists, social workers, paraprofessionals—need basic training in dealing with rape victims. Sensitive, sympathetic attitudes are essential in medical treatment. In addition, medical techniques for the gathering of evidentiary material must be improved. Empathetic emotional support for all sex assault victims—no matter what their age—is an essential part of rape reform. *Rape crisis centers* have made important contributions in this area, and now public institutions and mental health professionals are offering more support, often in conjunction with the centers. But limited funding for hospitals and centers still seriously handicaps these efforts.

Our *legal system* also needs overhauling in many aspects if victims—and rapists—are to receive justice and sex crimes are to be diminished. At present too many lawyers, judges, and juries operate according to ingrained prejudicial attitudes and outmoded procedures. While some state legislatures have done away with the inequitable corroboration restriction, other practices and procedures need to be changed. Again, fundamental to improvement are changes in the attitudes of the people who make and administer the law.

The reduction and eventual elimination of sex crimes depends, in the last analysis, on whether we can learn to recognize and rehabilitate the *rapists* in our communities. To date, the outlook is not hopeful. Far too little has been done to develop helpful, sound diagnoses and treatments for sex offenders. The paucity of useful research and the lack of treatment centers in prisons and mental hospitals mean that few assailants receive real help.

Again, we find the same basic problem underlying the lack of progress: systems are designed and administered largely by male-oriented professionals who have absorbed the sexist cultural prejudices which perpetuate rape. In addition to the very limited sample of rapists they are able to examine (due to ineffective reporting and legal procedures), the systems charged with handling rapists are not sufficiently funded to develop sophisticated, coordinated, and well-staffed programs of treatment, research, and rehabilitation.

All these problems come to the fact that, at present, our society, and the men who control its public policies, are still not concerned enough about the problem of rape. The core of the problem is indicated in Senator

Charles McC. Mathias's introduction to this book: while
some attitudes are changing, we still have a long way to
go. The Mathias provision for a national rape center to
help educate the public and administrative agencies is
an important step in this direction. But it is indicative of
the lack of Congressional sensitivity—which reflects to
a large degree the insensitivity of the nation—that the
authorized funding for the rape center is meager. The
latest House of Representative revision for the two-year
program sets the figure at $17,000,000—far less than it
costs to build a pair of F-15 fighter planes. Even this
authorization could be further reduced during Congressional appropriation battles.

Another ray of hope, however, is in the recent attention given to the possibility of *compensation* for rape
victims.

At least thirteen states (including California, Illinois,
New York, Massachusetts, Nevada, Maryland, Hawaii,
and Washington) now have laws providing payments to
the victims of crime, and Congress has been considering federal compensation bills for at least five years.
Yet most rape victims—indeed, the public at large—
seem unaware of the possibilities of compensation.

Obviously, money can never restore the personal security or psychological well-being lost when one is victimized, but monetary recompense could go part way
toward recognizing public responsibility for crimes of
violence. As Senate Majority Leader Mike Mansfield
said in introducing his federal bill in 1971 (reported in
U.S. News & World Report that April): "Society has
failed miserably in its obligation to the victim of crime.
. . . When the protection of society is not sufficient to
prevent a person from being victimized, society then
has the obligation to compensate the victim for that
failure of protection." Mansfield's bill, and others
which followed, were usually opposed on financial
grounds. As one unidentified opponent said: "Many
victims are too embarrassed to report rape. But if it
becomes *worth* several thousand dollars, the victim may

not mind having her name in the newspapers." (Italics added.)

But according to Illinois attorney Saul Wexler, who handles compensation cases in the state's attorney general's office: "The innocent victim often suffers more than the assailant who is sent to prison." This is especially true of the sex assault victim, who rarely comes forward to claim her due, even in the few states where it might be available. Victim compensation statutes do not usually cover "pain and suffering," nor do they honor claims unless the victim is considered "innocent"—in no way responsible for the assailant's crime. In cases where the jury acquits a defendant, though the rape victim may have suffered grievous injury, there is probably no way for her to claim compensation. His acquittal is "proof" of her lack of "innocence." In general, attacks by lovers or family members are excluded from most compensatory legislation; thus a woman raped by her fiancé, father, uncle, or brother would be ineligible. In most states, the victim's own insurance claims are deducted first, and benefits can range from a few thousand dollars to California's $23,000.

Despite dire predictions to the contrary, few crime victims come forward to assert a claim. Apparently the general public is not aware of compensation legislation; sex assault victims should seek information as to the laws in their states. It might even be faster than working through other channels; *vide* the gang rape victim in Kansas—repeatedly raped, sodomized, and publicly beaten by some eighteen men—who had to wait five years to recover damages under a local "mob action" statute.

Compensation can provide relief from the usual, long, frustrating judicial process, even though in some states it may depend upon the victim's cooperating with law enforcement officials, police, and prosecutors. But sex assault victims can then actively assist in apprehending and prosecuting rapists. Every state should offer such compensatory allowance, and Congress needs to share the responsibility for crime by passing and swiftly allocating funds for federal legislation.

The concept of compensation for victims is ancient, probably dating back to 1700 B.C. Under King Hammurabi's famous Babylonian code, citizens who had been robbed were supposed to be given public recompense. This system aimed at justice for the poor, the orphaned, and the widowed, but it incorporated the principle of an eye for an eye and a tooth for a tooth: the criminal, as punishment received the injury he had inflicted upon his victim. But the innocent also suffered; when a house fell and killed the son of the householder, the builder suffered the loss of his son, and a totally innocent human being was condemned to die. Anglo-Saxon laws evolved differently, incorporating the concept that crime is an offense against society instead of an individual. Control in our system was thus shifted to punishment of the criminal. Given the special plight of the rape victim—she is often poor, a member of a minority, inexperienced, and fearful—it is time to return to the ancient concern for those who have been injured.

The *prevention* of sex crimes is another area which has received too little public attention and action until recently. Crisis centers are working in their communities to educate the public and local institutions about the many precautions which can, and should, be taken to reduce rape. *Education* about sex assaults and assailants is an essential ingredient of all rape prevention. (This also is basic in the Mathias provision.) If state, county, city, and town authorities would launch continuous campaigns to prevent sex assaults, enormous changes could be effected. Such campaigns could include widespread dissemination of pamphlets with precautions, medical advice, and information about community resources for victims, to be given away in schools, libraries, churches, and stores; free *self-defense* training for girls and women through schools and adult education courses; rape warnings, including descriptions of assailants, hotline telephone numbers and recommended medical procedures regularly flashed on radio and television; more street lights in high-rape neighborhoods and shopping areas; and citizens' street call boxes to police stations.

State and local rape commissions could be created both for intensive rape research and to provide a means of tapping the vast number of unreported rapes. For example, a team of female professionals could receive calls from victims who do not want to go to the police. These professionals would also give medical and mental health aid. Regular liaison is important among all community groups concerned with rape, both official and unofficial. Local women's rape task forces and crisis centers could consult regularly with police, hospitals, courts, and legislatures, as well as conduct special publicly funded studies. The opening of *communication* channels and *coordination*, now seriously lacking, and the development of mutual trust among all official and community groups are vitally needed for a truly effective anti-rape campaign. And as always, rape must be seen and treated both by governments and individual citizens not as a silent, secret sexual crime, but as *an act of violence* directed specifically against females.

Rape as a Cultural Ideal

All through history, each culture has had its own conceptualization of rape, "idealized" in all its arts: painting, sculpture, literature, drama, dance, and film (as well as pornography). All through the centuries this idealized portrait has helped to shape the image of this crime. In Western cultures this portrait has been almost exclusively romantic with a total absence of pain or agony. The great rape paintings are indexed in art catalogs under "erotica," and the works of such great graphic artists as Rubens, Titian, Rembrandt, and others, which deal with the so-called "classic" rapes (the Sabines, Lucrece, Europa, Philomela, the daughters of Leucippus), show passion, excitement and even rapture, but no pain. (One eighteenth-century Zuccarelli version of the Europa rape can only be described as peacefully bucolic.) In one of the most famous Rubens paintings (the rape of Leucippus' daughters), there is even an enchanting little rosy cupid, helpfully hanging on to a horse's bridle while the rider does his dirty work. Rape is thus romantic, equated with love—with which it has nothing in common—and is divorced from its essential criminality.

The rape of the female is part of our universal heritage, a theme of poetic dimension as common to literature and art as war—though in rape, victors and victims never change identities. The conquerors are always men; the conquered are nearly always women. Art historians and literary critics, like the rest of our culture, explain away this romanticization of a grisly criminal theme by insisting that females really are "enjoying" it, or that they in some way "provoked" the attack and therefore "deserved" what they got.

What has also been absent in all these graphic portrayals of the conquest is the savagery with which it is accomplished. Today, that savagery is surfacing, especially in films, short stories, and novels. The savagery depicted in such film atrocities as *Straw Dogs* and *A Clockwork Orange* is part of the twentieth-century romantic image. The novel *A Clockwork Orange*, by the way, could be read as an attack on violence (even in the film a psychiatrist voices the theme that psychologically and morally healthy people find violence unbearable); but this pronunciamento is lost in director Kubrick's obsession with cruelty and brutality. In *Straw Dogs*, Sam Peckinpah's lust for violence all but wipes out the effect of the gang rape in the hideous blood bath which follows.

When sensitive persons, men as well as women, ask if anyone is shocked any more at such distorted portraits of rape, the answer is clearly yes. Anyone aware of women as individual entities, as persons, and as human beings with rights and the capacity for choices is shocked. And when more women wake up to the way in which we are used in the media of violence—always as victims, always degraded and demeaned—perhaps we will begin to understand the devastating effect of such material upon the public at large. For violence brutalizes the beholder as well as the actor; children of child batterers tend to batter their own children; men steeped in sexual violence tend to regard females as "things," disembodied four-letter words beginning with "c."

Unfortunately, too many women themselves accept this dangerous evaluation, often amending the external pressure with subjective disparagement and guilt. "I've been raped; I was raped at fifteen. It's no big deal," a black college student told us not long ago. "What's all the fuss about?" And a middle-aged friend, mother of three, is defensive about her husband's devotion to pornography: "Jack just loves his *Playboy* calendar. Who am I to say he can't hang his bunnies in the bathroom?" or "Phil adores all those big-breasted naked women magazines. He can't help if I'm flat chested, can he?" or "I figure if he's bringing all that porn stuff into the house at least he's doing it at home. After all, a man's home is his castle. He ought to be able to do what he likes."

None of these women has any identification with other women; none realizes that the degradation of a single female affects us all. Women's acceptance of demeaning sexuality—and only the woman herself can judge whether her situation *is* in that category—let alone their participation in it as performers, furthers the adoption of false standards by society at large. The ideal that *all* women, at *all* times, are ready to be "taken" sexually, by any and all takers (as rapists believe), is simply not true. This is male fantasy—or masculine ambition gone berserk, a patriarchal dreamland.

This attitude is prevalent in many contemporary films and books. Here it is presented by Irving Wallace, author of many bestsellers, in one of his heroes' flights of fancy: "She was just tits and ass and wanting it just like you wanted it. This was the big equalizer, wanting it and doing it, and nothing else counting more. The greatest leveler on earth, the greatest equality maker in the world was a man's cock. A good stiff eight inches did more to promote social justice than all the big brains in the world."

Such male attitudes are clearly illustrated in one of Wallace's novels, in which the intellectual writer-organizer of a gang rape, described on the book jacket as a "gentle idealist" and by the author, through his heroine, as "the dreamer," is allowed to go free by the movie star victim because "to transform this dark interlude in her life into a credibly romantic and plausible story that she could live with, the story must have a hero, even an anti-hero. . . . He and she had not been so different, after all." So, in order for women to live with male aggression, we must not only accept it but convert rape into "romance." If any more evidence were needed that we live in a patriarchy, this is it.

Once we believed that crime did not pay, that violent men were punished for their violence; today apparently that has changed. Through their stories and characterizations, writers such as Wallace perpetuate the fantasy that "intellectually" violent men, such as his "dreamer," should receive special dispensation because women need "heroes" and "romance." Women must wake up to the fact that *there are no heroes in rape.* There is no romance. There are only brutal, self-serving, and self-justifying male fantasies.

Rape is an atrocious crime, an act which violates a person's innermost physical and psychological being and can leave scars which may last a lifetime. Unlike victims of other crimes, the rape victim must prove she did not contribute to her assault. She is forced by society to pay for her victimization in humiliation and the loss of her self-image as a person. In court she has few of the legal protections accorded her assailant, although it is her credibility and reputation which are in effect on trial. Rape victims are considered guilty until proven innocent. Victims are denied their rights as humans by the attitudes of our society and institutions.

The statistics of rape, shocking as they are, fail to present a true picture of sex crimes against women and children in our society. Legal definitions are narrow and do not include the vast majority of sexual assaults against women, girls, and young children. Statistics can never reveal the countless ways in which every female's life is shaped by the persistent, inescapable threat of rape. Nor do they reveal the societal sexism perpetuating these crimes. And they ignore the prevailing misogyny entirely.

Rape is a crime which has thrived on misconceptions, prejudice, lies, indifference, and the past silence of victims. Today that silence is being broken, thanks to the courage and sacrifice of women acting alone and together. Women's voices are now being heard. They are determined to remain silent no longer.

APPENDIX

Sex Crime Report Forms

The following sample police report form for sex crimes (from Los Angeles) illustrates the sort of detailed information which should be routinely gathered by all departments on sex assailants and their *modus operandi*. Such compilations, if cross-indexed and computerized (at least by the larger departments) for inter- and intra-departmental use, can be of enormous assistance in apprehending sex criminals. The effectiveness of such forms, however, rests upon the attitudes, skills, and dedication of the police officers using them.

LOS ANGELES POLICE DEPARTMENT
SEX CRIME REPORT

☐ Shots Fired   ☐ Attempt

DR

PREMISES

13 Residence

01	SUSPECT'S
02	VICTIM'S
03	APT./PROJECT
04	HOTEL
05	MOTEL
07	SINGLE FAMILY
08	OTHER:

15 Miscellaneous

01	ALLEY
02	CARPORT
06	GARAGE
07	PARK
08	PARKING LOT
11	PED. OVERCROSSING
12	PED. TUNNEL
13	PLAYGROUND
14	SCHOOL
16	STREET
17	VACANT LOT
18	YARD
19	OTHER:
20	PUBLIC TOILET

11 Vehicle

01	SUSPECT'S
02	VICTIM'S
10	OTHER:

VICTIM'S NAME (LAST   FIRST   MIDDLE)

PHONES
RES.
BUS.

LOCATION OF OCCURRENCE   R.D.

TYPE OF CRIME

OCCURRED: MONTH   DAY   YEAR   DAY WEEK   TIME

REPORTED: MONTH   DAY   YEAR   TIME

VICT'S. SEX, DESCENT, AGE   VICT'S. CONDITION (NORMAL, HOSPITALIZED, ETC.)

JUV. VICT'S. BIRTHPLACE (CITY / STATE) & D.O.B.

INVESTIGATIVE DIVISION(S) & PERSON NOTIFIED

CONNECTED REPORTS – TYPE & DR. NO.

CODE: V–Victim   R–Person Reporting   W–Witness

V   Name & Phones Listed Above

	ADDRESS	CITY	PHONE Day Phone–X
RES.			
BUS.			
RES.			
BUS.			
RES.			
BUS.			

VEHICLE

LIC. NO.   STATE   MAKE/MODEL   MFG.   YEAR   TYPE   TOP – COLORS – BOTTOM

Modified	Body (CIRCLE IF APPL.)	Wheels	Windows (CIRCLE IF APPL.)
4 FRONT	4 DAMAGE 4 RIGHT	4 MAGS	4 DAMAGE 4 RIGHT 4 TINTED
2 REAR	2 SIDE 2 REAR	2 CHROME RIMS	2 SIDE 2 REAR 2 COVERED
1 OTHER	1 LEFT 1 FRONT	1 UNIQUE SIZE	1 LEFT 1 FRONT 1 DECAL / PLAQUE

FURTHER VEHICLE DESCRIPTION (INCLUDE INSIDE COLORS)

Upholstery	Interior	Exterior
4 UPHOLSTERY	4 STEREO TAPE	4 PAINTED INSCRP.
2 BUCKET SEATS	2 MIRROR ORNAM	2 STICKER/DECAL
1 HEADLINER	1 FLOOR SHIFT	1 RUST/PRIMER
(CIRCLE IF APPL.)	4 EQUIP. ADDED	4 VINYL TOP
4 CUSTOM	2 EQUIP. MISSING	2 DECORATIVE PAINT
2 TORN	1 UNIQUE ITEM	1 LEVEL ALTERED
1 COVER:OTHER		

SEX CRIME REPORT

Column headers: SEX | DESCENT | HAIR | EYES | HEIGHT | WEIGHT | AGE | CLOTHING

NAME & ADDRESS IF KNOWN: NAME, BKG. NO. & CHARGE IF ARRESTED.

SUSPECTS

PERSONAL ODDITIES

SUSP. NO. 1 2 3

300 Amputee
1 1 1 LEG
2 2 2 ARM
3 3 3 FOOT
4 4 4 HAND
5 5 5 EAR
6 6 6 FINGERS

301 Deformed
1 1 1 LEG
2 2 2 ARM
3 3 3 HAND
4 4 4 LIMP
5 5 5 FINGERS
6 6 6 BOWLEGGED

302 Tattoo
1 1 1 ARM
2 2 2 HAND
3 3 3 FINGERS
4 4 4 CHEST/NECK

303
1 1 1 PICTURES
2 2 2 DESIGNS

303 Tattoo (cont.)
3 3 3 NAMES
4 4 4 WORDS
5 5 5 INITIALS
6 6 6 PACHUCO

304 Facial Scars
1 1 1 CHEEK
2 2 2 CHIN
3 3 3 FOREHEAD
4 4 4 LIP
5 5 5 NOSE
6 6 6 EAR
7 7 7 EYEBROW

305 Facial Oddity
0 0 0 BIRTHMARKS
1 1 1 POCKMARKS
2 2 2 MOLES
3 3 3 FRECKLES
4 4 4 PIMPLES
5 5 5 LIPS - THICK
6 6 6 LIPS - THIN
7 7 7 CHIN - PROTRUDED
8 8 8 CHIN - RECEDES
9 9 9 HOLLOW CHEEK

307 Teeth
1 1 1 MISSING
2 2 2 GOLD
3 3 3 BROKEN
4 4 4 FALSE
5 5 5 STAIN/DECAY
6 6 6 PROTRUDING
7 7 7 IRREGULAR

308 Body Scars
1 1 1 ARM
2 2 2 HAND
3 3 3 WRIST
4 4 4 NECK
5 5 5 BURN
6 6 6 CHEST

309 Speech
0 0 0 IMPEDIMENT
1 1 1 ACCENT (U.S.)
2 2 2 ACCENT (OTHER)
3 3 3 LISPS
4 4 4 STUTTERS
5 5 5 HARE LIP
6 6 6 MUMBLES
7 7 7 RAPID
8 8 8 SOFT/LOW
9 9 9 REFINED

311 Eyes
1 1 1 MISSING
2 2 2 CROSSED
3 3 3 SUNGLASSES
4 4 4 GLASSES (PLAIN)
5 5 5 BULGING
6 6 6 SQUINT/BLINK
7 7 7 SLANTED

312 Hair Type
1 1 1 DYED
2 2 2 PROCESSED
3 3 3 WIG/TOUPEE
4 4 4 CREW CUT
5 5 5 BALD
6 6 6 AFRO
7 7 7 LONG
8 8 8 THIN/RECEDED
9 9 9 STRAIGHT

313
1 1 1 WAVY
2 2 2 BUSHY
3 3 3 CURLY

314 Facial Hair
1 1 1 MUST - CHINESE
2 2 2 GOATEE
3 3 3 BEARD - FULL
4 4 4 MUST - HEAVY
5 5 5 MUST - THIN
6 6 6 MUST - MEDIUM
7 7 7 BROWS - HEAVY
8 8 8 UNSHAVEN

315 Ears
1 1 1 CAULIFLOWER
2 2 2 PIERCED
3 3 3 PROTRUDING
4 4 4 CLOSE TO HEAD
5 5 5 LARGE
6 6 6 SMALL

316 Nose
1 1 1 CROOKED
2 2 2 HOOKED
3 3 3 UPTURNED
4 4 4 LONG
5 5 5 BROAD
6 6 6 FLAT
7 7 7 SMALL
8 8 8 THIN

317 Face
1 1 1 NEGRO W/CAUC. FEATURES
2 2 2 HI CHEEK BONE
3 3 3 LONG
4 4 4 BROAD
5 5 5 THIN
6 6 6 ROUND

318 Complexion
1 1 1 DARK
2 2 2 SALLOW
3 3 3 RUDDY
4 4 4 LIGHT/FAIR
5 5 5 MEDIUM

319 Other:
1 1 1

22 Initial Contact
06 BAR
08 INVITATION
11 PLACE OF ENTERTAINMENT
13 RESIDENCE
14 FORCED ENTRY
15 SUSPECT A PED.
16 SUSPECT A RELATIVE
18 VICTIM KNOWS SUSP.
17 SUSPECT IN VEH.
20 VICTIM A PED.
23 VICTIM IN VEH.

40 Weapon, Means
10 GUN
30 KNIFE
41 LIQUOR/DRUGS
28 BODILY FORCE
43 THREATS
03 MUTUAL CONSENT
70 OTHER/UNKNOWN:

CHECKED

SEX CRIME REPORT

Page ___ of ___   DR ___

23 Abnormal Acts

Code	
66	URINATION
52	DEFECATION
61	SADISM (PLEASURE FROM INFLICTING PAIN)
57	PUT OBJECT INTO VAGINA
55	SET FIRE
58	MASOCHISM (PLEASURE FROM HAVING PAIN INFLICTED)
65	PHOTOGRAPHED VICTIM
62	SODOMY
54	FETISHISM (EXCITED BY OBJECT -FOOT, HAIR, ETC.)
53	PORNOGRAPHY USED
51	TONGUE OR MOUTH TO ANUS
63	ASKED VICTIM TO COMMIT ABNORMAL ACT
56	PUT HAND INTO VAGINA
64	TALKED ABOUT BODY FUNCTION (SEMEN, ETC.)
59	MULTIPLE VICTIMS
60	OTHER UNUSUAL ACT:

23 288A Requested or 288A Forced

Code	
72	SUSPECT ON VICTIM
73	VICTIM ON SUSPECT

21 Type

Code	
21	CULT, RITUAL

22 Pretended To Be

Code	
41	GOD, SATAN, ETC.
31	POLICE
37	SEEKING SOMEONE
40	OTHER:

21 Statements

Code	
83	REMORSEFUL
84	EXTRAORDINARY
82	OBSCENE, PROFANE

24 Telephone

Code	
89	TORE FROM WALL
81	PULL/CUT/DIS-CONNECT WIRES
90	OTHER:

24 Suspect Wore

Code	
03	CLOTHES OF OPP. SEX
10	MASK, FACE COVER
04	UNUSUAL CLOTHES
07	NUDE
08	PARTLY NUDE

24 Lingerie Involved

Code	
41	CUT OR TORN
43	USED FOR MASTURBATION
44	OTHER:

24 Solicited/Offered

Code	
29	FOOD, DRINK (NOT LIQUOR), CANDY
36	RIDE
24	AMUSEMENT, GAME
25	ASSISTANCE
26	DIRECTIONS
34	MONEY
39	OTHER:

21 Masturbation

Code	
91	FORCED VICTIM TO MASTURBATE SELF
92	FORCED VICTIM TO MASTURBATE SUSP.
93	MASTURBATED SELF OR VICTIM

22 Victim Was

Code	
52	AGED, BLIND, CRIPPLED, ETC.

26 Theft Involved

Code	
00	

22 Shots Fired

Code	
90	

25 Force

Code	
54	HANDCUFFED
46	TIED TO OBJECT (BED, ETC.)
45	BOUND
47	BURNED VICTIM
49	COVERED VICTIM'S FACE
42	BIT
53	GAGGED
51	CUT, STABBED
52	WHIPPED (NOT WITH HANDS)
41	BRUTAL ASSAULT
50	COVER MOUTH WITH HANDS
65	THREATEN VICTIM'S FAMILY
48	CHOKED
55	HIT AFTER ACT
56	HIT DURING ACT
57	HIT PRIOR TO ACT
61	KIDNAPED
69	PULLED VICTIM'S HAIR
68	TWISTED ARM
66	TORE CLOTHES OFF VICTIM
43	BLINDFOLDED
70	OTHER:

22 Vehicle Involved

Code	
74	EXHIBIT SELF FROM VEHICLE
81	VICTIM PKG./GARAGING
83	OTHER:

26 Miscellaneous Sex Acts

Code	
30	RAPE OR ATTEMPT
29	OBSCENE, PROFANE WRITING
32	SIMULATED INTERCOURSE
36	UNABLE TO GET ERECTION
28	LOWERED PANTS/SHORTS (INDECENT EXPOSURE)
23	DESIRED TO SEE VICTIM'S GENITALS (CHILD MOLEST)
33	REACHED CLIMAX
21	MADE VICTIM TOUCH OWN GENITALS (CHILD MOLEST)
22	MADE VICTIM TOUCH SUSP'S. GENITALS (CHILD MOLEST)
31	HAD OBJECT OVER GENITALS (INDECENT EXPOSURE)
25	PUT FINGER IN VAGINA
24	HUGGED, PRESSED VICTIM (CHILD MOLEST)
26	KISSED VICTIM'S BODY
27	KISSED VICTIM'S FACE
34	TOUCH/FONDLE VICTIM'S BODY (CHILD MOLEST)
35	TOUCH/FONDLE VICTIM'S GENITALS (CHILD MOLEST)
37	OTHER:

25 Victim Forced To

Code	
11	DISROBE
19	OTHER:

TRADEMARKS

(1) IDENTIFY ADDITIONAL SUSPECTS ON A SECOND FACE SHEET. IDENTIFY ADDITIONAL WITNESSES. (2) RECONSTRUCT THE CRIME. (3) DESCRIBE PHYSICAL EVIDENCE-STATE LOCATION FOUND AND BY WHOM. GIVE DISPOSITION. (4) SUMMARIZE OTHER DETAILS RELATING TO CRIME. (5) INDICATE TIME AND LOCATION WHERE VICTIM AND WITNESSES CAN BE LOCATED BY DAY INVESTIGATORS IF NO AVAILABLE PHONE.

Graphs and Tables

Explanatory Note: **All data are taken from the Uniform Crime Reports, Department of Justice, Federal Bureau of Investigation, as issued. (Note: Uniform Crime Reports are usually published the year following; e.g., 1973 was issued in 1974)**

Two facts are worth noting from the Federal Bureau of investigation figures: over the seven-year period the rape rates were always highest in the West, and other violent crimes did not follow the same geographical distribution pattern over the same period. Increases in the rape rate may reflect increasing willingness of victims to report the crime and/or changes in statistical accounting within law enforcement areas.

1. Rape Rate (per 100,000 population) by U.S. Regions (1967–1973)

Regions: NE (Northeast); S (South); NC (Northcentral); W (West).

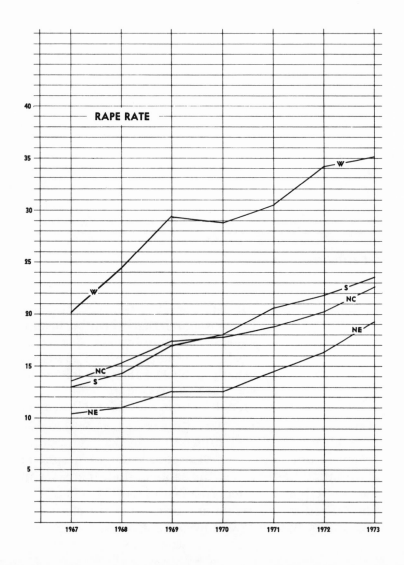

RAPE RATE

2. Total Violent Crime Rate (per 100,000 population) by U.S. Regions (1967–1973)

Violent crime = murder, rape, aggravated assault, and robbery. Regions: NE (Northeast); S (South); NC (North-central); W (West).

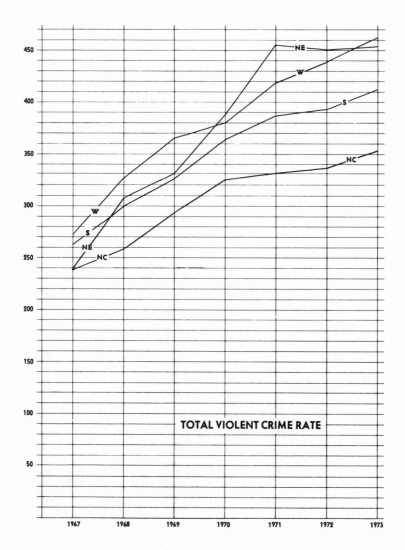

3. Total Aggravated Assault Rate (per 100,000 population) by U.S. Regions (1967–1973)

Aggravated Assault = assault involving severe bodily injury excluding rape, murder, and robbery.

Regions: NE (Northeast); S (South); NC (Northcentral); W (West).

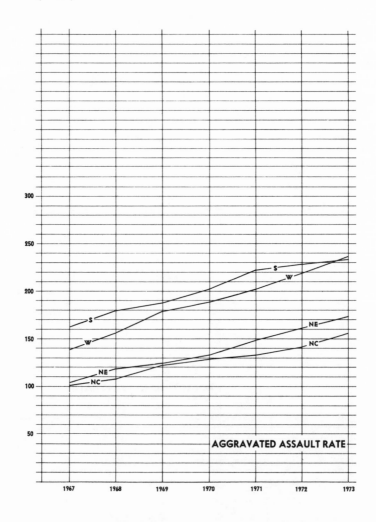

4. Rapes and Rape Convictions (1973)

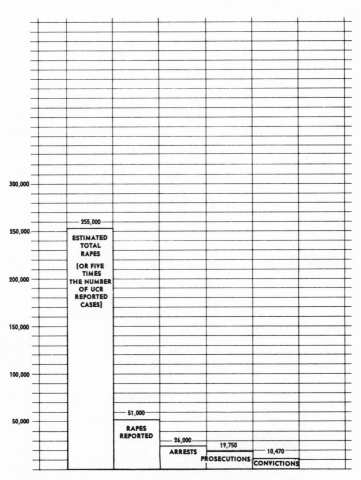

DATA FROM UCR 1973

5. **Rape Rates (per 100,000 population)—Top Ten in Metropolitan Cities (Standard Metropolitan Statistical Areas) with over 250,000 Population (1972–1973)**
Standard Metropolitan Statistical Areas: includes cities and suburban areas.

Number	1973	Rate
1	Memphis, Tennessee–Arkansas–Mississippi	64.6
2	Las Vegas, Nevada	62.2
3	Little Rock–North Little Rock, Arkansas	57.7
4	Albuquerque, New Mexico	57.0
5	Los Angeles–Long Beach, California	55.0
6	Jacksonville, Florida	52.9
7	Orlando, Florida	51.0
8	Denver–Boulder, Colorado	48.8
9	San Francisco–Oakland, California	44.9
10	Norfolk–Virginia Beach–Portsmouth, Virginia–North Carolina	44.7

Number	1972	Rate
1	Albuquerque, New Mexico	63.2
2	Los Angeles–Long Beach, California	56.0
3	Jacksonville, Florida	54.5
4	Colorado Springs, Colorado	53.1
5	Memphis, Tennessee–Arkansas–Mississippi	51.7
6	Denver–Boulder, Colorado	47.0
7	Little Rock–North Little Rock, Arkansas	46.0
8	Baton Rouge, Louisiana	45.5
9	San Francisco–Oakland, California	45.2
10	Las Vegas, Nevada	44.5

6. Rape Rates (per 100,000 population)—All Metropolitan Cities (Standard Metropolitan Statistical Areas) with over 2,000,000 Population (1973)
Standard Metropolitan Statistical Areas: includes cities and suburban areas.

Number	1973	Rate
1	Los Angeles–Long Beach, California	55.0
2	San Francisco–Oakland, California	44.9
3	Detroit, Michigan	43.2
4	New York, New York–New Jersey	38.9
5	Washington, District of Columbia–Maryland–Virginia	38.5
6	St. Louis, Missouri–Illinois	37.4
7	Baltimore, Maryland	34.4
8	Dallas–Fort Worth, Texas[1]	33.3
9	Houston, Texas	32.5
10	Chicago, Illinois	30.2
11	Cleveland, Ohio	27.1
12	Newark, New Jersey	26.1
13	Philadelphia, Pennsylvania–New Jersey	23.5
14	Minneapolis–St. Paul, Minnesota–Wisconsin	22.3
15	Boston, Massachusetts	19.6
16	Pittsburgh, Pennsylvania	16.0

[1]Estimated by combining separate figures for Dallas and Fort Worth.

(Continued)

6. Rape Rates (per 100,000 population)—All Metropolitan Cities (Standard Metropolitan Statistical Areas) with over 2,000,000 Population (1972)

Standard Metropolitan Statistical Areas: includes cities and suburban areas.

Number	1972	Rate
1	Los Angeles–Long Beach, California	56.0
2	San Francisco–Oakland, California	45.2
3	Washington, District of Columbia–Maryland–Virginia	42.0
4	New York, New York–New Jersey	37.0
5	St. Louis, Missouri–Illinois	34.5
6	Detroit, Michigan	33.1
7	Dallas–Fort Worth, Texas[1]	32.2
8	Baltimore, Maryland	31.4
9	Houston, Texas	30.1
10	Chicago, Illinois	28.5
11	Newark, New Jersey	28.5
12	Cleveland, Ohio	27.0
13	Minneapolis–St. Paul, Minnesota–Wisconsin	26.2
14	Philadelphia, Pennsylvania–New Jersey	19.9
15	Pittsburgh, Pennsylvania	19.1
16	Boston, Massachusetts	15.1

[1]Estimated by combining separate figures for Dallas and Fort Worth.

Bibliography

Books

Abrahamsen, David. *Our Violent Society.* New York: Funk and Wagnalls, 1970.
_____. *Who Are the Guilty?* New York: Grove Press, 1952.
Ahern, James F. *Police in Trouble: Our Frightening Crisis in Law Enforcement.* New York: Hawthorn Books, 1971.
Amir, Menachem. *Patterns in Forcible Rape.* Chicago: University of Chicago Press, 1971.
Arnold, Peter. *Lady Beware.* Garden City, N.Y.: Doubleday, 1974.
Astor, Gerald. *The Charge Is Rape.* New York: Playboy Press, 1974.
Baughman, Laurance E. *Southern Rape Complex.* Atlanta: Pendulum Books, 1966.
Bienen, Henry. *Violence and Social Change.* Chicago: University of Chicago Press, 1968.
Black, Charles L., Jr. *Capital Punishment: The Inevitability of Caprice and Mistake.* New York: W. W. Norton, 1974.
Blos, Peter. "Preoedipal Factors in the Etiology of Female Delinquency." In *The Psychoanalytic Study of the Child,* edited by Ruth S. Eissler et al. New York: International Universities Press, 1957.
Boston Women's Health Book Collective. *Our Bodies, Ourselves.* New York: Simon and Schuster, 1973; Boston: Boston's Women's Health Collective, 1971.
Botein, Bernard. *Our Cities Burn While We Play Cops and Robbers.* New York: Simon and Schuster, 1972.
Bremmer, Robert H., ed. *Children and Youth in America: A Documentary History.* Cambridge, Mass.: Harvard University Press, 1971.
Burgess, Ann Wolbert, and Holstrom, Lynda L. *Rape: Victims of Crisis.* Bowie, Md.: Robert J. Brady, 1974.
Burton, Lindy. *Vulnerable Children.* New York: Schocken Books, 1968.
Bychowski, Gustav. *Evil in Man: Anatomy of Hate and Violence.* New York: Grune & Stratton, 1968.

305

Caprio, Frank S. *Variations in Sexual Behavior*. London: Calder, 1957.

———, and Brenner, D. R. *Sexual Behavior: Psycho-legal Aspects*. New York: Citadel Press, 1961.

Chance, Michael R., and Lolly, Clifford. *Social Groups of Monkeys, Apes and Men*. New York: Dutton, 1971.

Chappell, Duncan, et al. "Forcible Rape: A Comparative Study of Offenses Known to the Police in Boston and Los Angeles." In *Studies in the Sociology of Sex*, edited by J. M. Heuslin. New York: Appleton-Century-Crofts, 1971.

Chesler, Phyllis. *Women and Madness*. Garden City, N.Y.: Doubleday, 1972.

Cleaver, Eldridge. *Soul on Ice*. New York: McGraw-Hill, 1970.

Csida, June Bundy, and Csida, Joseph. *Rape: How to Avoid It and What to Do about It If You Can't*. Chatsworth, Calif.: Books for Better Living, 1974.

DeFrancis, Vincent. *Child Abuse Legislation in the 1970's*. Denver: The American Humane Association, n.d.

———. *Protecting the Child Victim of Sex Crimes Committed by Adults*. Denver: The American Humane Association, 1969.

Dollard, John. *Caste and Class in a Southern Town*. New York: Doubleday/Anchor, 1949.

Dreifus, Claudia. *Women's Fate: Raps from a Feminist Consciousness-Raising Group*. New York: Bantam, 1973.

Eidelberg, Ludwig. *The Dark Urge*. New York: Pyramid Books, 1961.

Farson, Richard. *Birth Rights*. New York: Macmillan, 1974.

Firestone, Shulamith. *The Dialectic of Sex*. New York: Bantam, 1971.

Forer, Lois G. *No One Will Lissen: How Our Legal System Brutalizes the Youthful Poor*. New York: John Day, 1970.

Frank, Jerome. *Courts on Trial*. Princeton, N.J.: Princeton University Press, 1973.

———. *A Man's Reach*. New York: Macmillan, 1965.

———; and Frank, Barbara. *Not Guilty*. New York: Da Capo Press, 1971.

Frankel, Marvin E. *Criminal Sentences: Law Without Order*. New York: Hill & Wang, 1973.

Gagnon, John H., and Simon, William (eds.). *The Sexual Scene*. Chicago: Aldine, 1970.

Gebhard, Paul, et al. *Sex Offenders*. New York: Harper & Row, 1965.

Gelinas, N. J. *The Frightened Women*. New York: Tower, 1966.

Grimstad, Kirsten and Rennie, Susan (eds.). *The New*

Woman's Survival Catalog. New York: Coward, McCann & Geoghegan/Berkley, 1973.

Hartogs, Renatus, and Artzt, Eric. *Violence: Causes & Solutions.* New York: Dell, 1970.

Haskell, Molly. *From Reverence to Rape: The Treatment of Women in the Movies.* Baltimore: Penguin Books, Inc., 1974.

Hays, H. R. *The Dangerous Sex.* New York: Putnam, 1966.

Herschberger, Ruth. *Adam's Rib.* New York: Harper & Row, 1970.

Hume, Brit. *Inside Story.* New York: Doubleday, 1974.

Kalven, Harry, and Zeisel, Hans. *The American Jury.* Chicago: University of Chicago Press, 1971.

Kanowitz, Leo. *Sex Roles in Law and Society: Cases and Materials.* Albuquerque: University of New Mexico Press, 1973.

_____. *Women and the Law: The Unfinished Revolution.* Albuquerque: University of New Mexico Press, 1969.

Karpman, Benjamin. *The Sexual Offender and His Offenses.* New York: Julian Press, 1954.

Kinsey, Alfred Charles. *Sexual Behavior in the Human Female.* Bloomington: University of Indiana Press, 1948.

_____. *Sexual Behavior in the Human Male.* Bloomington: University of Indiana Press, 1948.

Kling, Samuel G. *Sexual Behavior and the Law.* New York: Random House, 1965.

Kronhausen, Phyllis, and Kronhausen, Eberhard. *Pornography and the Law.* New York: Ballantine Books, 1959.

Lewinsohn, Richard. *A History of Sexual Customs.* New York: Harper, 1959.

Lorenz, Konrad. *On Aggression.* New York: Harcourt, 1966.

Ludovici, L. J. *The Final Inequality: A Critical Assessment of Woman's Sexual Roles in Society.* New York: W. W. Norton, 1965.

McCord, William and McCord, Joan. *The Psychopath: An Essay on the Criminal Mind.* Princeton, N.J.: D. Van Nostrand, 1964.

MacDonald, John M. *Rape Offenders and Their Victims.* Springfield, Ill.: C. C. Thomas, 1971.

Marshall, D., and Suggs, Robert (eds.). *Human Sexual Behavior: Variations in the Ethnographic Spectrum.* New York: Basic Books, 1971.

Medea, Andrea, and Thompson, Kathleen. *Against Rape.* New York: Farrar, Straus & Giroux, 1974.

Mehrhof, Barbara, and Kearon, Pamela. "Rape: An Act of

Terror." In Notes from the Third Year: Women's Liberation, edited by Anne Koedt. New York, 1971.

Milton, Catherine. Women in Policing. Washington, D.C.: Police Foundation, 1972.

Offstein, Jerrold N. Self-Defense for Women. Palo Alto, Calif.: National Press Books, 1972.

Parker, T. Hidden World of Sex Offenders. Indianapolis: Bobbs-Merrill, 1969.

Perkins, Rollin M. Criminal Law. New York: Foundation Press, 1969.

Piercy, Marge. Living in the Open. New York: Knopf, 1975.

Reik, Theodore. The Many Faces of Sex. New York: Farrar, Straus & Giroux, 1966.

Rose, Thomas (ed.). Violence in America. New York: Random House, 1969.

Rosenblatt, Stanley. Justice Denied. Los Angeles: Nash, 1971.

Rubinstein, Jonathan. City Police. New York: Farrar, Straus & Giroux, 1974.

Ryan, William. Blaming the Victim. New York: Pantheon, 1970.

Sherfey, Mary Jane. The Nature and Evolution of Female Sexuality. New York: Random House, 1972.

Shiloh, Ailon (ed.). Studies in Human Sexual Behavior, the American Scene. Springfield, Ill.: C. C. Thomas, 1970.

Shultz, Gladys Denny. How Many More Victims? Society and the Sex Criminal. Philadelphia: J. B. Lippincott Company, 1965.

Slovenko, Ralph (ed.). Sexual Behavior and the Law. Springfield, Ill.: C. C. Thomas, 1965.

The Supreme Court Obscenity Decisions. San Diego, Calif.: Greenleaf Classics, 1973.

Tappan, Paul. Crime, Justice, and Correction. New York: McGraw-Hill, 1960.

Taylor, G. Rattray. Sex in History. New York: Vanguard, 1954.

Thompson, Hunter S. Hell's Angels. New York: Random House, 1966.

Toch, Hans. Violent Men: An Inquiry into the Psychology of Violence. Chicago: Aldine, 1969.

Tormes, Yvonne M. Child Victims of Incest. Denver: The American Humane Association, 1968.

———. The Victim: Child Victims of Incest. Washington, D.C.: U.S. Children's Bureau, 1968.

Uhnak, Dorothy. Policewoman. New York: Simon & Schuster, 1964.

Van Vogt, A. E. The Violent Man. New York: Farrar, Straus & Giroux, 1962.

Von Hentig, Hans. *Crime Causes and Conditions.* New York: McGraw-Hill, 1947.
_____. *The Criminal and His Victim.* New Haven, Conn.: Yale University Press, 1948.
Vuocolo, Alfred. *The Repetitive Sex Offender.* N.J.: Quality Printing, 1969.
Wecht, Cyril H., and Collom, Wellon D. "Medical Evidence in Alleged Rape." In *Legal Medicine Annual.* New York: Appleton-Century-Crofts, 1969.
Wickler, Wolfgang. *The Sexual Code: The Social Behavior of Animals and Men.* New York: Doubleday, 1972.
Wigmore, John Henry. *A Treatise on the Anglo-American System of Evidence in Trials at Common Law, including the Statutes and Judicial Decisions of all Jurisdictions of the United States and Canada.* Edited by James H. Chadbourne. 10 vols. 3d ed. Boston: Little, Brown, 1940.
Wilson, Colin. *Lingard.* New York: Pocket Books, 1972.
Wolfgang, Marvin E. (ed.). *Patterns of Violence.* Philadelphia: American Academy of Political and Social Science, 1966.
_____, and Short, James, Jr. (eds.). *Collective Violence.* Philadelphia: American Academy of Political and Social Sciences, 1970.
Woodbury, John, and Schwartz, Elroy. *The Silent Sin.* New York: New American Library, 1971.

Articles

Aarons, Leroy F. "Rape as Murder Defense." *Washington Post,* September 22, 1974.
Adams, Nathan M. "Hitchhiking—Too Often the Last Ride." *Reader's Digest,* July 1973.
"Alleged Rape: An Invitational Symposium." *Journal of Reproductive Medicine,* April 1974.
Altman, Jack, and Ziporyn, Marvin. "The Mind of a Murderer." *Saturday Evening Post,* July 1, 1967.
American College of Obstetricians and Gynecologists. "Medical Procedures in Cases of Suspected Rape." *Medical Aspects of Human Sexuality,* September 1973.
_____. "Prevention of Pregnancy in Cases of Suspected Rape: Modification of A.C.O.G. Recommendations." *Medical Aspects of Human Sexuality,* December 1973.
Apfelberg, Benjamin; Sugar, Carl; and Pfeffer, Arnold Z. "Psychiatric Study of 250 Sex Offenders." *American Journal of Psychiatry* (1944).

Bagley, Christopher. "Incest Behavior and Incest Taboo." *Social Problems*, Spring 1969.

Banay, Ralph S. "Police Dilemma with Sexual Crimes." *Medical Aspects of Human Sexuality*, September 1971.

Barnes, Bart. "Girls Taught 'Passivity,' Panel Hears." *Washington Post*, November 26, 1972.

Barnes, Josephine. "Rape and Other Sexual Offenses." *British Medical Journal*, April 1967.

Barry, M. J., and Johnson, A. J. "The Incest Barrier." *Psychoanalytic Quarterly* (1958).

Bayne, Sheila. "An Answer to Rape and Other Violent Crimes." *University of Washington Daily*, January 24, 1974.

Bender, L., and Blau, A. "The Reaction of Children to Sexual Relations with Adults." *American Journal of Orthopsychiatry* (October 1937).

————, and Grugett, A. E. "A Follow-Up Report on Children Who Had Atypical Sexual Experience." *American Journal of Orthopsychiatry* (October 1952).

Berkowitz, Leonard. "The Effects of Observing Violence." *Scientific American*, June 1964.

Berlin, Abby. "Treatment for the Violent Offender." *Crime and Delinquency Literature*, March 1972.

Blades, Nancy. "Lobby for Protection Laws Zeros In on Rape Victims." *Home News* (New Brunswick, N.J.), February 26, 1973.

Blanchard, W. H. "The Group Process in Gang Rape." *Journal of Social Psychology* (May 1959).

Blitman, Nan, and Green, Robin. "Inez Garcia on Trial." *Ms.*, May 1975.

Bohmer, Carol. "Judicial Attitudes toward Rape Victims." *Judicature*, February 1974.

————. "Judicial Use of Psychiatric Reports in the Sentencing of Sex Offenders." *Journal of Psychiatry and Law*, Summer 1973.

Brabec, Dette Dewing. "Rape: The Ultimate Violence." *Prime Time*, September 1974.

Breen, James L.; Greenwald, Earl; and Gregori, Caterine A. "The Molested Young Female: Evaluation and Therapy of Alleged Rape." *Pediatric Clinics of North America*, August 1972.

Bright-Sagnier, Barbara. "50 Turn Out to Protest Calif. Sentence." *Washington Post*, October 22, 1974.

Brown, William P. "Police-Victim Relationships in Sex Crime Investigations." *Police Chief*, January 1970.

Burgess, Ann W., and Holstrom, Lynda L. "The Rape Victim in the Emergency Ward." *American Journal of Nursing,* October 1973.

Capraro, Vincent J. "Sexual Assault of Female Children." *Annals of the New York Academy of Sciences,* May 1967.

Cavallin, H. "Incestuous Fathers: A Clinical Report." *American Journal of Psychiatry* (1966).

Chriss, Nicholas C. "Can a Black Be Acquitted?" *The Nation,* December 18, 1970.

Cohen, Murray L., and Boucher, Richard J. "Misunderstandings about Sex Criminals." *Sexual Behavior,* March 1972.

Cohen, Murray L., et al. "The Psychology of Rapists." *Seminars in Psychiatry,* August 1971.

Colen, B. D. "County to Open Rape Unit." *Washington Post,* September 7, 1974.

Colianni, Eileen. "How They Caught the Oakland-Shadyside Rapist." *Pittsburgh Forum,* July 19, 1974.

"Cops Build Solid Rape Case; State Settles for Probation." *The Blue Light,* June 1974.

Cormier, Bruno, and Simons, Siebert P. "The Problem of the Dangerous Sexual Offender." *Canadian Psychiatric Association Journal,* August 1969.

"Corroborating Charges of Rape." *Columbia Law Review,* June 1967.

"Corroboration Rule and Crimes Accompanying a Rape." *University of Pennsylvania Law Review,* January 1970.

"Crime Statistics: Let the Buyer Beware." *Washington Post,* August 31, 1972.

"Crime Victims Compensation." *Time,* October 14, 1974.

Daley, Robert. "Inside the Criminal-Informant Business." *New York,* March 24, 1975.

Davenport, Diana. "White Slave Trade, Circa 1973." *Cosmopolitan,* August 1973.

Davis, Angela. "Joanne Little, the Dialectics of Rape." *Ms.,* June 1975.

Dejanikus, Tacie and Kelly, Janis. "WASP: On Target." *Off Our Backs,* January 1975.

Del Drago, Maria. "The Pride of Inez Garcia." *Ms.,* May 1975.

Densmore, Dana. "On Rape." *No More Fun and Games: A Journal of Female Liberation,* May 1973.

_____. "On Self-Defense." *No More Fun and Games: A Journal of Female Liberation,* May 1973.

Dubrow, Marsha. "Women Organize to Combat Rapists and Counsel Victims." *Washington Post,* December 21, 1972.

Dworkin, Roger B. "The Resistance Standard in Rape Legislation." *Stanford Law Review*, February 1966.

E. D. G. "Age No Barrier to Rape." *Prime Time*, September 1974.

Emergency Department Protocol for Management of Rape Cases." *Journal of the American Medical Association*, December 24, 1973.

Enos, William F., and Beyer, James C. "A Standard Rape Investigation Form." *Virginia Medical Monthly*, January 1974.

————, and Mann, Geoffrey T. "The Medical Examination of Cases of Rape." *Medico-Legal Bulletin*, July 1972.

Enos, William F.; Mann, Geoffrey T.; and Dolan, William D. "A Laboratory Procedure for the Identification of Semen." *American Journal of Clinical Pathology*, March 1963.

Evrard, John R. "Rape: The Medical, Social, and Legal Implications." *American Journal of Obstetrics and Gynecology*, September 15, 1971.

"The Facts on Rape." *Human Behavior*, June 1973.

Feegel, M. D. "Synopsis of Rape for the Florida Examiner." *Florida Medical*, September 1969.

"The Female Fuzz." *Newsweek*, October 23, 1972.

Fields, Sidney. "Tracks Down Rapists." *New York Daily News*, February 20, 1973.

F. M. "Coming to Terms." *Off Our Backs*, January 1975.

————. "Reforms." *Off Our Backs*, January 1975.

"Forcible and Statutory Rape: An Exploration of the Operation and Objectives of the Consent Standard." *Yale Law Journal* (December 1952).

Fox, Sandra Sutherland, and Scherl, Donald J. "Crisis Intervention with Victims of Rape." *Social Work*, January 1972.

Foxe, Arthur N. "Rape, Rats, and Reflection. Crime: The Broad View." *Corrective Psychiatry and Journal of Social Therapy* (1968).

Fromm, Erich. "Man Would as Soon Flee as Fight." *Psychology Today*, August 1973.

Fulman, Ricki. "Crimes Unit Still Faces Some Flack." *New York Daily News*, December 21, 1973.

Gaensbauer, Theodore J. "Castration in Treatment of Sex Offenders: An Appraisal." *Rocky Mountain Medical Journal*, April 1973.

Gager, Nancy and Schurr, Cathleen. "Rape." *Washingtonian*, June 1973.

Gagnon, John H. "Female Child Victims of Sex Offenses." *Social Problems* (1965).

Geis, Gilbert, and Chappell, Duncan. "Forcible Rape by Multiple Offenders." *Abstracts on Criminology and Penology,* July–August 1971.

"Give Rapists Brain Surgery!" *Confidential Flash,* May 28, 1974.

Godwin, Ira D., and Seitz, George K. "Vaginal Acid Phosphatase." *Medical Annals of D.C.,* March 1970.

Goldfarb, Ronald. "Rape and Law Reform." *Washington Post,* August 2, 1973.

Goldner, Norman S. "Rape as a Heinous but Understudied Offense." *Journal of Criminal Law, Criminology and Police Science* (1972).

Graham, Loral. "Defend Yourself!" *Canadian Nurse,* August 1968.

Graves, Lester R., and Francisco, J. T. "Medicolegal Aspects of Rape." *Medical Aspects of Human Sexuality,* April 1970.

Gribbin, August. "The Cop-Out Cops." *National Observer,* August 3, 1974.

Griffins, Susan. "Rape: The All-American Crime." *Ramparts,* September 1971.

"Guilty Victims, Theories of M. Symonds." *Newsweek,* June 17, 1974.

Halleck, S. L. "The Physician's Role in Management of Victims of Sex Offenders." *Journal of the American Medical Association,* April 28, 1962.

Hayman, Charles R. "Increasing Rape Reflects Increasing Violence." *Sexual Behavior,* November 1971.

———. "Victimology of Sexual Assault." *Medical Aspects of Human Sexuality,* October 1971.

Hayman, Charles R., et al. "Rape and Its Consequences." *Medical Aspects of Human Sexuality,* February 1972.

———, and Lanza, Charlene. "Sexual Assault on Women and Girls." *American Journal of Obstetrics and Gynecology,* February 1, 1971.

———; Lanza, Charlene; Fuentes, Roberto; and Algor, Kathe. "Rape in the District of Columbia." *American Journal of Obstetrics and Gynecology,* May 1, 1972.

———; Lanza, Charlene; and Noel, Essex C., III. "What to Do for Victims of Rape." *Resident and Staff Physician,* August 1973.

———; Stewart, William F.; Lewis, Frances R.; and Grant, Murray. "Sexual Assault on Women and Children in the District of Columbia." *Public Health Reports,* December 1968.

314   Bibliography

"Healthy Rise in Rape." *Newsweek*, July 31, 1972.

Heimel, Cyndy. "I Should Have Known: It's August." *Majority Report*, August 22, 1974.

Heinz, H. John, III. "Rape: Society's Crime against Women." *Congressional Record*, May 6, 1974.

Helpern, Milton. "Sexual Crimes and the Medical Examiner." *Medical Aspects of Human Sexuality*, April 1974.

Hendrix, Kathleen. "Women Take the Offensive on Rapists." *Los Angeles Times*, December 8, 1974.

Henley, Arthur. "The Mind of the Victim." *Physician's World*, August 1973.

Hibey, Richard A. "The Trial of a Rape Case: An Advocate's Analysis of Corroboration, Consent and Character." *American Criminal Law Review* (1973).

"Hijackers Had Accused Michigan Police of Brutality." *Washington Post*, November 13, 1972.

Holt, Brad. "The Rapist Could Be Standing Right Here." *Washington Star-News*, May 10, 1974.

Horin, Adele. "Rape: How Women Can Stop It." *Pageant*, February 1975.

Jarrett, Tommy W. "Criminal Law: Psychiatric Examination of Prosecutrix in Rape Case." *North Carolina Law Review*, December 1966.

"Joanne Little: No Escape Yet." *Off Our Backs*, January 1975.

"Joanne Little Released." *Poverty Law Report*, March 1975.

Kanin, Eugene J. "Male Aggression in Dating-Courtship Relations." *American Journal of Sociology*, September 1957.

KGO-Radio San Francisco. "I Never Set Out to Rape Anybody." *Ms.*, December 1972.

Kiefer, C. Raymond. "Sexual Molestation of a Child." *Medical Aspects of Human Sexuality*, December 1973.

Kiernan, Laura A. "Sex Crime: No Easy Answer." *Washington Post*, January 20, 1974.

King, Carl K. "Police Discretion and the Judgment That a Crime Has Been Committed: Rape in Philadelphia." *University of Pennsylvania Law Review* (1968).

Kirkpatrick, Clifford, and Kanin, Eugene. "Male Sex Aggression on a University Campus." *American Sociological Review*, February 1957.

Koenig, Joseph L. "Terror City for Girls." *Front Page Detective*, June 1973.

Kopp, Sheldon B. "The Character Structure of Sex Offenders." *American Journal of Psychotherapy* (January, 1962).

Kozol, Harry L. "Myths about the Sex Offender." *Medical Aspects of Human Sexuality*, June 1971.

———; Boucher, Richard J.; and Garofalo, Ralph F. "The

Diagnosis and Treatment of Dangerousness." *Crime and Delinquency,* October 1972.

Kramer, Linda. "The Case of Inez Garcia: Woman vs. Assailant. Is Murder of Rapist Justified?" *Boston Sunday Globe,* October 27, 1974.

Krause, Charles A. "Area Police Handling of Rape Scored." *Washington Post,* March 20, 1973.

Lake, Alice. "Rape: The Unmentionable Crime." *Good Housekeeping,* November 1971.

Lanham, David A. "The Dangerous Sex Offender." *Medical Annals of the District of Columbia,* February 1974.

Lanza, Charlene. "Nursing Support for the Victim of Sexual Assault." *The Quarterly Review,* Summer 1971.

Lear, Martha Weinman. "If You Rape a Woman and Steal Her TV, What Can They Get You for in New York? Stealing Her TV." *New York Times Magazine,* January 30, 1972.

———. "What Can You Say about Laws That Tell a Man: If You Rob a Woman, You Might as Well Rape Her Too—The Rape Is Free." *Redbook,* September 1972.

"The Least Punished Crime." *National Affairs,* December 18, 1972.

Leblanc, Renee Dictor. "Rape Squad: Women Avengers Take the Law into Their Own Hands." *Coronet,* October 1972.

Le Grand, Camille. "Rape and Rape Laws: Sexism in Society and Law." *California Law Review,* May 1973.

"Letters to the Editor: Some Reactions to the G. W. Rape Case and the Post's Editorial." *Washington Post,* December 21, 1972.

LeVine, Robert. "Gusii Sex Offenses: A Study in Social Control." *American Anthropologist* (1959).

Lewis, M. "Some Psychological Aspects of Seduction, Incest, and Rape in Childhood." *Journal of the American Academy of Child Psychiatry,* October 1969.

Lewis, Nancy. "The Behind-the-Scenes Story of the Unanimous Repeal Bill Victory." *Majority Report,* March 1974.

Lichtenstein, Grace. "Rape Squad." *New York Times Magazine,* March 3, 1974.

Lipton, G. L. "Rape: A Complex Management Problem in the Pediatric Emergency Room." *Journal of Pediatrics,* November 1969.

McCubbin, Jack H., and Scott, Daniel E. "Management of Alleged Sexual Assault." *Texas Medicine,* September 1973.

McDermott, Shirley; Himmelman, Audrey; Lopez, Juanita; and Ride, Barbara. "Letter to the Editor." *Denver Post,* July 26, 1973.

Maitland, Leslie. "Rape Study Details the How, the Why and the Who." *New York Times*, July 29, 1974.

Margolin, Debbie. "Rape: The Facts." *Women: A Journal of Liberation* (1972) Vol. 3, no. 1.

Massey, Joseph B.; Garcia, Celso-Ramon; and Emich, John P., Jr. "Management of Sexually Assaulted Females." *Obstetrics and Gynecology*, July 1971.

Mathias, Charles McC. "Statement by Senator Mathias, Title VIII of S. 3280, 'Rape Prevention and Control.' " *Congressional Record*, September 10, 1974.

Matthews, Robert B. "Protest." *Glamour*, February 1972.

Mead, Margaret. "Must Men Be Violent?" *Redbook*, September 1972.

"Medical Procedures in Cases of Suspected Rape." *American College of Obstetricians and Gynecologists Technical Bulletin* No. 14, September 1973.

Meyer, Eugene. " 'Green Car' Rapist Gets Life in Jail." *Washington Post*, December 19, 1973.

Meyer, Lawrence. "GWU Rape Case Figure Held in Catholic U. Theft." *Washington Post*, March 20, 1973.

Miron, Charles. "The Sex Crimes That Women Fear Most." *The Woman*, August 1970.

Montgomery, Paul L. "New Drive On in State to Ease Rape Convictions." *New York Times*, November 13, 1973.

Mosse, Hilde L. "The Influence of Mass Media on the Sex Problems of Teenagers." *Journal of Sex Research*, April 1966.

Moyer, K. E. "The Physiology of Violence." *Psychology Today*, July 1973.

Mulligan, Elizabeth. "Fight Rape or Do What?" *Girl Talk*, January 1974.

"The Myth: Women Want It." *Crawdaddy*, June 1974.

Oelsner, Lesley. "Law of Rape: 'Because Ladies Lie.' " *New York Times*, May 14, 1972.

O'Hara, Mary. "He Had a Knife in His Right Hand . . . Then I Screamed!" *Pittsburgh Press*, February 29, 1972.

Pacht, Asher R.; Halleck, Seymour L.; and Ehrmann, John C. "Diagnosis and Treatment of the Sexual Offender: A Nine-Year Study." *American Journal of Psychiatry*, March 1962, 118:802–808.

Packard, Alice. "New Questions about Birth Control." *The Woman*, August 1973.

Peters, Joseph J. "Child Rape: Defusing a Psychological Time Bomb." *Hospital Physician*, February 1973.

———. "Emotional Recovery from Rape." *Medical Aspects of Human Sexuality*, October 1973.

_____, and Roether, Hermann A. "Group Psychotherapy for Probationed Sex Offenders." *International Psychiatry Clinics*, 1972, 8:69–80.

_____, and Sadoff, Robert L. "Psychiatric Services for Sex Offenders on Probation." *Federal Probation*, September 1971.

"Public Pay for Crime Victims: An Idea That Is Spreading." *U.S. News and World Report*, April 5, 1971.

"Questions and Answers on Sexual Offenses." *Medical Aspects of Human Sexuality*, April 1974.

Randal, Judith. "Rape: An Analysis." *Washington Evening Star*, November 12, 1971.

"Rape." *The Monthly Extract*, December–January, 1974–75.

"Rape and Battery Between Husband and Wife." *Stanford Law Review*, July 1954.

"Rape Corroboration Requirement: Repeal Not Reform." *Yale Law Journal*, June 1972.

"Rape in the Courtroom." *Off Our Backs*, December 1972.

"Rape: The Experience." *Women: A Journal of Liberation* (1972), Vol. 3, no. 1.

"Rape! These Women Say They Will Stop It!" *National Examiner*, September 23, 1974.

"Rape: Trend an Expression of Hostility, Violence." *Washington Evening Star*, November 12, 1971.

Reiss, Albert J. "Sex Offenses: The Marginal Status of the Adolescent." *Law and Contemporary Problems* (1960).

Roberts, Eleanor. "Help for Rape Victims." *Sunday Herald Advertiser*, Boston, April 15, 1973.

Robinson, Timothy S. "Settlements Reached in Two Rape Suits." *Washington Post*, October 10, 1974.

Rowan, Carl T., and Mazie, David M. "The Terrible Trauma of Rape." *Reader's Digest*, March 1974.

Rupp, Joseph C. "Sperm Survival and Prostatic Acid Phosphatase Activity in Victims of Sexual Assault." *Journal of Forensic Sciences*, April 1969.

Rush, Florence. "The Sexual Abuse of Children: A Feminist Point of View." *The Radical Therapist*, December 1971.

Russell, Bruce. "Sex Offenders Helping Each Other." *Washington Post*, June 16, 1974.

"S." "The Civilized Rapist: Checkmate in Bed." *Village Voice*, September 9, 1971.

Schiff, Arthur F. "Examining the Sexual Assault Victim." *Journal of the Florida Medical Association*, September 1966.

_____. "Modification of the Berg Acid Phosphatase Test." *Journal of Forensic Sciences*, October 1969.

————. "Rape." *Medical Aspects of Human Sexuality,* May 1972.

————. "Rape in Other Countries." *Medicine, Science, and the Law* (London), July 1971.

————. "Statistical Features of Rape." *Journal of Forensic Science,* October 1968.

Schmidt, Peggy. "Rape Crisis Centers." *Ms.,* September 1973.

Schultz, Leroy G. "Psychotherapeutic and Legal Approaches to the Sexually Victimized Child." *International Journal of Child Psychotherapy.* 1972.

Schurr, Cathleen. "Rape: Victim as Criminal." *Pittsburgh Forum,* November 1971; *Know, Inc.,* 1972.

Schwartz, B. "The Effect in Philadelphia of Pennsylvania's Increased Penalties for Rape." *Journal of Criminal Law* 1968.

Seawell, Mary Ann. "Rape—The Myth and the Reality." Five Part Series. *Palo Alto Times,* June 1972.

Selkin, James. "Rape: When to Fight Back." *Psychology Today,* January 1975.

"Sex Assaults and the Equal Rights Amendment." *Yale Law Journal,* April 1971.

"Sexual Assaults on Women and Girls." *Annals of Internal Medicine,* February 1970.

Seyfert, Sheryl. "Help for the Rape Victim." *Parade,* May 26, 1974.

Shaffer, Helen B. "Crime of Rape." *Editorial Research Reports,* January 19, 1972.

Shah, Diane K. "Women Attack Rape Justice," *National Observer,* October 9, 1971.

Shearer, Lloyd. "Defend Yourself with a Whistle." *Parade,* June 2, 1974.

————. "Our Sex Laws—Should They Be Changed?" *Parade,* January 7, 1973.

————. "Reducing the Sex Urge." *Parade,* August 11, 1974.

Sheehy, Gail. "Nice Girls Don't Get into Trouble." *New York,* February 15, 1971.

Sheldon, Ann. "Rape: A Solution." *Women: A Journal of Liberation* 1972, vol. 3, no. 1.

Shultz, Gladys Denny. "Society and the Sex Criminal." *Reader's Digest,* November 1966.

————. "What Sex Offenders Say about Pornography." *Reader's Digest,* July 1971.

Sidley, Nathan T., and Stolarz, Francis J. "A Proposed 'Dangerous Sex Offender' Law." *American Journal of Psychiatry,* July 1973.

"Special Problems of Sexually Assaulted Females." *Modern Medicine,* October 4, 1971.

Steadman, Henry J., and Cocozza, Joseph J. "We Can't Predict Who Is Dangerous." *Psychology Today,* January 1975.

Steinem, Gloria. "But What Do We Do with Our Rage?" *Ms.,* May 1975.

Stickney, John. "A Gang-Rape Trial (1): It Seemed Like an Open-&-Shut Case." *Village Voice,* April 19, 1973.

_____. "A Gang-Rape Trial (2): How Do You Corroborate a Rape?" *Village Voice,* April 26, 1973.

"The Story of Morris Kent—Rapist." *Washington Post,* June 18, 1967.

Stuart, Roger. "City Police Steal a Bow as Crime Rate Here Drops 10%." *Pittsburgh Press,* March 29, 1973.

Stumbo, Bella. "Rape: Does Justice Turn Its Head?" *Los Angeles Times,* March 12, 1972.

Sturup, Georg K. "Sex Offenses, the Scandinavian Experience." *Law and Contemporary Problems,* Spring 1960.

Sullivan, Gail Bernice. "Rape and Its Neglected Victims." *San Francisco Chronicle,* April 9, 1972.

"Suspected Rape." *Medical Legal Bulletin,* September 1970.

Sutherland, Sandra, and Scherl, Donald J. "Patterns of Response among Victims of Rape." *American Journal of Orthopsychiatry,* April 1970.

Szumski, Gerald J. "A New Law Shields Rape Victims' Private Lives." *National Observer,* May 25, 1974.

Theoharis, Saghorn, and Calmas, Wilfred. "Sociometric Study of the Sex Offender," *Journal of Abnormal Psychology,* 1964.

"Three Women Report Being Raped." *Fort Lauderdale Sun Sentinel,* May 21, 1973.

"Victim Still Fears Attacker." *Kansas City Star,* February 13, 1974.

Von Hoffman, Nicholas. "A Natural Crime for an Unnatural Society." *Washington Post,* August 17, 1971.

_____. "Perils and Humiliation." *Washington Post,* November 22, 1971.

Wainwright, Loudon. "The Nine Nurses." *Life,* July 29, 1966.

Walker, Mae. "Rape and the Harlem Woman: 'She Asked for It'—Or Did She?" *Majority Report,* August 22, 1974.

Warden, Rob, and Saperstein, Saundra. "Study Reveals Rapists Follow a Background Pattern." *Denver Post,* February 1, 1973.

Wasserman, Michelle. "Rape: Breaking the Silence." *Progressive,* November, 1973.

Weisman, Joel D. "New Rape Laws Urged by ABA." *Washington Post,* February 25, 1975.

Weiss, Edward H.; Taub, Norman; and Rosenthal, Jesse. "The Mental Health Committee Report of the Subcommittee on the Problem of Rape in the District of Columbia." *Medical Annals of the District of Columbia,* 1972.

"When Crime Victims Are Paid for Losses." *Good Housekeeping.* February 1971.

Wolfgang, Marvin E., and Risdel, Marc. "Race, Judicial Discretion, and the Death Penalty." *Annals of the American Academy of Political and Social Science,* May 1973.

"Woman Raped as She Obeys Sign to Stop Car." *Washington Post,* March 20, 1973.

"Women Cops Make Better Police Executives Than Men, Study Shows." *National Enquirer,* April 29, 1974.

"Women and the Criminal Law." *American Criminal Law Reporter,* Winter 1973.

"Women and Rape." *Pittsburgh Fair Witness,* July 28, 1972.

Wood, Pamela Lakes. "The Victim in a Forcible Rape Case: A Feminist View." *American Criminal Law Review,* Winter 1973.

Government Publications

Los Angeles Police Department. "Lady Beware." 1974.

Maryland, State of, Prince George's County. "Report of the Task Force to Study the Treatment of the Victims of Sexual Assault." March 1973.

Michigan, State of, Department of Corrections, State Prison of Southern Michigan. Program Description: SONAR. Prepared by Barry Minzes. November 1973.

New York City, Police Department, Sex Crimes Analysts Unit. "Sex Crimes—Scientific Aids." March 1974.

New York, State of, Department of Mental Hygiene. "Report on Study of 102 Sex Offenders at Sing Sing Prison." 1950.

U.S., Congress, Senate, Committee on the Judiciary, Subcommittee on Criminal Laws and Procedures. *Hearing on Victims of Crime.* 92d Cong., 1st sess. September 29, November 30, 1971; March 27, 1972.

U.S., Congress, Senate, Committee on Labor and Public Welfare, Subcommittee on Children and Youth. *Hearing on Child Abuse Prevention Act.* 93d Cong., 1st sess. March 26, 27, 31; April 24, 1973.

U.S., Department of Health, Education, and Welfare, Social and Rehabilitation Service. *The Violent Offender.* Prepared by Daniel Glaser, Donald Kenefick, and Vincent O'Leary. Washington, D.C.: Government Printing Office, 1968.

U.S., Department of Justice, Federal Bureau of Investigation. *Crime in the United States.* Uniform Crime Reports. Washington, D.C.: Government Printing Office, 1968–73.

U.S., Department of Justice, National Institute of Law Enforcement and Criminal Justice, Law Enforcement Assistance Administration. "Forcible Rape: A Consideration of the Basic Issues." Prepared by Cynthia S. Jackson. Washington, D.C.: Government Printing Office, August 1973.

U.S., Department of Justice, National Commission on the Causes and Prevention of Violence. *Crimes of Violence.* Prepared by Donald J. Mulvihill, Melvin M. Tumin, and Lynn A. Curtis. Washington, D.C.: Government Printing Office, 1969.

U.S., Department of Justice, National Commission on the Causes and Prevention of Violence. Final Report: "To Establish Justice, to Insure Domestic Tranquility." Washington, D.C.: Government Printing Office, 1969.

U.S., Department of Justice, President's Commission on Law Enforcement and Administration of Justice. *The Challenge of Crime in a Free Society.* Washington, D.C.: Government Printing Office, 1967.

_____. *Corrections.* Washington, D.C.: Government Printing Office, 1967.

_____. *The Courts.* Washington, D.C.: Government Printing Office, 1967.

_____. *Crime and Its Impact: An Assessment.* Washington, D.C.: Government Printing Office, 1967.

_____. *The Police.* Washington, D.C.: Government Printing Office, 1967.

Washington, D.C., City Council, Public Safety Committee Task Force on Rape. Report. July 9, 1973.

Washington, D.C., City Council, Subcommittee on the Problem of Rape in the District. Report. Prepared by Norman Taub, Jesse Rosenthal, and Edward Weiss. January 1973.

Washington, D.C., Metropolitan Police Department, Sex Offense Branch. Procedures for Sexually Assaulted Persons. 1974.

Pamphlets, Speeches, and Unpublished Resources

Agopian, Michael W.; Chappell, Duncan; and Geis, Gilbert. "Interracial Forcible Rape in a North American City: An

Analysis of Sixty-three Cases." Address given at the American Society of Criminology Conference, Caracas, Venezuela, November, 1972.

Ann Arbor, Michigan, Women's Crisis Center. "Freedom From Rape." Pamphlet. 1974.

————. *How to Organize a Women's Crisis-Service Center.* 1974.

Barry, Kathy; Fredrick, Debbie; *et al.* "Stop Rape." Pamphlet. Detroit Women's Liberation, Women Against Rape, 1972.

Boston Rape Crisis Center. "Rape: Medical and Legal Information." Pamphlet. 1973.

Boston Women's Health Collective. "Crimes Against Women: Rape." In *Women's Yellow Pages.* Published by The Sanctuary, Inc., Cambridge, 1972.

Buffalo (N.Y.) Police Department. "Preliminary Results of 1972 Forcible Rape Cases."

Carlson, Nancy. "Psychological Implications." A speech at Rape Training Session at the University of Maryland, April 30, 1973.

Central New Jersey NOW. Newsletter: Special Issue on Rape. May 1971.

Chapel Hill, N.C., Women's Assault Line. "Medical Procedure." Mimeographed. 1973.

Easton, Todd. "The Crime of Rape: A Social Dilemma." Pamphlet. National Public Radio, New York, 1973.

Gager, Nancy. "Rape and Society: Possibilities for Change." Testimony given before the Public Safety Committee Hearings on Rape, District of Columbia City Council, September 18, 1973.

Harvey, Jean Campbell. Unpublished article on Rape in Washington, D.C. March 1973.

Joy, Linda. "The Majority Wins." Pamphlet. Lansing, Michigan: Lansing Chapter of the National Organization for Women, 1974.

Largen, Mary Ann. "History of Woman's Movement in Changing Attitudes, Laws, and Treatment toward Rape Victims." A speech delivered at Rape-Research, Action, Prevention, the Sixth Alabama Symposium on Justice and the Behavioral Sciences, University of Alabama, January 22, 1975.

————. "National Organization for Women Hospital Questionnaire, with Instructions for Use." Mimeographed. 1973.

————. "Telephone Counseling of Rape Victims." Mimeographed. National Organization for Women, 1973.

Miami/Dade County Rape Task Force. "An open letter to that

person out there who's concerned enough ABOUT RAPE to do something about it." Mimeographed. May 1974.

————. "Medical Treatment of the Rape Victim." Mimeographed. Jackson Memorial Hospital, Rape Treatment Center, Miami, Florida, 1973.

Minneapolis, Minnesota, Rape Counseling Center, Neighborhood Involvement Program (NIP). "Stop Rape." Brochure. 1974.

National Organization for Women (NOW). "Rape Task Force Project." Mimeographed. 1974.

————, Legislative Office. "Rape-Revenue Sharing Project." Mimeographed. 1974.

————, 6th National Conference (Washington, D.C.). "Workshop on Prostitution and Rape." Mimeographed. 1973.

————, National Office (Chicago, Ill.): "A Report on Rape in the Suburbs." Booklet. 1973.

————, Northern Virginia Chapter. "Rape: Facts Every Victim Should Know." Pamphlet. 1973.

New Mexico, University of and Associated Students of. "Women's Law: Or How to Stop the Most Commonly Committed Violent Crime: RAPE." Brochure. 1974.

New York City Police Department. "Sex Crimes—Scientific Aids." 1973.

New York Women Against Rape (NYWAR). "A Description of a Women's Anti-Rape Group." Mimeographed. n.d.

————. "Facts About Rape." Mimeographed. n.d.

————. "Orientation Guide for Counselors." Mimeographed. November 1973.

————. "Psychology of Rape." Mimeographed. n.d.

————. "Self-Defense." Mimeographed. n.d.

————. "The Police—and the Rape Victim." Manuscript. 1973.

Nijhof, Collette. "Open Season on Women: The Press and the Sociology of Rape in the U.S.A." American University. Manuscript. April 1972.

Peters, Joseph J. "The Philadelphia Rape Victim Study." Center for Studies in Sexual Deviance, Philadelphia General Hospital. A paper prepared for the First International Symposium on Victimology, Jerusalem, September 2–6, 1973.

————. "The Psychological Effects of Childhood Rape." A paper presented at the annual meeting of the American Psychiatric Association, Honolulu, May 9, 1973.

Philadelphia Women Organized Against Rape (WOAR). "Child Rape Victims and Their Families." Mimeographed. 1973.

————. "Handbook . . . Medical and Legal Aspects of Rape." Mimeographed. 1973.

————. "Medical Fact Sheet." Mimeographed. 1973.

"Proposed Reform of Michigan's 117 Year-Old Rape Law." Michigan Women's Task Force on Rape. Sexual Assault Legislation. S. B. 1207 Summary & Test.

Rape Relief (Seattle, Washington). "Information, Counseling, Advocacy, Third Part Reporting, Referrals." Mimeographed. 1974.

Schurr, Cathleen. "The Myths of Rape." Testimony given before the Public Safety Committee Hearings on Rape, District of Columbia City Council, September 18, 1973.

Seattle, Washington. "Rape Reduction Project: A Fact Sheet." Mimeographed. 1974.

Sex Problems Court Digest. New York: Juridical Digests Institute, January 1970–April 1974.

Shultz, Gladys Denny. Unpublished manuscript, personal communications. March 1973.

Washington, D.C., General Hospital. "Procedures for Management of Alleged Sexually Assaulted Persons in the Emergency and Admitting Service." Mimeographed. 1973.

Washington, D.C., Rape Crisis Center. "How to Start a Rape Crisis Center." Mimeographed. 1972.

————. "Medical Procedures in Treating Rape Victims." Newsletter. November–December, 1973.

————. "Protection Tactics." Mimeographed. n.d.

Webbink, Patricia, and Herman, Michael Harway. "Statement." Testimony given to the Public Safety Committee Hearings on Rape, District of Columbia City Council, September 1973.

Women Organized Against Rape. "Child Rape Victims and Their Families." Mimeographed. Philadelphia, 1973.

Yapp, Shelly. "Advocacy Service and Third Party Reporting for Rape Victims." Rape Relief, University YWCA, Seattle, Washington, March 12, 1973.

INDEX